Coal from Camerton

NEIL MACMILLEN AND MIKE CHAPMAN

Lightmoor Press

New Pit from the east, with train of coal tubs in front of the workshops. *Radstock Museum Archive*

CONTENTS

First published 1990, reprinted 2000, this edition
Published by Lightmoor Press

British Library Cataloguing-in-Publication Data.
A catalogue record for this book is available from the British Library

ISBN 13: 9781899889 86 0

Lightmoor Press
Unit 144b, Lydney Trading Estate, Harbour Road, Lydney, Gloucestershire GL15 5EJ
www.lightmoor.co.uk

Lightmoor Press is an imprint of Black Dwarf Lightmoor Publications Ltd

Designed by Alan Kittridge

PREFACE TO THIS NEW EDITION

Coal from Camerton was first published in 1990 as a result of a request to Avon Industrial Buildings Trust from Camerton Parish Council to record the history of the coal pits within the parish. The book followed the purchase of the area of Old Pit for use by the public in 1987.

In the years that have followed more information and photographs have become available, not least from the material which is now catalogued and recorded at the Radstock and Midsomer Norton and District Museum.

We are extremely grateful to the many people who, over the years, have contributed to this new and enlarged edition by way of encouragement, information and photographs. Penny Bonsall has read the manuscript and been most helpful with information on the local coal industry.

It is our hope that this edition will give the reader better insight into the conditions under which ordinary men hewed the coal and the lives of their families. For many people it was a harsh life amid the green hills of Somerset.

Neil Macmillen
Mike Chapman
2014

DEDICATION

This book is dedicated to all those who, through the centuries, lived and worked in the North Somerset Coalfield.

A COALFIELD WITH CHARACTER

AN INTRODUCTION

This is the story of one village, in the context of the whole coalfield, which reflected life in this part of Somerset for over two hundred years. The North Somerset Coalfield is situated in an Arcadian landscape of valleys and streams, woods and fields only a few miles to the south west of Bath. Even today it is a somewhat secluded area, where access from neighbouring towns has always been difficult. It was an area isolated from the other coalfields in the Midlands and South Wales until the coming of the railways. The populations of Bristol and Bath were growing at the end of the 18th century increasing the need for easily accessible coal and in this unlikely area, amid the green hills of

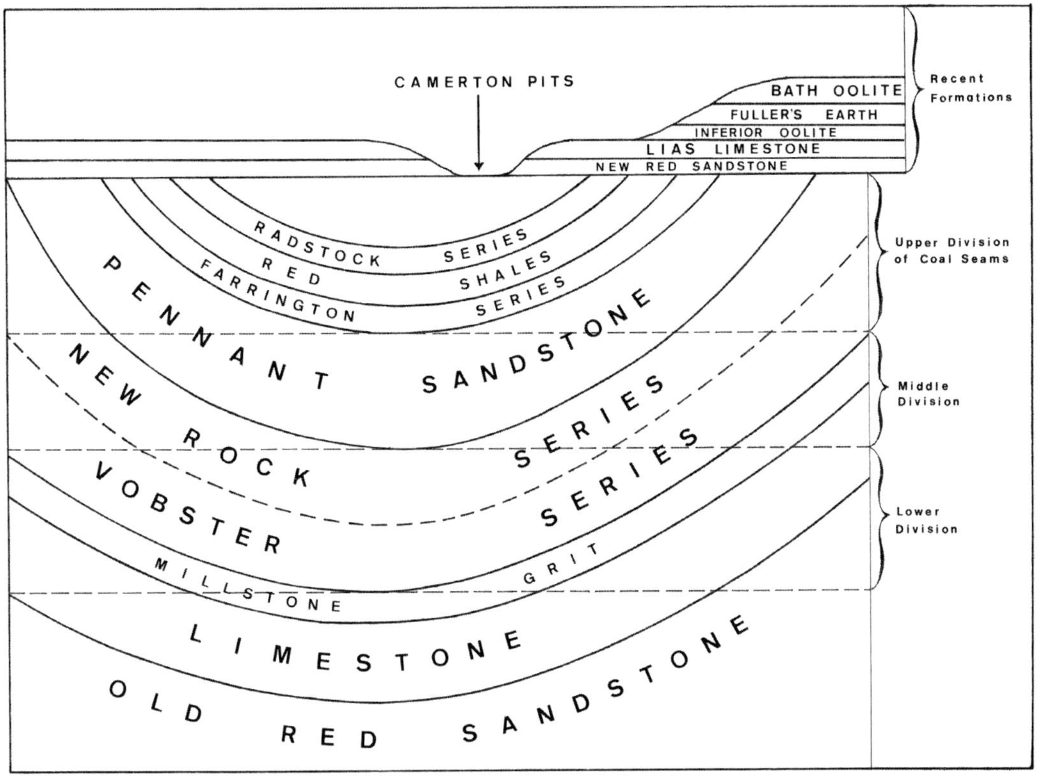

The Geological Strata of the North Somerset Coalfield.

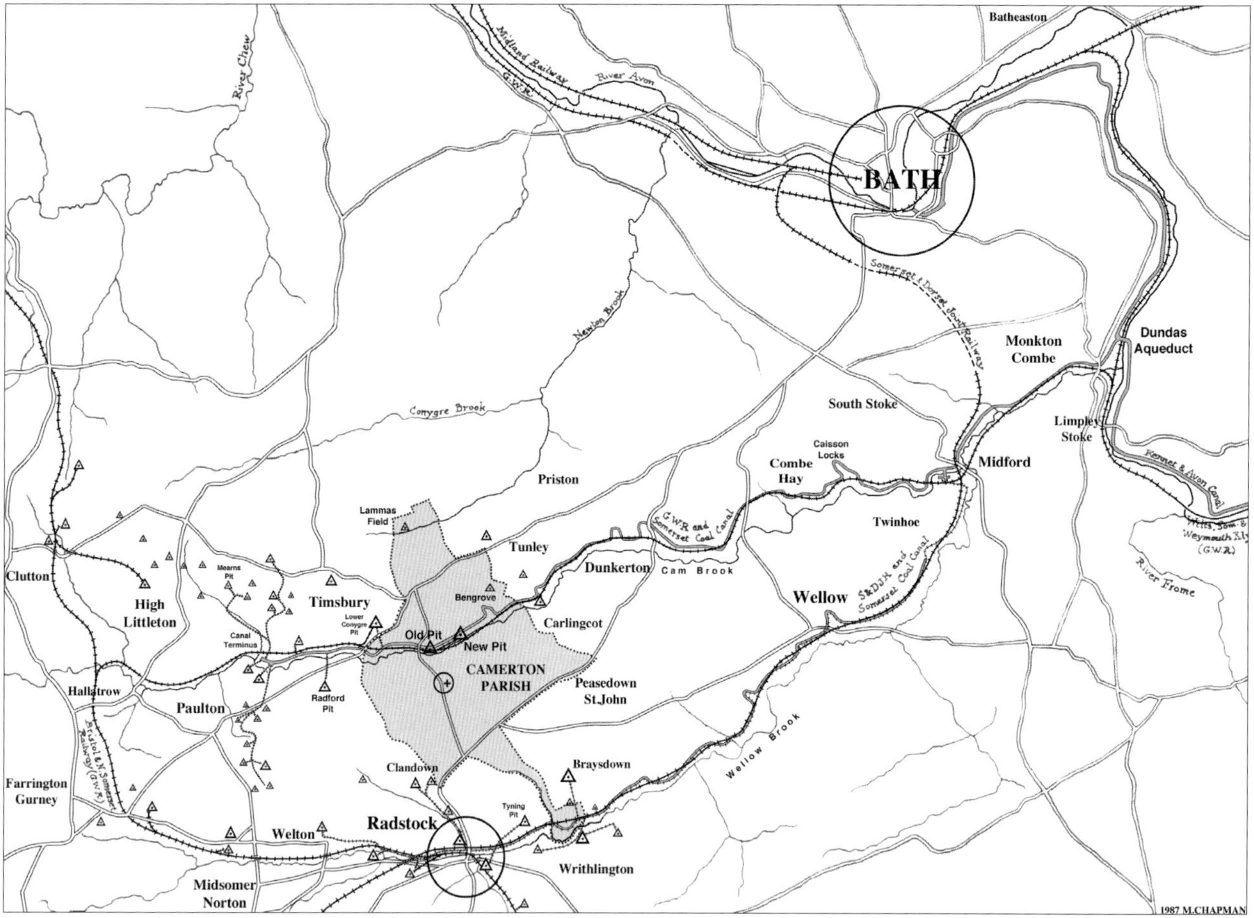

Map of the North Somerset Coalfield.

Somerset, there were real possibilities of meeting that demand. Furthermore, the coal owners were men of vision and enterprise. They were prepared to take risks to exploit the coal beneath their land and to look for the possibility of markets beyond their immediate area.

There were difficulties to overcome. The coalfield would prove to be one of the most contorted and faulted in the United Kingdom, the seams of coal being thin and rarely level, although mostly free from the dangers of firedamp. Mining here would call for different methods from other coalfields. The whole area is best understood as being distorted into the shape of a basin, tilted to the east, in which the seams of coal and rock form a series of layers which lie parallel to the shape of the bowl. This symmetrical model is, however, seriously disturbed by the faults and folds which have been caused by the northward movement of the Mendip Hills.

Only a small portion of the coal measures are exposed at the surface as outcrops, due to the covering of secondary limestone rocks, the Lias and Oolite, which lie above the coal measures. The seams themselves fall into three distinct groups separated by beds of unproductive sandstones and shales, but only the Upper Coal Group was mined at Camerton at the northern eastern edge of the coalfield. This group contains two well-known series of coal-bearing rocks, the first, known as the Radstock series being worked at Camerton, known as the 'Camerton' series by the local miners. Lying between 500-700 feet below the surface, it forms a layer about 13½ feet thick containing six veins which vary in thickness from 9ins to 2ft 4ins, each known by its own local name. The coal from the Radstock series was known to burn clearly and brightly, giving out a good heat and leaving little ash, useful for household purposes. Camerton was the last pit in Somerset to bring coal to the surface from this series.

As a result of the difficulties caused by the coalfield being heavily faulted the introduction of underground machinery and other improvements was often delayed although, for the same reason, Somerset miners were regarded as the most skilful and resourceful in the country. This is well illustrated by the comments made by William Smith in his correspondence in 1804, included below. Consequently, extraction became increasingly uneconomic during the early 20th century, even though it has been estimated that some four thousand million tons of coal still remain untapped in the Somerset coalfield. Nevertheless, the vision, determination and exploration of the strata came together to enable this coalfield with character to be mined for almost two hundred years.

Notes to the Introduction

Further Reading

'Rambles to Camerton' Dennis Chedgy and Dick Graham in *Five Arches, The Journal of the Radstock, Midsomer Norton & District Museum Society* Issue 12, 1991 (Hereafter *Five Arches*)

The seams or 'veins' in the Camerton (Radstock) Series

Great
Top Little
Middle Little
Slyving or Slyven
Under Little Seam New or Little Under
Bull Seam –hardly known at Old Pit

Letters to and from William Smith

On 26th December 1804 Thomas Walters Esqr, of Batheaston, writing to Wm Smith about the Colliery at Batheaston, referred to 'Joseph Rose, our present Foreman, who you probably remember at the Camerton & Newton Works, & I dare say is pretty accurate [regarding the exact depths of the Batheaston Colliery].' Joseph Rose is listed as one of the shareholders at Camerton Colliery in 1781. In his reply on 31st December 1804 Smith stated that:

> '... Few Collieries can now be carried on without a Steam Engine and the additional draught from a deep Pit is not of much consequence to Such Machinery. Nor is there any more Expense in getting Coal in a deep Pit than a shallow one. The Expense of filling or Emptying the Buckets &c &c is all the same & I have observed that deep Pits are generally freer from Water'.

Smith continued by emphasising the abilities of the Somerset miners who had to work such difficult seams of coal:

> 'And one of your most intelligent Colliers in the Country agrees with me in opining that "the Coal which may be found farther in the deep" (as you are) will lye much Flatter than it does where it is now working. Radford [adjacent to Camerton in the adjoining parish of Paulton] is the deepest Pit in Your Neighbourhood & there the Coal lies nearly level.
>
> I am glad you have got a Foreman who has been used to the sinkings of the Country for I have not seen many places where they manage these matters as well as in Somersetshire, & Rose has had as much Experience as any man in the Country ...'.

Smith MS, Oxford University

CHAPTER ONE

MINING IN SOMERSET BEFORE 1790

Coal has been mined in the northern part of Somerset since the time of the Roman occupation of these islands. Traces of coal were found by the Rev. John Skinner[1] Rector of Camerton, when he excavated the Romano-British site nearby on the Fosse Way, at the beginning of the 19th century. It is probable that the coal would have been used for the smelting of lead, which had been brought from the Mendips, and tin to make pewter. The remains of a substantial industry dating from the third century, including a coal store, were found at the smelting site during the extensive excavations carried out by the archaeologist William Wedlake[2] in the 1950s. The source of the coal cannot be determined with accuracy. The Roman historian Solinus[3], writing in the third century, mentioned that coal was used in the Temple in Bath where it was burned on the altar of the Goddess Sul Minerva. Some geologists believe that the Romans may have used drifts or shafts to obtain the coal and not merely outcrops.[4]

Early Mining in the Area

There is little evidence of the development of mining in the area during the next thousand years but by the 14th century mining had started in Somerset. These were shallow or open cast workings on land rented from the owner. The earliest date known for this is 1305[5] and it is believed that for the next three hundred years much the same methods would have been used locally to win coal. The earliest mining in North Somerset probably relied on drifts or sloping passageways into the coal deposits. They had the added advantage that they would also drain the workings as adits. Later, shallow shafts were

The Camerton area as shown on the border of Benjamin Donne's *Map of the Country Eleven Miles around the City of Bristol*, 1769, just before the 18th century expansion of coal mining in the Cam valley. Although many details are only sketched in, the mines around Paulton are included (indicated by triangles surrounded with fragments), particularly at Paulton Engine Pit where the two Newcomen Engines are also shown. The names Stephens and Palmer, later to have considerable influence, have already appeared.

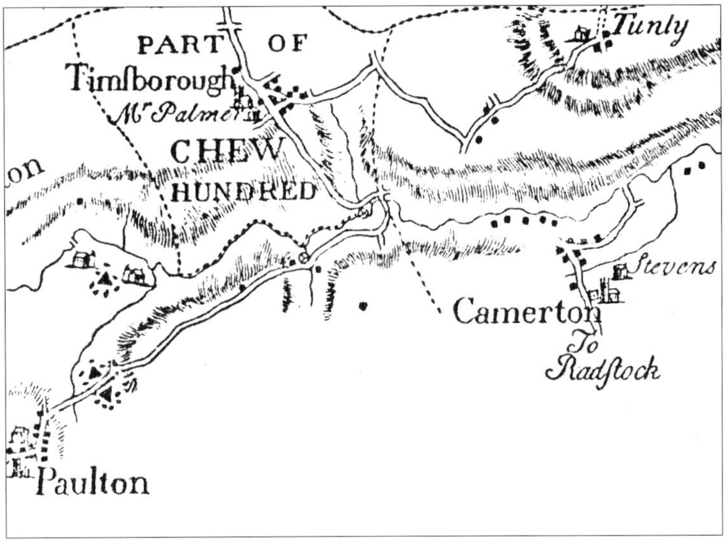

probably sunk, and the coal, carried in a wicker basket or corve, was winched up the shaft, by men or boys using a windlass.

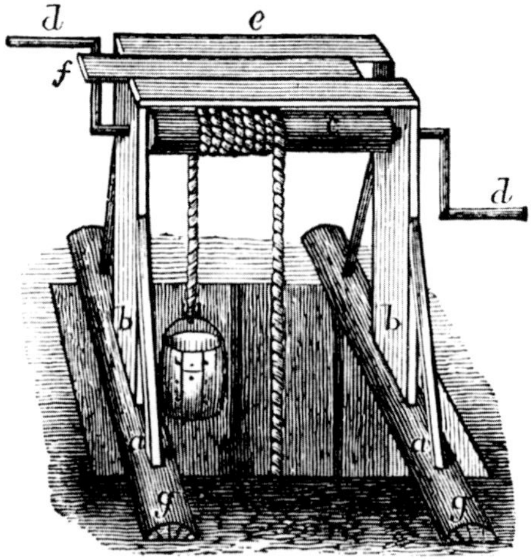

An early mining windlass.

By the year 1437 the pit at Kilmersdon, near Radstock, was deep enough to have an adit or drainage channel, and surveying to determine the extent of the underlying coal was done by sinking adjacent pits.[6] Six years later serious coal mining started at Stratton-on-the-Fosse.[7] Coal mined at Timsbury by the 16th century[8] was finding a good market in Bath and coal from the area was also being used in Wells by 1590.[9]

A good picture of the great activity in the mining parishes of this area is contained in the *Victoria History of the Counties of England.* During the 17th century shafts were already being introduced to reach the coal and men were recruited from among the former lead miners of Mendip whose industry had come to an end. These men introduced their own nomenclature, e.g. a 'batch' for a pile of dirt or spoil from the workings, and 'veins' instead of seams. Coalface workers were known as 'breakers' and they worked by 'turn' or 'tasks'. They would cut into the seams with a mattock and break very large pieces of coal away with a wedge. The corve was replaced later by the wreath cart. This consisted of a circular wooden base about two feet in diameter around which a number of vertical iron rods, about two feet in length, were bolted. These were then interwoven with hazel rods and at the top the metal rods were joined by an iron ring, to which the winding rope was attached.[10] This implies that wooden rails were being introduced underground, so that the corves could be put on a carriage or cart to take them to the bottom of the shaft. More sophisticated methods were being introduced to bring the coal to the surface using a horse gin or drum under the direction of boys. The buildings and works around a mineshaft would be situated on a raised platform consisting of coal shale and material from the sinking. This was known as the heapstead and it avoided lifting the coal twice into wagons at that time.

A corve or wreath-cart.

A two-horse coal-winding 'whim gin' or drum, operating sheaves over a shaft (right), as illustrated in W.Pyne's *Rustic Vignettes for Artists and Craftsmen*, 1808. Note the size of the coal in the foreground.

A contemporary account states:

> 'They usually or always sink one pit first; when the air is bad they sink another pit about six yards distant on the same course as near as can, and cut a lane of communication from one pit to another, to give air, or else, when one pit is sinking they put down trunks, and make a trunk-hole to let the air to the nose of the shides or pipes, and so carry the air into the lane. About Midsummer the air is usually bad when the hedges are full of leaves, then they sink an iron grate about ten yards into the pit with burning coals, which draws the stenched or stagnated air from the bottom and lane.' [11]

Despite the serious problems posed by ventilation, it appears that true underground working for coal started about this time.[12] In the manuscript 'Observations on Coalworks' by James Twyford, in the Ammerdown Collection, he advised owners of coal-bearing land to adventure for coal on their own account and to get a skilled collier as a manager.[13] Water mills were also being used to pump water from

Operation of a mine pump by water wheel, crank and beam.

A water-driven pump engine in use in the 1840s in the north of England.

the workings by 1610;[14] there was one at Timsbury by 1697.[15] One of these mills is described in 1700: 'Paulton Wheel at Mr.Brewers' works draws about 17 fathoms deep. The wheel, of 8 feet diameter, 3 feet broad with two cranks, water troughs 20 inches broad, 10 inches deep.'[16] The spread of new techniques in mining led eventually to the use of steam power for drainage from the pits, resulting in more efficient production.

The Mid 18th century Increase in Output

After 1750 coal mining began to expand in this area for a number of reasons.[17] First, the population was growing, due partly to natural increase but also to new pits attracting labour from the agricultural sector and the declining woollen industry. This growth, which was to be found in rural areas as well as cities, produced a greater demand for coal. Between the years 1750 and 1800 the growth of population in this area was above the natural increase common in the rest of Britain. The parish records at Camerton show that there were sixty baptisms between 1751 and 1758, while a few years later the number has risen to seventy five in the period from 1775 to 1781.[18]

Second, coal was being increasingly used to fire lime kilns and for the growing needs other industries. The collieries themselves consumed greater amounts with the increasing use of steam power for pumping. In 1698 Thomas Savery (1650-1715) invented a type of steam engine which was suitable for pumping water from mines. It was the beginning of the application of steam to the problems of drainage and winding in the coal pits. Some fourteen years later, in 1712, Thomas Newcomen (1736-1819) built an engine with a piston and cylinder. Steam from the boiler was admitted beneath a piston in a vertical cylinder. When cold water was squirted into the cylinder it condensed the steam and caused a reduction in the pressure. This enabled the atmospheric pressure outside to force the piston down again. The Newcomen engines were widely used in mines throughout the country from about 1720 until 1800, but, like Savery's engine, they were inefficient, wasting a lot of steam and a great deal of coal.[19]

The first atmospheric Newcomen pumping engine in this area was introduced at Paulton Engine Pit in 1738, and although it is impossible to say how many steam engines were at work in the Somerset coalfield by the end of the 18th century, it is evident they were already becoming a familiar feature.[20] As the century progressed, however, improvements to the Newcomen Engine were already being introduced. In 1763, when mending a Newcomen Engine, James Watt noticed the waste of steam caused by alternately heating and cooling the cylinder. He therefore improved the basic design by cooling the steam in a separate condenser and put a steam jacket around the cylinder.[21] His more efficient design, patented in 1769, provided a much greater impetus to the use of steam power, and engines erected at the end of the century in Somerset would have been of this type. While the transport of coal from the pits was to be dependent on horse power for many years to come, the use of the horse at the pit head was becoming less important as the 18th century drew to a close. The horse gin had been the main aid for winding the coal to the surface and for lifting and lowering the miners to the pit bottom, but the age of steam was about to change this picture significantly.

Principal features of the Newcomen Engine.

Third, there were improved road and river communications. Once the coal had been brought to the surface there was the problem of transportation to the markets. In the early days the condition of the local roads was so poor that most coal could only be taken, at great expense, to nearby markets by pack-horses. The maximum load possible was about two and a half hundredweights.

Improvements had begun with the passing of Turnpike Acts in 1621 and 1662, and in 1707-08 the Bath Turnpike Trust was established with the result that over the next fifty years all the main roads around and out of Bath were turnpiked.[22]

A pack-horse train.

Such was the improvement that a single horse could now pull a load of ten hundredweights instead of the previous two and a half.[23] These Acts banned the more damaging waggons from the roads by setting weight limits and stipulating the width of tread on the wheels and the number of horses in draught. The Act of 1662 had set the maximum weight that waggons could carry as twenty hundredweights in winter and thirty in summer.[24] The Act of 1719 restricted the minimum tread to two and a half inches and that of 1741 exempted waggons from this provision during the summer months. The maximum load that was now permissible was fixed at sixty hundredweights, three tons, and in order to make sure that this was enforced the Trustees were empowered to erect weighing machines and to charge twenty shillings for every hundredweight over the prescribed limit.[25] All these improvements would have contributed to the cheaper transportation of coal into the expanding markets in Bath and Wells.

The coal trade now put a severe strain on the road surfaces, however, and there were frequent complaints about the damage caused by the constant stream of horses and coal carts. The coal trade was the principal user of the local roads during this period. The miners themselves were often resentful of the tolls charged and yet it was this traffic which was responsible for the appalling state of the roads that led to the pits.[26] In the Bristol area the miners actually delayed the provision of adequate roads by their hostility and were powerful enough to ensure that the Trusts granted them special rates for the carriage of coal.[27] The Act of 1727 gives the tolls that were charged on the Bristol Turnpike as: 'A packhorse 1d, but with coals 1/2d'. Under the Act of 1749 coal carts were exempted, no doubt as a result of the prolonged hostility of the colliers.[28] The Turnpike Trusts did what they could to increase their revenue, often moving the toll gates to sites where they could tap as much of the coal traffic as possible as it entered the system, so ensuring the maximum income possible from these elusive customers.[29]

During 1750-1760 the local Turnpike Trustees had been active, improving the road at Dunkerton, which was the eastern outlet for much of the coal from the area, the main gate controlling this road being at the Burnt House, Odd Down near Bath.[30] By this time the coal masters had come to realise that money spent on road repair and maintenance was well spent. It is known that the Timsbury proprietors made frequent payments towards the upkeep of the Timsbury to Bath road via Tunley, but, of course, these improvements resulted in land carriage becoming more expensive due to the increase in the tolls.[31] In May of 1789 a letter appeared in the *Bath Chronicle* signed by various coal proprietors, among them those at Camerton, in which they opposed the increase of tolls as this was pushing up the price of coal to their customers.[32] This was to be one of the factors which was to lead to the movement towards the establishing of a coal canal which, it was believed, would better serve the coal owners and their customers in Bath and later markets further to the east in Wiltshire and beyond.

The fourth factor that contributed to the expansion of the industry was greater investment and organisation among the wealthier partnerships of coal masters. Before 1750 most mines were small enterprises but after that date there was increasing co-operation between the coal owners and partnerships became more common. In 1787, when John Collinson was writing his *History of Somerset* he commented that the Manor at Camerton had been sold by Thomas Carew to Philip Stephens, who had bought the Camerton estate in 1750 'for the purpose of winning coal,'[33] although it was his son James who actually started the mining. 'In the valley at RODFORD [*sic*] is a coal-mine belonging to the said James Stephens, esq; and other gentlemen, which has been worked for some years with much success.'[34] Furthermore, the coal masters played their own part in the distribution of the coal which was now of a larger size and greater quantity, by using their own or hired waggons. In 1792 they combined to

A Bath Turnpike Trust boundary post (left) which stood next to the Burnt House turnpike gate on Odd Down. The original gate, until c.1810, was situated on the old road below the trees on the right.

raise the price of coal, as by this time they felt they had a secure market for their saleable coal.[35]

Another result of investment was the search for new reserves of coal, particularly on the eastern edge of the coalfield:

> 'The possible existence of coal beneath the surface rocks of the Radstock-Camerton area had long been a matter of speculation, although discounted by most local miners. One old collier is quoted as having said '...if ever coal was found in Radstock he would get on the top of Norton tower and flee down'. The discovery of coal in the upper series at Radstock with the sinking of Old Pit there in 1763 marked an important break-through in the development of the coalfield. It was followed by a rapid extension of mining activity in the valleys of north Somerset, particularly in the valleys of the Cam and Wellow brooks.'[36]

It was about this time that various pits were sunk which later became closely associated with the Camerton coalworks, although these did not last for long. The opening of Bengrove Pit above Bengrove Wood in Camerton, dates from this period, as also another at Lammas Field in the northern part of the parish.

Mining starts at Camerton

The significant year for Camerton was 1781, because on the 13th November the lease for coalmining was granted by James Stephens of the manor at Camerton for the sinking of Camerton 'Upper' Coalworks, or Camerton 'Old' Pit. The original shareholders were James Stephens himself, Zachary Bailey (a banker) and Peter Fry, with lesser shares being held by Thomas Tyley, Moses Reynolds and Joseph Rose.[37]

The first compound steam engine erected by Hornblower and Winwood at Radstock in 1781-2, as illustrated in Rees's *Cyclopaedia*, 1797.

It was also in that year, coincidentally, that a completely new design of steam pumping engine made its first appearance in the Somerset coalfield, at Middle Pit in Radstock.[38] This was designed by Jonathan Hornblower, a Cornish engineer, and was the first to use the expansive power of steam, together with the ability to extract further energy in a second cylinder, and known as a compound steam engine. It was reported in April 1785 that James Stephens was about to erect an engine at Camerton, but, with his neighbours, '... the Gentlemen will not let Hornblower put them up', probably in anticipation of legal action from Boulton and Watt who considered Hornblower to have infringed their patent.[39] Although the informant suggested to Boulton and Watt that they might have more success in obtaining the contract, Stephens was probably not in a hurry, as he seems to have already installed a water wheel. However, there is every indication that a steam pumping engine was installed at Old Pit at an early stage.

John Wesley, who was a frequent visitor to these parts in the latter half of the 18th century, was more concerned with the hewers of coal and their families than the latest developments in coalmining. He visited Paulton, possibly for the first time, in January 1747 and was there again in April 1750. When he came in September 1776 he wrote in his Journal 'I preached in the new house at Paulton to a plain, simple, loving people...' From 1778 he was back in the area in the autumn of every year, save for a few exceptions, until 1788. In March 1779 he recorded 'At Paulton ... the liveliest people in all the circuit. This people are now just of the same spirit as those of Bristol were forty years ago'. He was obviously pleased with the results of the work that had been done in this area over the years. When he preached at Midsomer Norton in 1789, two years before his death, he wrote in his Journal of the 16th September 'I never saw the church so full before. In the evening I preached to the honest, earnest colliers at Coleford, most of whom attended again at five in the morning.'[40]

Notes to Chapter One

Further Reading

Stephen Clewes, *Roman Life in North East Somerset, Five Arches*, Issue 25, 1996.

Population Growth

Population Growth in North Somerset 1701-1800, Five Arches, Issue 5, 1987.

Measures and Units

Twenty hundredweights (cwts) = one ton
One bushel = eight gallons = approx 80lbs of coal
One quarter = 8 bushels
8 bushels = $^1/_4$cwt = 28lbs
One fathom = six feet, approximately two metres
One hogshead= 52.5 imperial gallons

The Savery Engine

Savery's 'fire engine', as it was called, was based on the principle that when steam is cooled it condenses. In his engine steam was admitted into an egg-shaped vessel which was then cooled with water. The partial vacuum thus created, together with the air pressure outside, forced water, for example from the bottom of the mine, into the vessel. This water was then expelled by the admission of more steam which blew the water out into the waste system. It was the beginning of a mechanical pumping method which would be developed throughout the 18th century.
Children's Britannica, Encyclopaedia Britannica International Ltd. Volume 17, 1970.

The Newcomen Engine

> 'A pit called Brewer's Pit at Paulton was in existence c.1700, when it was about 100 ft deep and using an eight-ft wheel for drainage. It may have been the same pit which in 1736 was being worked by a partnership of Elizabeth Brewer of Winchester, Robert Houlton of Trowbridge, and Richard Hewish, clothier and Joseph Hill and Jacob Carter, coal miners, all of Paulton. They took a lease of water-rights in Littleton Brook, but water-power probably proved insufficient, for two years later a 21$^1/_2$-in cylinder was cast at Coalbrookdale for Hewish and Co. of 'Polton'. Dr Mott assigned this tentatively to Polton, Midlothian, but there can be no doubt that the reference was to Paulton.'

K.H. Rogers, *The Newcomen Engine in the West of England*, 1976.

The Compound Engine

In the compound steam engine the exhaust steam from a small high pressure cylinder is made to do further work by admitting it to another larger low pressure cylinder. This second cylinder has to be larger than the first to ensure that the thrust produced in each cylinder is the same as both pistons are connected to the same shaft driving the machinery. In other words, the amount of energy, and hence its capacity to do work, in the high pressure steam has to be balanced by a greater amount of steam at low pressure to have the same amount of energy, and so achieve equal thrusts from each cylinder.

It is quite possible that the principle of the compound engine was first put forward by Hornblower in a patent of 1781. 'The patentee says:

1. I use two vessels, in which the steam is to act, and which in other steam-engines are generally called cylinders.
2. I employ the steam after it has acted in the first vessel, to operate a second time in the other, by permitting it to expand itself, which I do by connecting the vessels together, and forming proper channels and apertures, whereby the steam shall occasionally go in a out of the said vessels.
3. I condense the steam by causing it to pass in contact with metalline surfaces while water is applied to the opposite side.'

T.M. Goodeve, *Textbook on the Steam Engine and on Gas Engines*, 1888.

Philip and James Stephens

Philip Stephens appears to have been the son of a wealthy and eminent London physician, from whom he acquired a 'scientific' education and an interest in agricultural improvement, becoming one of the founder members of the Bath and West Society in Bath in 1777. Although he is said to have purchased Camerton manor in 1750 'for the purpose of winning coal', he appears to have spent his time establishing himself as a local dignitary, becoming Sheriff of Somerset in 1758, and leaving his son James to develop the coal interests of the Camerton estate. He died in 1781, the year Camerton Old Pit was opened by James (1748-1816) who continued to maintain an interest in scientific improvement. In 1784 James became an honorary member of the Society for Promoting Natural History in London (founded 1782) to whom he sent geological specimens, and it was through his contact with Billingsley and other eminent 'improvers' in Wiltshire that he was among the first to recognise William Smith's ideas, employing him to put his knowledge of drainage into practice on his own estates at Camerton in 1786. In Smith's words:

> '.. drained a piece of clayey and stony ground, which was levelled by James Stephens Esq. in his park at Camerton, on whose estates I first put into practice my ideas of draining derived from a knowledge of the strata, … by moving the soil and laying the sod on again'.

Like his father, James also was a well respected figure in Somerset, becoming Sheriff in 1786, but was perhaps more important for the leading role he played in the building of the Somersetshire Coal Canal as Chairman of the Management Committee from 1794.

See Hugh Torrens, 'Geological Communication in the Bath Area in the last half of the 18th century', *Images of the Earth, essays in the history of the environmental sciences*, British Society for the History of Science 1978;

and 'The water-related work of William Smith', *200 Years of British Hydrogeology* (ed. J.D. Mather), Geological Society Special Publication, 225, pp.15-30, 2004.

Jonathan Hornblower 1753-1815

Although from Penrhyn, Cornwall, Hornblower seems to have chosen the North Somerset Coalfield to launch his engine partly for the ready availability of coal, but mainly through his business connection with the Winwood family who produced the engine parts at their iron foundry in Bristol. Although not taken up in Somerset, the Hornblower engine received greater success in Cornwall, where the

compound engine made an important contribution to the perfection of the Cornish beam engine.
Hugh Torrens, 'Winwoods of Bristol Part 1, 1767-1788', *Bristol Industrial Archaeological Journal* Vol.13, pp.9-17, 1980.

John Wesley 1703-1791
Wesley identified with ordinary people who were untouched by the more formal rules, regulations and worship of the Church of England. Finding the churches closed to him he began field-preaching to the Kingswood colliers in 1739. As a result of his methods he was forbidden from preaching in the churches and did so in the fields and on the moors.

Wesley was a man of the greatest courage and persistence, with a vast capacity for leadership and organisation. His personality was magnetic, his piety and charity uncontestable. Common people could understand his approach and message. He had great sympathy for the poor, depressed and hopeless. His mission coincided with the start of the Industrial Revolution when those who moved into new factory towns often experienced dreadful conditions in housing and at work. Much the same situation would have existed in the growing mining communities of North Somerset.
Adapted from F.L. Cross, *The Oxford Dictionary of the Christian Church*, 1961
See also Dr.R.C. Chillcott, 'John Wesley and North Somerset', *Five Arches*, Part 1, Issue 13; Part 2, Issue 14, 1992.

The Burnt House Turnpike Gate, Odd Down
This was located on Bloomfield Road (then the main Wells Road on the south side of Bath) at the junction of Old Fosse Road, until the new Wellsway (A367) became the main road in c.1810. It was then moved to the corner of the new road where it could control both roads.

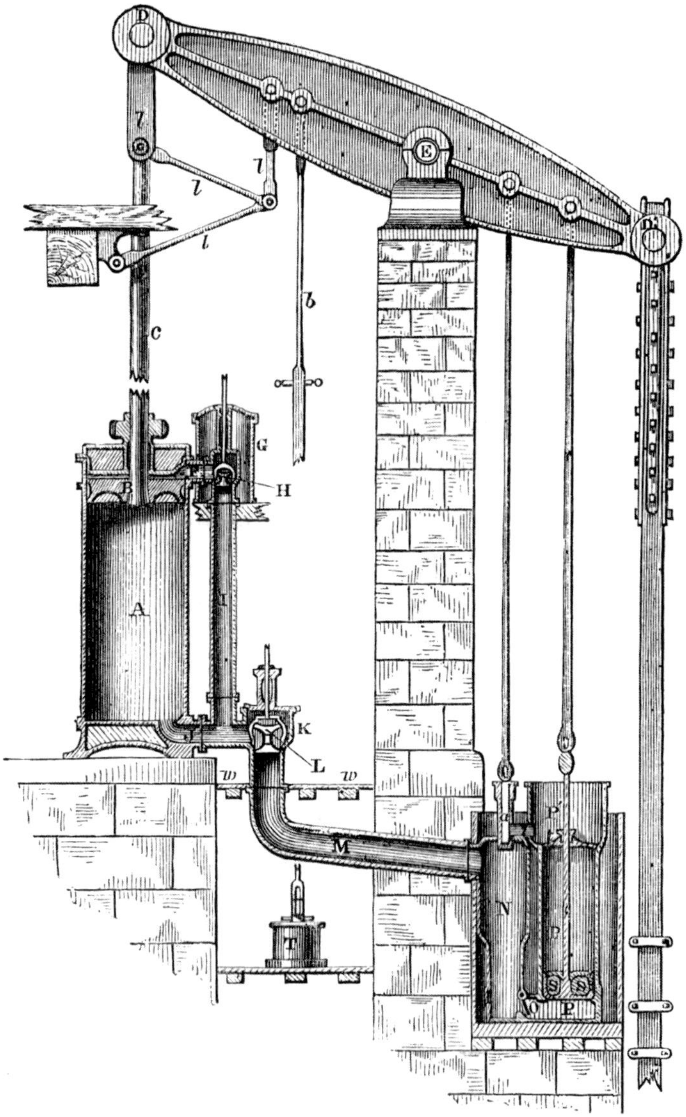

Fig. 67.—ELEVATION (part sectional) of a CORNISH PUMPING ENGINE

Principal features of the Cornish pumping engine which eventually became standard in mining.

Camerton Shareholders

The original shares in 1781 were allocated as follows:

James Stephens*	5/22
Zachary Bailey	8/22
Peter Fry	5/22
Thomas Tyley	2/22
Moses Reynolds	1/22
Joseph Rose	1/22

* who also received a freeshare of 1/8 as the lessor.

Down & Warrington *op.cit.* p.113

Old Pits adjacent to Camerton

Radford Pit

This colliery, on the eastern boundary of Paulton, was the nearest large pit adjoining Camerton, and appears to have opened about the same time. Radford is included, for example, among the collieries that agreed to the regulation of miners' wages in 1792, and is still marked as 'Radford New Coal Work' on John Rennie's plan of the proposed Coal Canal of 1793. Besides James Stephens, the shareholders of the 'Radford Coal Company' are unknown, but likely to be the same as at Camerton. As Collinson states, it was a successful venture, and was linked to the Coal Canal by a tramroad in 1799, but by the 1840s was exhausted, the equipment being sold by auction in 1853.

Bengrove Pit, also known as Cuckoo Pit.

By the time the two pits were sunk at Camerton, other pits nearby had already been opened. Although close to the Camerton Pits, Bengrove pit above Bengrove Wood actually lay just over the boundary in the manor of Dunkerton which, in the late 18th century, belonged to Sir Richard Warwick Bampfylde, bart. It was therefore known simply as 'Dunkerton Coalworks', run by the Dunkerton Coal Company. According to the Radstock Notebooks it was sunk in 1764-65, but about 1792 a second shaft was opened a few hundred yards further east called 'Dunkerton New Coalwork', mentioned in the *Bath Herald* of 2nd June. A plan of the proposed Somersetshire Coal Canal shows that both were intended to be connected to the canal by a tramway, but this did not occur. Modified plans of the canal show that by 1809 the 'new' works had closed and that Bengrove had road access instead to Tunley via Stone Edge Lane. An advertisement in 1819 for the sale of the engine house belonging to the pit in the valley below suggests that the pumping had ceased by then and that the mine was no longer in use. Presumably the mine would have filled with water from hereon, which may

A watercolour sketch by the Rev. John Skinner of the ruined pumping engine house belonging to Bengrove Pit in Dunkerton, abandoned in 1819. *Rev.D.E. Cooper*

The Old Down Inn, Chilcompton, with 8-horse power heavy goods vehicle. The inn was a popular venue for business meetings in the North Somerset Coalfield.

explain Anstie's statement that the closure was caused by flooding. A group of miners' cottages nearby remained inhabited until demolished in the late 20th century, and an 'airshaft' on the site today suggests that the workings may have been reopened for ventilation. No explanation has so far been found as to why it was known as Cuckoo Pit.

When the pumping engine to drain Bengrove Pit at Hopyard became redundant by 1819, the engine house at Hay Meadow was put up for sale along with some workshops in Wick Lane which had been converted to cottages. The abandoned engine house is illustrated in one of John Skinner's watercolour sketches, but appears to have been completely demolished, although the cottages still exist. *Bath Chronicle*, 3 June 1819.

Lammasfield

Lammasfield is an area on the north side of Camerton which originated as a freehold property belonging to the manor of Priston, but became associated with the parish of Camerton at the end of the middle ages. In 1757 the manor of Priston was purchased by William Jenkins, a commissioner of HM victualling office, who carried out exploration for coal throughout the manor in 1764 with some success, presumably at Lammasfield. Jenkins died in 1774, and his daughter and her husband, William Davies (also a victualling agent) sold off Lammasfield soon after. It is not clear who the purchaser was, but the pit at Lammasfield is one of those named in August 1792 in the agreement drawn up at the Old Down Inn that month between the coal owners and the miners. The estate was again put up for sale in 1804, and was evidently considered to be worth developing. A freehold estate there was offered 'all in a ring fence, and well worth the attention of a person desirous of entering on the Coal-Mine Concern, as there is already a Pit sunk, which has produced the finest kind of coal in that neighbourhood. Further details from Mr. Tiley on the premises.' Thomas Tiley is listed as one of the original shareholders at Camerton in 1781. However nothing further is heard of it.

References to Chapter One

1. W.J. Wedlake, *Excavations at Camerton*, Camerton Excavation Club, 1958, p.82f.
2. *Ibid.*, p.94f.
3. C.G. Down & A.J. Warrington, *The History of the Somerset Coalfield*, David & Charles 1970, p.16.
4. H.K. Bluhm, *A Bibliography of the Somerset Coalfield*, Library Association 1968, p.9f.
5. A.W. Coysh, E. Mason & V. Waite, *The Mendips*, Robert Hale 1971, p.208.
6. J. Bulley, 'To Mendip for Coal', *Journal of the Somerset Archaeological and Natural History Society* 1952-53, I, p.61f.
7. Bluhm, *op.cit.*, p.9.
8. *Victoria History of the Counties of England: Somerset*, Volume II, Oxford University Press 1911,

p.382.

9. Bluhm, *op.cit.*, p.9.
10. *Victoria History*, *op.cit.*, pp.379-388.
11. Coysh, *op.cit.*, p.209.
12. *Ibid.*, p.208.
13. *Ibid.*, p.209.
14. Bulley, *op.cit.*, p.70.
15. Bluhm, *op.cit.*, p.173.
16. Coysh, *op.cit.*, p.209
17. Bulley, *op.cit.*, p.55f. and note to author from Penny Bonsall.
18. J. Collinson, *The History of Somersetshire*, 1791, Camerton Parish entry.
19. *Children's Britannica*, Encyclopaedia Britannica International Ltd. 1970, Volume 17 p.5.
20. R.K. Bluhm, 'The Somerset Coalfield 1790-1820', *A Second North Somerset Miscellany*, 1971, Bath and Camerton Archaeological Society, p.57.
21. *Children's Britannica op.cit.*
22. R.W. Dunning, *A History of Somerset*, Somerset County Library, 1978, p.80f.
23. Coysh, *op.cit.*, p.210.
24. W. Albert, *The Turnpike Road System in England 1663-1840*, Cambridge University Press 1972, p.133f.
25. Albert, *op.cit.*, p.133.
26. R. Atthill, *Old Mendip*, David & Charles 1971, p.120.
27. *Ibid.*, p.126.
28. *Ibid.*, p.121.
29. *Ibid.*, p.127.
30. *Ibid.*, p.131.
31. Bulley, *op.cit.*, p.54f.
32. *Ibid.*
33. W.J. Wedlake, 'Tithe Disputes at Camerton, Somerset, 1800-1839', *A Second North Somerset Miscellany, op.cit.*, p.37.
34. Collinson *op.cit.*
35. Bulley, *op.cit.*, p.58f.
36. A. Buchanan & N. Cossons, *Industrial Archaeology of the Bristol Region*, David & Charles 1969, p.78.
37. Down & Warrington *op.cit* p.113.
38. *Ibid.*, p.161.
39. Hugh Torrens, 'Winwoods of Bristol Part 1, 1767-1788', *Bristol Industrial Archaeological Journal* Vol.13, 1980, pp.9-17.
40. John Wesley, *The Journals of the Revd. John Wesley*, edition 1909-1916.

CHAPTER TWO

STEAM WINDING AND A NEW CANAL FOR COAL 1790-1800

One of the greatest periods in the history of the Somerset coal industry began about 1790. During the next forty years the coalfield was of greater relative importance in the national economy than at any other period. This success was in no small way due to the initiative of the local coal owners and gentry who introduced new technology in the pits and pioneered and promoted their own canal to carry the coal to the most important markets.[1]

Steam Winding comes to Somerset

By this time the coal workings in Somerset were among the deepest in the country, and although methods of pumping were sufficient to cope with the drainage, raising the coal to the surface became increasingly slower and more difficult. It was fortunate therefore that steam power for winding, then still at an experimental stage, was introduced, and new pits opened up, just as the demand for coal

An early steam winding engine, c.1790. *Walker Art Gallery, Liverpool*

increased. During the summer of 1791, Samborne Palmer and Jacob Mogg, partners in the Timsbury Collieries, travelled to Coalbrookdale to inspect steam winding engines in operation there and to enquire the price of engine castings.[2] In the following spring the first steam winding engine in Somerset duly appeared at the newly-opened Conygre Pit in Timsbury, as reported in March 1792 by the *Bath Herald*:

> 'It is with pleasure we announce to the public, that the late complaints of the scarcity of Coal, are now done away, by the opening of a new coal-work in the parish of Timsbury, whence 75 quarters, or above 12 waggon load of coal, are daily brought to market, in addition to the former quantity raised in the neighbourhood. By the ingenuity of the engineer, a new application of the power of steam has been invented, by which, at this new work, two bushels of coal are raised to the mouth of the pit from a depth of ninety fathoms, in a minute and forty-five seconds. Notwithstanding the great powers of this steam engine, they may be wholly suspended by a boy in less than three seconds, for as long a time as may be thought proper; and in the same space may be made to recommence their operations, only by the turn of a small wheel. From the great superiority of this discovery, to the common method of raising coal with horses, both as to œconomy and expedition, it may be fairly presumed, that its use will soon become very general, for the savings are not less than £40 per cent. and any given quantity of coal may be raised, and for any continuance in the same space of time, by increasing the powers of the engine.'

The newspaper also remarked on the increased population of Bath which was requiring more coal, noting that: '

> Within the last seven months new coal works have opened at Dunkerton and Timsbury. Each sent ten waggons per day. The demand was so great that the teams [of horses] were obliged to wait several hours before they could be supplied.'[3]

Only three months later, in June 1792, steam power for winding also came to Camerton, installed by James Stephens, Samborne Palmer's neighbour. The *Bath Herald* again carried the story:

> 'At Camerton a steam engine for raising the coal has been lately erected on the model of that at Timsbury but on a more improved plan. Fifteen baskets of Coal, each containing three bushels, are hourly raised to the mouth of the pit from a depth of one hundred and forty fathoms. The engineer, to whom the greatest praise is due for the discovery, will, in a few years, render the use of horses in coal works altogether unnecessary.'

The paper went on to call the steam engine 'an excellent invention'.[4]

Collaboration between Palmer and Stephens seems highly probable, as these two gentlemen were not only the first to introduce steam winding in the area, but were at the same time also leaders in the promotion of a coal canal. The winder at Camerton was probably at Old Pit, although by 1793 Stephens had opened a second shaft nearby known as Camerton Lower Coalworks or New Pit. Within a few years, John Billingsley of Ashwick near Oakhill, an authority on the economic resources of Somerset, was able to report that, in the northern sector of the coalfield, 'Coal is now working generally from seventy to eighty fathom in depth. In a few places deeper; and by a late introduction of machinery to raise it by the steam engine, a much greater depth of working will be obtained'.[5] In 1795 the *Herald* observed that there had been 'great progress of mechanics within the last twenty years in this kingdom and that proof of it can be seen at the Timsbury coal works where not ten years since, no more than one bushel of coal was brought to land at the same time, by the power then in use, which was that of horses: whereas at present, by the application of steam, not less than fourteen or fifteen bushels are landed with the same facility.'[6]

Another innovation, coinciding with the introduction of steam winding, was the use of the 'hudge'. Somerset pits were unusual in that their shafts were narrow, often being only four and a half feet in diameter and seldom over ten. This put severe limits on the capacity of the wreath carts, which were replaced with iron tubs or barrels known as hudges in about 1800. Initially they could only carry about three hundredweight of coal but when larger bores were introduced their capacity increased to over a ton. This method was to remain in use until the introduction of cages around 1850.[7]

The Guss & Crook.

As to the transport of men between the surface and pit bottom, this had first been by means of a rope and chain onto which they hung themselves so that they were described as looking like 'a string of onions'. One hand held on to the rope and the other fended off the walls of the shaft. Each miner would often have a boy sitting on his lap. It was known as the hooker system or 'man-riding', whereby the hook of the man's 'guss & crook' was attached to the chain enabling him to sit in the loop of the guss. Later this very dangerous method was replaced by a 'man-hudge' which was able to carry two or three men. The man-hudge resembled the coal hudge but had a roof and a hole in the side though which the miners entered. In some pits they were called 'hoppits'.[8] Shafts were the source of many accidents in the earlier days. People fell down them, others fell out of the hudge or the chain broke.

It was eventually the practice to have two shafts at each pit situated fairly close together. In the latter part of the 19th century these were required by law to be at least fifteen yards apart. In the early years the shafts had passing places so that the corves could pass each other.[9] They were nearly always brick-lined, although local Lias stone was sometimes used.[10] Fresh air from the surface reached the workings by way of the Downcast shaft, the presence of some water leaking down the inside of the shaft assisting the airflow. This was the shaft which was used to wind the coal and by which the miners reached the pit bottom. Stale air from underground returned to the surface by way of the Upcast shaft, being assisted by a furnace at some convenient point near the top or bottom of the shaft to draw the air from the workings. In most pits this shaft was also used for pumping. Underground the airflow was controlled by two common methods. One was the use of a hessian-type material called Brattice cloth in the form of sheets or curtains to block off the passageways and so divert or direct the flow of air. The other method was to use timber doors on the main roads, often opened and shut by young boys, perhaps their first job underground. They opened them for the passage of the carts and had to ensure that at all other times they were kept shut.[11]

The introduction of new technology must have stretched local finances considerably. Most of the collieries in this area were small and needed a fair concentration of capital, which was raised locally, and often within a small closed circle of the leading local families. Partnerships, rather than companies, were the rule and a favourite number for this was seven because royalty payments were often one eighth of the value of the coal raised. It made the calculations easier. In Somerset the common term for a royalty payment was "freeshare".[12] When the mines increased in size and activity, local tradesmen and professional men were still involved in partnerships. At Camerton in 1792 shares were held by Thomas Flower, a Timsbury carpenter, and James Flower, a Chilcompton apothecary. The proprietors always lived locally, usually no further away than Bath or Bristol.[13]

The Threat of Competition

These were the years of 'canal mania' in Britain, and it was in 1792, following the authorisation of the Monmouthshire Canal between Newport and Pontypool, that a visit was again made by some of the Somerset colliery owners, perhaps including Palmer, to view the situation there. They realised that there was a real threat of Welsh coal coming into Bath and Wiltshire at a cheaper price than that from Somerset, which they themselves were unable to reduce at the pithead.

> 'If, therefore, a canal would lower the price of carriage (which, on an average, amounts at Bath to five-sixths of the value at the pits, and at other places in proportion to the distance) the trade might be preserved ... but so serious were the apprehensions of the coal proprietors, as to the Bath trade, that, determined at all events to secure the supplying of Wiltshire, they resolved not to cut their canal direct from the collieries to Bath, but to join the Kennet and Avon Canal at Limpley Stoke that they might from Bath gain six or seven miles of the Pontypool coal in the Wiltshire market, and thus at least continue one branch of their former trade.' [14]

However it was soon realised that what was feared by the coal owners 'will in all probability turn out a source of an extended sale of their coals ... and will impart the blessing of excellent and cheap fuel to many districts of the county of Wiltshire ... the inhabitants in the neighbourhood of the Kennet & Avon and the Wiltshire & Berkshire Canals will be enabled to purchase their coals from fifty to eighty per cent cheaper than by land carriage where their distance is more than ten miles from the collieries, with the exception of the City of Bath, which will not reap so much of the benefit from the reduced price on account of the circuitous route of the canal.' [15] In effect, '... the Somersetshire Coal Canal was intended primarily to secure existing markets in Wiltshire against the threatened competition from Welsh coal, and secondarily to expand those markets into Berkshire. Any chance of cheapening prices in Bath was incidental and there was no chance of getting into the Bristol market.' [16]

At the end of December 1792 a meeting was held at the Old Down Inn near Chilcompton to consider the idea of a canal and a committee headed by John Billingsley was formed. At a second meeting on 4th February 1793, attended by representatives of the coal mines in the Cam valley including Camerton, Dunkerton, Timsbury and Paulton, as well as Radstock and others to the south,

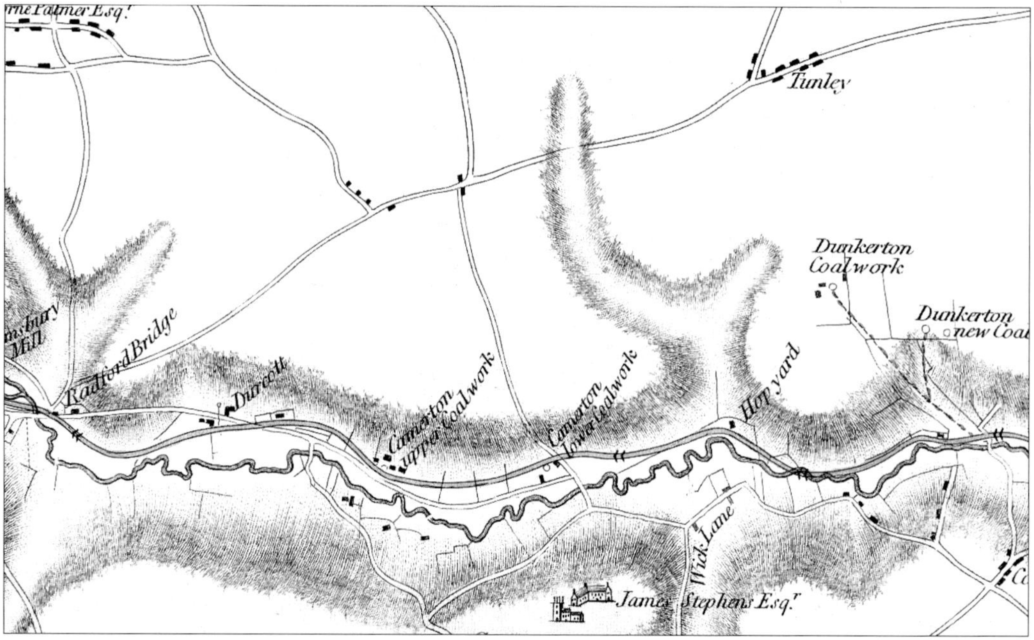

Part of Rennie's 1793 plan for the proposed Somersetshire Coal Canal running through Camerton parish. The route, part of which was intended to follow the line of the leat for the water wheel pumps from Radford, was modified to pass along the north side of the hamlet of Durcott and Camerton Upper Coalwork (Old Pit). The tramways to the canal from the Dunkerton Coalworks were never built.

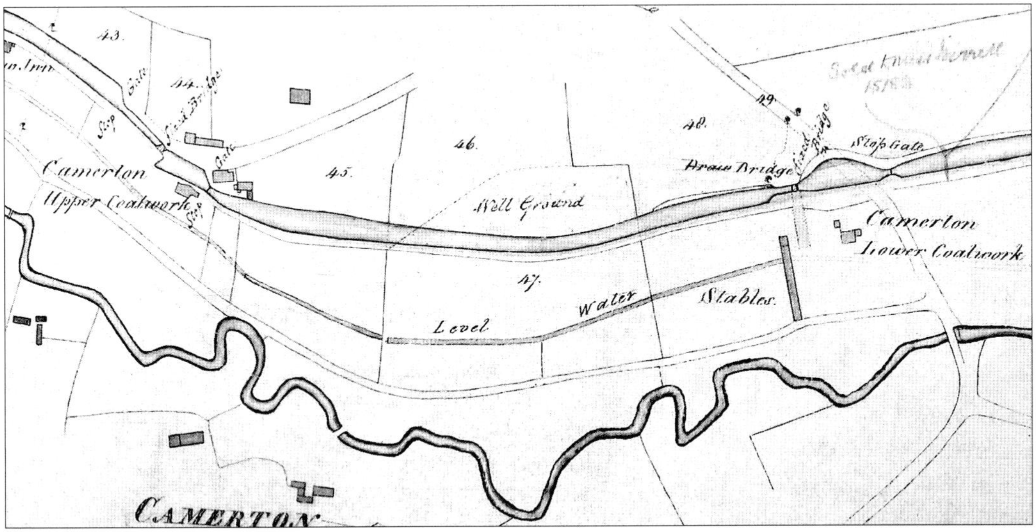

Part of Rennie's 1793 plan for the proposed Somersetshire Coal Canal running through Camerton parish. The route, part of which was intended to follow the line of the leat for the water wheel pumps from Radford, was modified to pass along the north side of the hamlet of Durcott and Camerton Upper Coalwork (Old Pit). The tramways to the canal from the Dunkerton Coalworks were never built.Detail of the Camerton collieries from a map compiled during the construction of the canal. The leat supplying the water wheel pumps (here marked 'Level Water') is shown open as far as the Lower Coalworks, where it continues in a culvert (shown as a dotted line) to its outfall into the Cam Brook near Wick Lane. The building marked 'Stables' later became the site of New Pit Cottages. The old road to Camerton from the north has been diverted to cross the canal by a 'Draw Bridge' (later 'fixed'), with a new road (Red Hill) leading off to the Upper Coalworks. On the extreme left, the New Inn (later the Jolly Collier) has already been built. *Public Record Office*

a resolution was passed supporting the building of a canal.[17] John Rennie was chosen to make a survey of the proposed route as he was already in the area working on the early stages of the canal later known as the Kennet & Avon Canal. Appointed to assist Rennie in taking the levels was William Smith, later known as the 'Father of English Geology', but then a land surveyor, whose ability had come to the notice of two members of the committee, Jacob Mogg and James Stephens about 1792. In 1795 Smith became the official surveyor and sub-engineer of the canal company.[18] When the plans for the Canal were deposited by Smith later in 1793 they listed twenty six pits adjoining or near the proposed navigation, including the 'new coal works at Camerton' (New Pit).[19]

A Committee of Management was then set up with James Stephens of Camerton as chairman, the rest of the members, except John Billingsley, also being connected with the coal industry. In April 1794 an Act was passed for 'making and maintaining a Navigable Canal, with certain Rail Ways, and stone Roads, from several Collieries'. It was to consist of a northern branch from Paulton down the Cam valley as far as Midford, where a southern branch from Radstock would meet it. The canal would then pass through Monkton Combe before joining the planned Kennet and Avon Canal at the Dundas Aqueduct near Limpley Stoke. The final details of the canal were settled in a second Act of March 1796, which was necessary because of changing the line of the canal to a higher level.

In August 1794, to find the best methods of canal construction, a delegation from the committee headed by Samborne Palmer, and including William Smith was sent on a nationwide survey of canal and railway technology. This tour, which covered a distance of 900 miles, included a visit to Shropshire. Palmer had already made enquiries during his visit to Coalbrookdale in 1791 on the methods employed on the Shropshire Canal at Brierly Hill to overcome the difference in level between the canal and the Coalbrookdale Ironworks. This was a problem which also had to be solved on the Somerset Coal Canal, which had to overcome a drop in level of 134ft in order to reach the Kennet & Avon Canal.

In May 1795 advertisements began to appear in the local papers for contractors to cut the sections between Paulton Engine Pit and Hopyard in the parish of Camerton, and for 'laying out the proposed railroads from the different collieries to the canal'. Another two-mile section from Hopyard to the turnpike road at Dunkerton was agreed with a contractor called Hodge for the sum of £4,000. On the Radstock branch the section between there and Peglinch Farm in the parish of Wellow was also started.[20]

The First Cargo of Canal Coal

Some idea of the work involved even on a short section of the canal can be gained when it is remembered that between Hopyard and Dunkerton the canal had to cross two aqueducts over the Severcombe valley and the Hollow between Longhouse and Dunkerton village. This section was ready by October 1798 and the *Bath Herald* reported:

> '.. five vessels, loaded with coal, were conveyed on the Somersetshire Coal Canal to Dunkerton, from Camerton Coalworks on Monday. Mr. [Eleazer] Pickwick, of the White-Hart [in Bath], brought the first two loads to Bath the same day with the same team. In the course of three weeks, or a month, we understand, a wharf will be opened, for handling of coal on the Wells road, near Dunkerton, about three and a half miles from this city, from whence a team can bring two loads a day with great ease. This will make a reduction of eight shillings per load in the carriage only.' [21]

The first of many thousands of tons of coal had been carried on the canal. The northern branch was extended westwards from Camerton during 1799, first to Radford in May and by November to Paulton. As a result a considerable quantity of coal was reaching the turnpike road at Dunkerton from the pits in the Cam valley as the century was ending.[22]

The *Gloucester Journal* commented that Bath was feeling the benefit of the coal canal 'which is enabled to render the coal at Dunkerton wharf, within less than four miles from hence, on a good turnpike road, at only two shillings per ton freight and tonnage, thus is a waggon or cart capable of going twice a day to Dunkerton wharf, with more ease to the horses than once to the coal-works, from this place.' [23]

A watercolour sketch by the Rev.John Skinner of the canal at Durcott. *Rev. D.E. Cooper*

The Turnpike Roads

It was about this time that most turnpike trusts ceased making any distinction between winter and summer rates. This may have been due to the improved state of the roads and the more regular freight trade.[24] 'Before the Turnpike was established coal was carried on horses' back to a distance of fifteen to twenty miles from the collieries; each horse carried about two and a half hundredweights. Now one horse with a light cart will draw ten hundredweight … Can an insignificant toll be put in competition with this saving?' So wrote John Billingsley at the close of the century, also reporting that the roads in north Somerset were pretty good considering the traffic that they had to carry. Furthermore he estimated that the output of coal worked in the area was about 130,000 tons every year.[25]

Others, such as the Rev. Richard Warner in Bath, were hoping that the new canal would considerably reduce the amount of coal carried by road. 'Bath is chiefly supplied from mines to the south and south west of the city, and the product as till now comes in waggons and on the backs of colliers horses and asses. But the Somersetshire Coal Canal, which is nearly completed, will speedily supersede the use of other modes of carriage … it will relieve humanity from the pain of contemplating the multiplied instances of cruelty which the barbarity of the collier inflicts on his wretched animals.'[26]

Although Somerset miners were considered the best in the country at that time, it has been pointed out that at the end of the 18th and the beginning of the 19th centuries the mines in Somerset were considered to be technically backward.[27] The complex geological nature of the coalfield made mechanical improvements difficult to apply. Billingsley acknowledged the introduction of machinery for winding the coal in 1795 and thought that the days of horses in the coal industry were numbered. It appears that about 1,500 men and boys were employed in the area and they were able to produce between 1,500 and 2,000 tons of coal a week. Most of the coal owners were receiving an eighth of the gross receipt of the sales. 'Many people are under alarming apprehensions lest the coal mines may be exhausted by the extra demand produced by the extension of sale established by the canals.' He went on to point out that there were plenty of reserves to meet any future demand.[28]

The market was already becoming extensive, eventually reaching into adjacent parts of Somerset and the western areas of Wiltshire. It was found that the coal travelled well so that it arrived at its destination still high in quality. 'Nor must it be forgotten, that on both lines of the Coal Canal there is abundance of limestone, which may together with small coal be transferred to any part of Wiltshire … it may be burnt on the spot, and sent either in bulk, or in boxes proper for the purpose…'[29]

Conditions

Despite these improvements, conditions in the pits were extremely hard and in the summer of 1792 some four thousand miners in Timsbury, Paulton and Radstock came out on strike. The situation was resolved by the Somerset colliery owners in an 'Agreement for the regulation of miners' wages' made at the Old Down Inn on 22nd August 1792. This document gives the rates that were agreed for all the grades of worker:

> 'Breaker (coalgetter): For every turn carrying in his wall and turning his own dung [OE – a heap] and breaking the coal for tale of the vein, 1/8d.
>
> Carting Boy: For carting the tale of the vein seventy yards to be measured straight to the head, 1/3d. The carting boy to keep his way good and make his wall and haul what stones may be in his road for that purpose, upon the distance increasing, for every thirty yards, 5d.

Sinkers: For each turn of 6 hours, 1/8d. For working under a pump, 1/9d.
Resolved that the foregoing Regulation of wages shall be adopted in the several collieries … Camerton, Dunkerton, Lammas Field, Priston, Radford … and that the same be printed and dispersed at these collieries.' [30]

Camerton Old Pit, with a shaft of 7 feet in diameter, had been sunk to a depth of between 900ft and 921 feet, sources vary in the figures they give, near the lane from Red Hill. About half a mile to the east James Stephens had opened the New Pit by 1793, reaching a depth of between 1,818ft and 1,836ft, with a diameter of 8ft. Both pits were connected underground and on the surface.[31] Two new veins of coal were found at Camerton early in 1795 and it was reported: 'The great vein of coal has baffled the miners for more than twelve months. Several times there was the prospect of rich treasure, but then they have been deceived. The seam is between two and three feet thick, of excellent quality and about sixty yards from the bottom of the Pit'.[32]

Accidents

Articles concerning two accidents at Camerton were in the newspapers of 1792. James Parfitt, the father of ten children, was dashed to pieces, when the rope broke.[33] In June a seventeen year old called Joseph Payne caught his thumb in the clasp that attached the rope to the basket, which was used to haul up the coal. In this way he was lifted through one hundred and forty fathoms to the surface, holding onto the basket with his other hand. Halfway up he dreaded being hit by the descending basket and so he shouted out and was heard by the people above. Consequently, they moderated the speed of winding so that he was able to push the empty basket aside as he passed. The newspaper remarked that his thumb was 'as flat as a knife.' [34]

Over a year later there was a serious explosion above ground. A lad of sixteen had gone into the gunpowder room where between six and seven barrels were stored at the time. The scattered powder on the floor took fire and the boy was killed, two others being injured in the accident. The thatch and the works around the coal pit took fire, according to the paper, but fortunately it was soon extinguished by the miners. 'The nails in the shoes of the lad striking against those in the floor must be the means by which this accident was occasioned.' [35]

Gunpowder had already been introduced in coal mining by the early 18th century to blast away the rocks to get at the coal. It was accidents such as this that were to lead to regulations being passed which insisted that all stores for explosives be well away from the pithead and that they be lined throughout in wood. The Explosives Act was passed in 1875 to try to prevent this kind of accident. The Powder House at Camerton still stands some two hundred yards from the site of Old Pit.

As the 18th century drew to its close the Camerton pits were well established. The coal canal was in use between Camerton and Dunkerton and prospects for the next century looked encouraging.

Notes to Chapter Two

Steam Winding

By the 1770s there was a great deal of interest in the idea of converting the reciprocating action of the beam engine into rotary motion, and many experiments were tried. Although an effective method using a crank was developed by the Bristol engineer, Matthew Wasborough, in collaboration with a Birmingham button manufacturer, James Pickard, no agreement could be made with James Watt for its use with his engines. When Pickard patented the crank mechanism in 1780, it could only be adapted to the old and inefficient Newcomen Engine. In response, in 1781 Watt patented a number of rotary devices of his own design which, though more complicated, were quickly seized upon by industrialists who preferred the Watt engines, and within a year or so these were already being used for winding purposes. It was two of Watt's designs that Palmer and Mogg witnessed when they made their visit to Coalbrookdale in 1791, one of which was presumably installed at Timsbury. Whether the one adopted by James Stephens at Camerton 'on a more improved plan' was the same is not known, but in any case, as soon as Pickard's crank patent expired in 1794, followed by Watt's engine patent in 1800, the way was open for the rapid development of the crank and flywheel and its adaptation to any engine, particularly to the high pressure engine introduced by Trevithick a few year later.

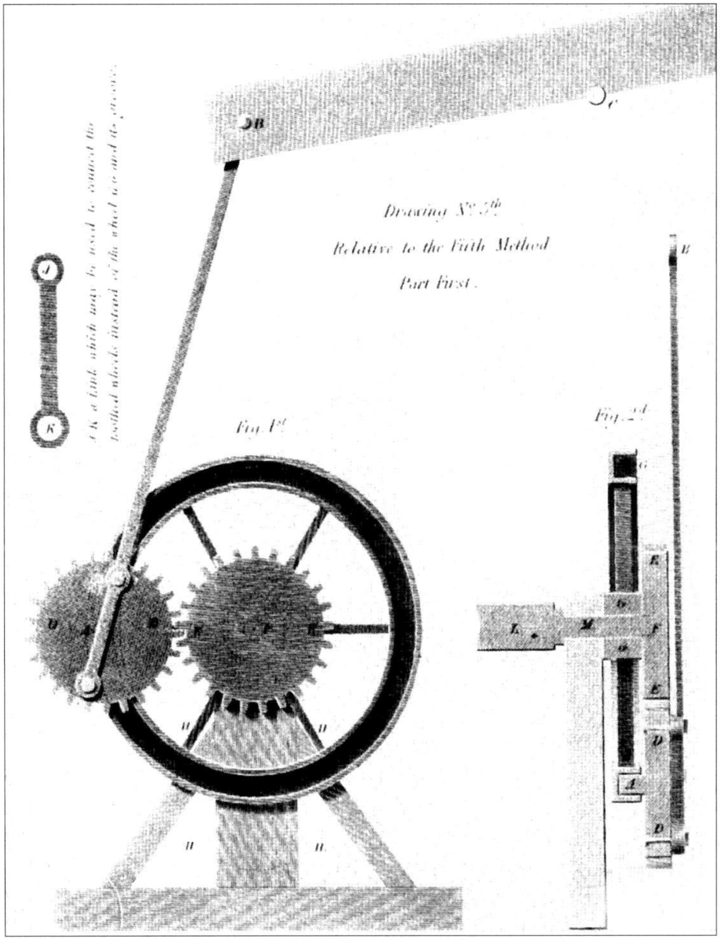

Rotary Sun and Planet gear patented by James Watt for his engines.

The Freeshare System

Royalties – A payment made by coal companies to the owners of the mineral rights in the area in which they operate. The coal company mined and sold its landlord's coal, and paid him so much a ton for the right, i.e. the royalty. The system ended in 1938 when the Government, in taking over ownership of the country's coal deposits, bought the rights of the royalty owners.

The following example is from Down & Warrington (pp.25-26) to explain how the system of freeshare, which was peculiar to Somerset, was operated:

> 'At Camerton in 1921, 4,084 tons of coal were mined under the land leased from Sir Frank Beauchamp; five per cent of this weight was, by the terms of the lease, deducted for colliery consumption, but on the remaining 3,879 tons Sir Frank was credited with a royalty of 6d per ton, i.e. £97. The average selling price of the coal was 29s.5 $^{1}/_{2}$ d per ton, which totals £5,714.14s. On this value, Sir Frank was credited with his freeshare of one-twentieth, i.e. £285.14s. However, from this sum was deducted the £97 royalty payment so that Sir Frank actually received £188.14s. In earlier days the usual rate of freeshare was an eighth or a tenth, which represented a good source of income for the mineral lords.'

The Ventilation of Pits

The introduction of water in the Downcast shaft increased the downward flow of fresh air because it increased the density of the air as it was cooled. The water was applied so that it scattered and fell fall like rain, sometimes being called a water fall or cascade. The air passing through the workings became warmed by the heat of the strata, the miners' bodies, the ponies and the lights. A furnace at the bottom of the Upcast shaft reduced the density of the air as it was further warmed, so increasing the flow of this air upwards towards the surface.
Adapted from Robert Peel *Coal Mining* 1912

Underground Doors

Boys employed from the age of eight opening the doors underground were known as 'trappers' in some South Gloucestershire and North Somerset mines and could work from ten to twelve hours. They would live on bread and cheese, eating two to three times during their shift.
R.Meurig Evans, *Children Working Underground*, National Museum of Wales, 1979.

Guss and Crook

This consisted of either a piece of tarred rope or leather forming a loop or girdle. At the front a 15-inch long chain was attached with an elongated s-shaped hook or crook at the other end. This was a very useful device for pulling heavy objects in confined spaces. Throughout the country this device was of fair antiquity, with a variety of local names. In Somerset it was used into the 20th century, and became the hallmark of this coalfield.

The Rev. Richard Warner 1763-1857

He was an antiquarian and topographical writer who moved to this area in 1794 to become the officiating minister of St. James's Church in Bath. His best-known work, the *History of Bath* was published in 1801. He wrote to a friend about his visit to the canal; 'At a short distance from hence [i.e. South Stoke] in a bottom below we meet with a canal, a recent undertaking, intended to convey the coals of Timsbury, Paulton, Camerton and Dunkerton pits to Bath. The course of this cut, which is not yet completed, will embrace in its various windings to its junction with the Radstock cut, a distance of ten miles, and pass through a country as highly picturesque as any in the kingdom.' He commended canal travel as the way to see 'romantic scenery'. In *A Walk through some of the Western Counties of England*, 1800, he wrote of Dunkerton; 'a small and retired village, five miles from Bath, bedded in the bosom of a deep valley, and only to be discerned by the tower of its church peeping through the woods.' However, at Radstock he was struck by the noises of curses, the dingy tenants and the threat of violence. About the Radstock branch of the Somersetshire Coal Canal he wrote: 'A Canal terminating at this place is now cutting, and in great forwardness, intended to convey the produce of the mines to Bath and more distant places. This is very considerable, amounting on an average to 10,000 bushels per week, and sold at the pit's mouth at the rate of 5d per bushel.'
A Walk through some of the Western Counties of England 1800 p.16

The mines at Camerton are mentioned specifically by Warner in his *History of Bath*, where he lists among the principal coal works those at Radstock, Camerton and Dunkerton. 'The coal works with which Bath is chiefly connected lie on the north and south side of the Somersetshire Coal Canal, in a

direction from south west to the north east dipping about nine inches in the yard, frequently interrupted by faults. Most of the works are from ninety to one hundred and thirty fathoms deep and extend in some distances nearly a mile from the bottom of the shaft ... Water appears at a depth of a few fathoms, but workmen, on opening the shaft contrived to get rid of 283 hogshead [14,858 gallons] in an hour. There are about ten coal works in the northern line of the coal canal ... The hard, compact and solid coal is preferred to every sort.'
History of Bath, 1801 p.398f.

Richard Warner's concern for the welfare of animals
So strongly did Warner feel about this subject that he returned to it in another of his books *Excursions from Bath*, dated 1801, in which he wrote:

> 'Holloway [on the outskirts of Bath] affords a nocturnal retreat for a much more useful class of beings (than beggars), the animals employed in the conveyance of coals from the pits to Bath. Wearied and panting with the labour of the day, here the wretched beasts are driven by crouds, as the evening closes, into Yards hired for the purpose, not so much for the sake of rewarding their services with rest, as to prevent their escape from the toil of the morrow ... The inhuman master never removes from their backs the heavy and incumbering wooden saddle in which the coals are packed ... Full oft has my heart bled for this little, wasted, panting wretch staggering under its unconscionable burthen, and labouring up the steep streets of Bath, now dropping with fatigue and again urged to exertion by reiterated blows. No provision for the punishment of those who force their beasts to disproportionate labour ... all we can do is to endeavour to persuade the proprietors that their interest is connected with the better treatment of the beasts.'

Excursions from Bath, 1801, p.9f.

John Rennie 1761-1821
He was born at Phantassie, East Lothian in Scotland, the son of a farmer. In 1791 he set up his own business as an engineer in London. His first important work in England was the Kennet & Avon Canal but he went on to build bridges and harbours, as well as canals, throughout the United Kingdom. (Phantassie probably *fan taise*, 'slope of softness', i.e. wetness.)
W.W. Watson, *The History of the Celtic Place-Names of Scotland*, W.Blackwood & Sons 1928

John Rennie in later life.

William Smith 1769-1839
Known to his friends and associates as 'Strata Smith', was initially a land surveyor, but his work with the Somersetshire Coal Canal Company led to him to be appointed as its sub-engineer. It was during the excavation of the canal that his interest in geology enabled him to discover the basic principles of the order of rock formations and their identification by the species of fossils found in them. His work meant that there was a much greater understanding of the strata underlying the surface and hence a more economical exploitation of minerals could be developed. It was about this time also that the proprietors were using boring rods to search for coal, and specialist firms were employed to sink shafts. The fruit of Smith's research was published in 1815 as his *General map of Strata found in England and Wales*. It was the first geological map of its kind. (See Simon Winchester, *The Map that Changed the World*, Viking-Penguin 2001.)
Dr. H. Woodward, *William Smith Father of British Geology*, Bath Field Club Vol. 10.

William Smith in later life. *Victoria Art Gallery, Bath*

The Value of Somerset Miners

The conditions in the Somerset pits at this time may have compared unfavourably with other parts of the country. This may be reflected in the advertisement that was placed in the *Bath Herald* by some Staffordshire coal owners for several hundred miners to go from Somerset 'Who will find constant employment, wages from 2/6d to 3/6d per day, with two quarts of ale.'
Bath Herald 19 Dec 1795.

Eleazer Pickwick 1748-1837

Eleazer Pickwick.
Victoria Art Gallery, Bath

In 1779 Eleazer Pickwick started a stage-coach business from Bath to London based on the White Hart Inn in Stall Street, the latter being run in partnership with his nephew Moses Pickwick. The coaching business quickly became one of the largest and most successful in the West of England, from which Eleazer made a considerable private fortune over a period of 40 years. The fame of the White Hart and the name of Pickwick remain immortalised in the works of Jane Austen and Charles Dickens.

Eleazer was also one of the original proprietors named in the first Somersetshire Coal Canal Act of Parliament in 1794, and it was he who supplied the team of horses (from his stable of 300) that hauled the first shipment of coal from Camerton into Bath via the canal in 1798. Being a member the Canal Committee, meetings were often convened at the White Hart, but his rôle in the construction of the canal was crucial; without him it is possible that it would not have been finished due to rising costs. Fortunately Eleazer came to the rescue with a loan of £10,000, and after being appointed treasurer in 1803 made a further advance of £11,000. By the time of his death, he owned £20,000 of shares in the Canal.

The Pickwick connection with the coalfield continued, it appears, at Camerton, where he (or perhaps his son, also Eleazer) is named as one of the proprietors in 1816. This connection passed on to his grandson, William Eleazer ('Major') Pickwick, who became joint proprietor of the coalworks with 'Mr. Bailey' (possibly Zachary, an original shareholder and Bath banker) up to the 1830s, and Horatio Davis in the 1840s.

John Billingsley 1747-1811

John Billingsley.

Born into a wealthy family at Ashwick Grove, Oakhill, he became an active and prominent pioneer of improvement and innovation in agriculture, industry and transport. These he demonstrated in his own business interests, such as farming, brewing and coalmining, as well as in active involvement in the Somersetshire Coal Canal, Kennet & Avon Canal, Dorset & Somerset Canal and the regional turnpike trusts. He was the Chairman of the Committee which launched the Somersetshire Coal Canal in 1792, and later a member of the management committee in 1794.

He became an outstanding agricultural expert, his major innovation being the introduction of the double-furrow plough, and a founding member of the Bath & West of England Society. He is best known for his monumental paper *General View of the Agriculture of the County of Somerset with Observations on the Means of its Improvement* written for the newly-formed Board of Agriculture in 1794 in view of concerns about food supply following the outbreak of war with France. In that book he mentioned that 'The coal is prime quality; pure and durable in burning; firm, large and of a strong grain; which ensures its conveyance to almost any distance, without injury to its appearance or quality, which cannot be exceeded in any part of the kingdom.' This work is also of particular interest for its description of the experimental Caisson Lock introduced on the Somersetshire Coal Canal.

References to Chapter Two

1 Bluhm, article, *op.cit.*, p.52.
2. Doughty, M. W., 'Samborne Palmer's Diary: Technological innovation by a Somerset coal-mine owner', *Industrial Archaeology Review*, Vol. 3, no. 1, 1978, pp.17-28.
3. *Bath Herald*, 10 March 1792.
4. *Bath Herald*, 2 June 1792.
5. John Billingsley, *A General View of the Agriculture of the County of Somerset*, 1797, p.26f.
6. *Bath Herald*, 28 February 1795.
7. Down & Warrington *op.cit.*,44.
8. *Ibid.*, p.46.
9. *Victoria History op.cit.*, II. P.382.
10. Lecture given by Alec Hann November 1986.
11. Williams, W.J., *Coalmining in Bishop Sutton - North Somerset*, c.1799-1929, p.8.
12. Bluhm, article, *op.cit.*, p.58ff.
13. Bulley, *op.cit.*, II, p.19.
14 Warner, *The History of Bath*, 1801, footnote p.397.
15. *Ibid.*
16. Bluhm, article, *op.cit.*, p.55.
17. Kenneth R. Clew, *The Somersetshire Coal Canal and Railways*, Bran's Head 1986, p.15.
18. Clew, *op.cit.*, p.19.
19. Bluhm, article, *op.cit.*, p.53.
20. Clew, *op.cit.*, p.26 & 28.
21. *Bath Herald*, 6 October 1798.
22. Clew, *op.cit.*, p.39.
23. Clew, *op.cit.*, p.34.
24. Albert, *op.cit.* p.175
25. Billingsley, *op.cit.*, p.26f.
26. Warner, *op.cit.*, p.397.
27. Bulley, *op.cit.*, I, p.76f.
28. Billingsley, *op.cit.*, p.26f.
29. Warner, *op.cit.*, p.397.
30. Bulley, *op.cit.*, II, p.39.
31. Down & Warrington *op.cit.*, p.112 & p.273.
32. *Bath Herald*, 7 and 14 February 1795.
33. *Bath Herald*, 26 May 1792.
34. *Bath Herald*, 2 June 1792.
35. *Bath Herald*, 14 September 1793.

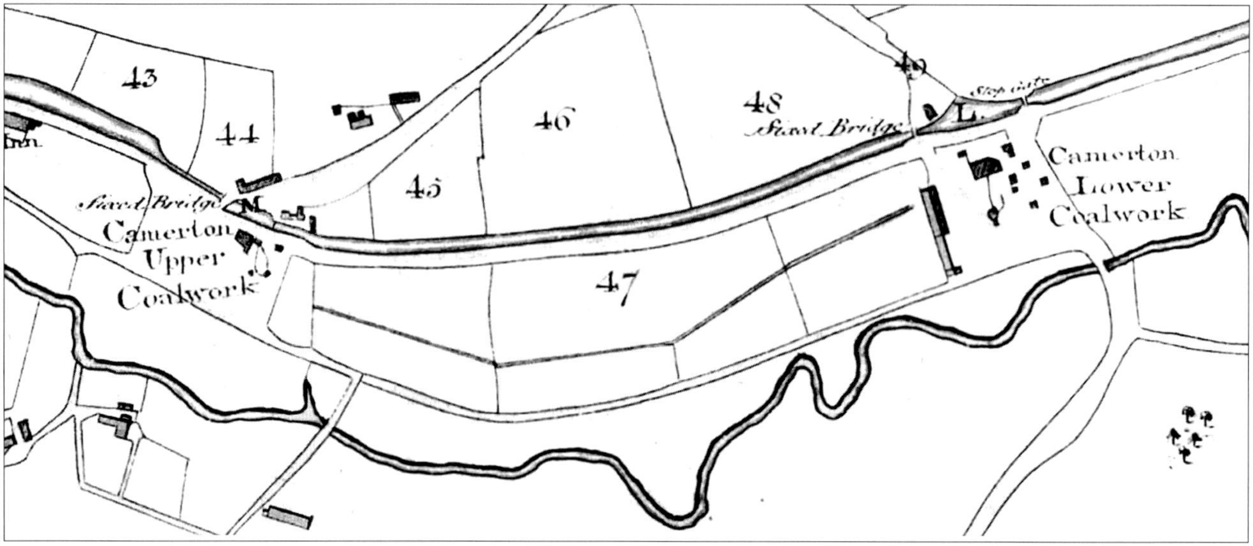

Detail of the Camerton Collieries from the Coal Canal Company map, c.1810. By this time much of the leat to the pumps on the west side has been buried to permit access between the Upper Coalwork and the Durcott Road. The bends in the Cam Brook have also been straightened for a new bridge from Durcott Road over the brook to the 'Bridge Place' cottages and Camerton Village. The 'Stables' building on the previous map has been enlarged, presumably for conversion to the dwellings known as Collier's Row or New Pit Cottages. *Bath Royal Literary and Scientific Institution*

CHAPTER THREE

A TIME OF EXPANSION 1800-1810

Problems on the Canal

There was a great deal of activity during the first five years of the 19th century in order to complete the Somersetshire Coal Canal throughout its length. There were troubles of a serious nature in the section between Dunkerton and Midford as the navigators had to overcome a difference in level of about 130 feet. The first idea was to use an experimental 'Hydrostatic Caisson Lock' at Combe Hay to raise and lower the boats from one level to another. This invention was successful when the initial trials were carried out in 1798, but within a short time the masonry walls of the cistern began to bulge. At the time it was believed that the cause of the resulting leaks was bad workmanship, but more recently it has been pointed out that the Caisson Lock had been built through Lower Fuller's Earth clay. In wet weather the clay would have absorbed water, causing it to expand and exert pressure on the cistern walls. This would have destroyed 'the essential geometry of the cistern causing the caisson to jam in transit as in fact happened. The distorted cistern wall would be almost incapable of remaining water-tight under these conditions.'[1]

The plan to have a system of caisson locks to lift the boats from one level to another was finally abandoned in 1800, and while a better substitute was being decided, the two levels were connected with a temporary inclined plane. In November 1801 this was finished and it enabled coal from pits in the Cam Valley to reach the Kennet & Avon Canal near Limpley Stoke.[2] The arrangement was not ideal because of the inconvenience involved in transhipping the coal at the top and bottom of the plane. A boat reached the top of the plane with three large boxes of coal, each weighing a ton. These were unloaded by a crane onto a carriage for transporting down the plane to the lower level of the canal.[3] It is not surprising that the Kennet & Avon Canal Committee report of the time

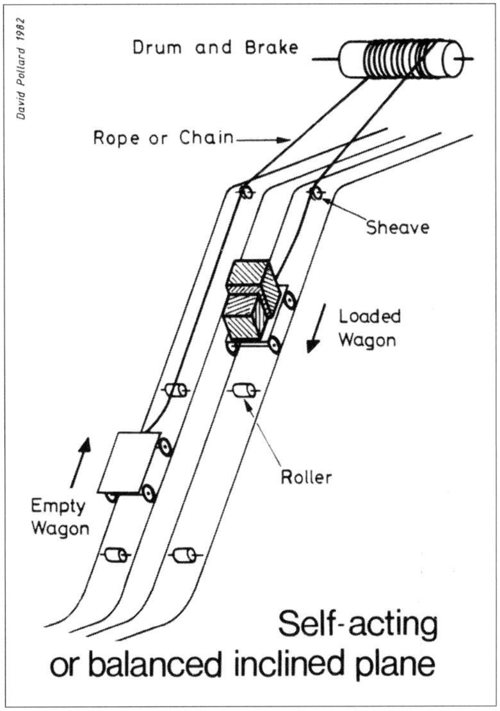

Operation of the self-acting Inclined Plane.

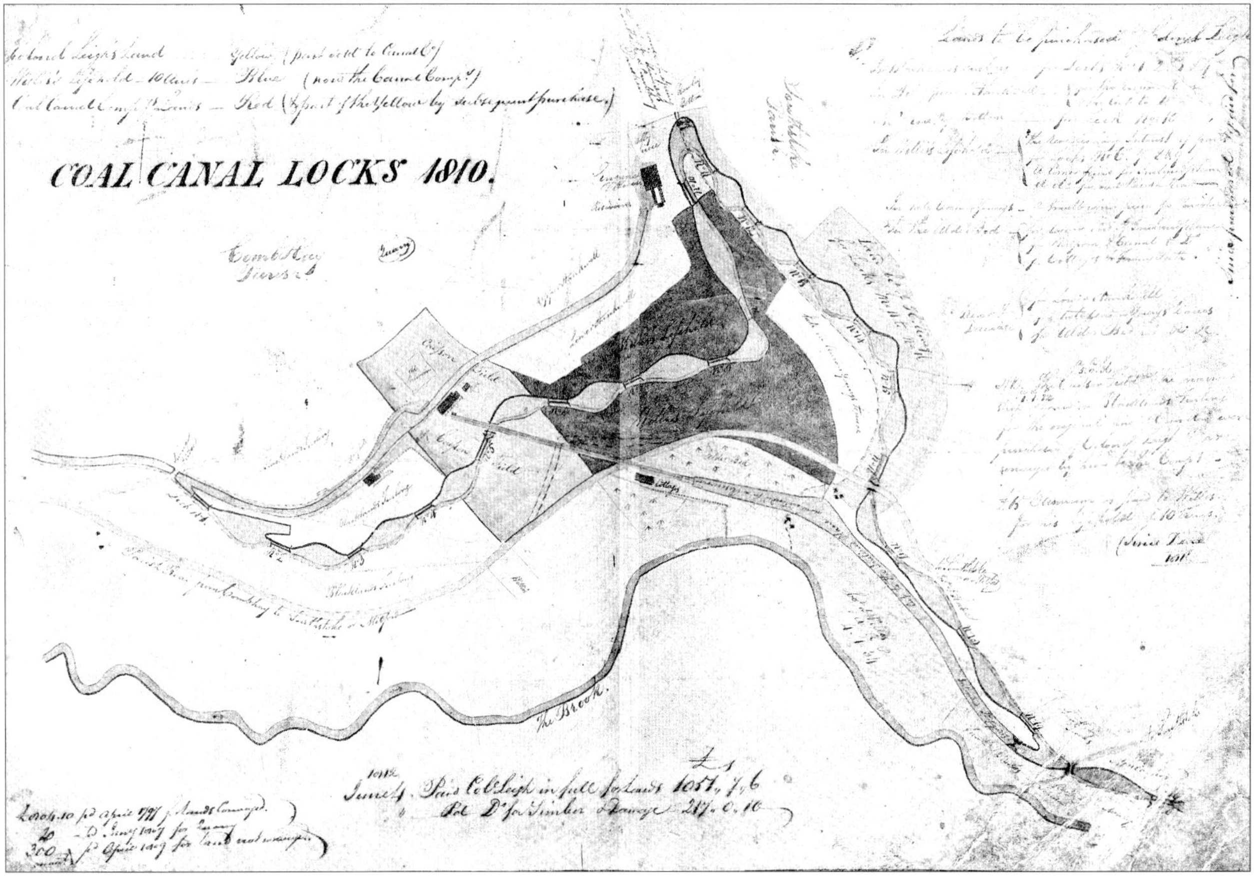

Map of the Combe Hay Lock Flight, 1810.
Bath Royal Literary and Scientific Institution

Remains of the Lock Flight today.

described it as 'extremely inconvenient and difficult to pass'[4]. The main problem was that it did not allow enough coal to pass through the canal in a steady stream, even though the canal was capable of accommodating boats carrying twenty-five tons of coal. In the meantime the Company had finally decided to replace the Caisson with a flight of conventional locks, and tenders were invited for the construction of these locks in August 1802, and also for an aqueduct at Midford joining the two branches of the canal.[5]

The Pumping Station at Dunkerton.

Water Sources for the Canal

The large number of locks created a further problem. The upper level was fed by the River Cam through a leat at Paulton Basin and by a spring at Dunkerton but these would not now provide sufficient water, and already in September 1801 an advertisement appeared in the press for a pumping engine. This was installed at Dunkerton in May 1802.[6] It raised water from the River Cam and remained in use during the working life of the canal. A representation of the Dunkerton Pumping Station appeared in the second quarter of the Somersetshire Coal Canal Company's coat of arms.[7]

The system of twenty-two locks at Combe Hay were officially opened on the 5th April 1805. The *Bath Journal* recorded the event: 'on the 5th instant, the proprietors of the Somersetshire Coal Canal opened their locks (twenty-two in number) at Combehay, which produces a water communication between the Coal Pits, the Kennet & Avon, and the Wiltshire & Berkshire Canals. It being a day of festivity, the parties, consisting of ladies and gentlemen, attended by the Bath Forum Band, proceeded by water from Timsbury Bason [*sic*], through all the locks to Sydney Gardens [in Bath], (a distance of about 16 miles) where they partook of a good dinner and in the evening concluded with a ball'.[8]

By the spring of 1806 a second pumping engine was working at Combe Hay, enabling the locks to operate fully.[9] At last all the major difficulties had been solved and the completed canal was able to play a significant role in carrying the coal from the Cam Valley to distant markets for many years to come.

> 'The canal pursues its course from hence through Dunkerton to the inexhaustible coal-mines at Paulton, Timsbury, etc., which constantly supplies the county eastward and the city of Bath with the finest coals. Another line of the canal and a rail-way path, convey the produce of the Radstock pits into the same channel, forming a junction at Midford.'[10]

Most of the collieries in the neighbourhood were now being connected by tramways, in some cases more than a mile in length, to wharfs on the new canal. It was only at Camerton that the canal ran immediately alongside the pits. This meant that the coal could be delivered almost directly from the pit mouth to the waiting boats, and screens could later be erected over the canal itself. Although the canal was situated along the north side of the pits through shallow cuttings, plans of the canal show that it was originally intended to run along the south side, following the route of a pre-existing leat from the Cam Brook to the water-engines which operated the pumps. These pumps were retained, and were still in use in 1811 when mentioned by John Skinner in the case of an accusation of rape by a woman who claimed that her screams were unheard owing to the noise of the water wheels.

The Network of Canals and Prices of Coal

The Coal Canal acted as a feeder to the two longer canals to the east. The Wiltshire & Berkshire Canal was completed in September 1810 when it reached the River Thames at Abingdon, via Melksham, Dauntsey, Wootton Bassett and Swindon. There were branches from this canal to Calne, Chippenham and Wantage. The Kennet & Avon Canal linked Devizes, Pewsey, Hungerford and Newbury to Reading. It was completed in December 1810.[11] The Coal Canal was the key to such prosperity as these two canals enjoyed, so great a part of their revenue did they draw from the carriage of coal.[12]

After 1805 coal could make the entire journey by canal from its junction at Dundas Aquaduct, with the completed section of the Kennet & Avon Canal, to coal wharves being established within the city of Bath. The *Bath Journal* reported early in 1807 that the canal company had just erected a powerful steam engine (i.e. at Combe Hay) to 'secure for the canal a regular and constant supply of water. They now want to establish a Coal Wharf near Sydney Gardens. Price at all seasons is to be 11d per cwt at the Wharf and if conveyed to the consumer's cellar the charge will be:

> l/- per cart load
> 2/- per waggon load (extra for distance and trouble)'[13]

The paper printed the comparative charges for conveying the coal from the pits to Bath by land and water, showing that the latter was more economical. It was claimed that one horse would convey as much, by canal, as forty-eight horses could draw by waggon. The public were assured that there was a weighbridge at the wharf under the supervision of a trustworthy agent. The Coal Canal Company's offices were located at 6 Trim Street in Bath. The names of the Committee of Management at this stage were:

James Stephens	Eleazer Pickwick
James Savage	John Crang
John Billingsley	Joseph Penny
Sambourne Palmer	Richard Bowsher[14]

The threat of Welsh coal in Bath was never far away and later in 1807 an advertisement appeared in the *Bath Journal* to the effect that coal from Newport was now available. It was claimed that this was less sulphurous, longer burning and produced less dust than coal from other areas. The merchants also offered small coals for smiths and factories of all kinds. The notice suggests that this was an attempt by Welsh coal to break into the Bath markets and it was considered to be something of a novelty.[15] The invariable price of Somerset coal was twelve shillings a ton at the pithead, and this was probably higher than the cost in most other parts of the country.[16]

After some three years the Canal Company lost interest in selling coal in Bath. The *Bath Chronicle* of August 1810 carried the following advertisement:

> 'R. Carpenter and Co. having taken the coal trade carried on by the Coal Canal Company respectfully solicit the favours of their friends and the public which will endeavour permanently to secure by having a regular supply of the best coal that can be procured and which they will retail on fair terms, and they have the satisfaction to state, they commence trade with an entire new stock fresh from Timsbury and Camerton Pits.'

This new company gave the prices of the coal at the wharf as follows:

June to September	13d/ cwt
October, November, April, May	14d/ cwt
December to March	15d/ cwt.[17]

With the opening of the Somersetshire Coal Canal and the resulting increase in the export of coal, landowners in the areas where coal was to be found were conscious of the potential for development. James Stephens, the squire of Camerton writing about 1800, described the Particulars of the Camerton Living, prior to the induction of the Rev. John Skinner:

> 'The Parish of Camerton abounds in coal of the very first quality, where considerable works are now carrying on, and when taken from under the Glebe, which it will be in the process of working, the Rector will be entitled to his free share (they have purposely avoided the Glebe and Churchyard).'[18]

Increase in Population

The increase in mining activity in North Somerset stimulated a rise in the population. Between 1801 and 1831 the population of Dunkerton increased by 200% and that of Camerton by 100%. This was probably the result of both natural increase and an influx of people from neighbouring areas, from the less prosperous southern parts of the coalfield around Mells, as well as from the surrounding agricultural districts. 'The discontents of the wage-earning agricultural community in the early 19th century, and the decline in the cloth-making industry of East Somerset may have assisted in the achievement of this transfer of population.'[19] Indeed, the pits in Somerset were considered to be better places in which to work than in some areas of the country such as Yorkshire. It is probable that no women or girls were employed in Somerset pits and, it was claimed, boys did not go underground at eight years of age but more usually at ten. The competition to work in the pits was keen, probably due to the low agricultural wages, and the two groups, colliers and farm workers seem to have had little to do with each other.[20]

This increase in population at Camerton can be seen in the figures from a number of sources. In 1801 the figure is given as 594 and according to Skinner around five hundred newcomers made their home in the parish because of the developing local industry.[21] By 1811 the population had risen to 786 and ten years later it stood at 1004. At that time, of the one hundred and eighty families in the parish thirty-two were employed in agriculture, and it can be assumed that the majority of the remainder were linked with the pits.[22] The change from an agricultural to an industrial base meant considerable social and economic instability in the area, frequently resulting in great hardship for the population.

Meanwhile, on the 20th April 1801, a marriage settlement was made between James Stephens and the Jarrett family on the occasion of the marriage of his daughter Anne to Herbert Jarrett. As a result of this settlement the Jarretts were eventually to inherit both the manor of Camerton and the mines.[23] Three years later James Stephens now a widower, married the widow of Hugh Boyde, a niece of Viscount Gressford.[24]

The writings of John Skinner, who became the Rector of the parish in 1800, provide an interesting account of life in Camerton during the early years of the l9th century, until his death in 1839. For most of that period, he kept a diary in which he noted a number of events concerned with the pits, the colliers and the canal. It appears that in the year of his induction he started a school for the colliers' children which he supported at his own expense until the 1820s when it was closed due to the interference of the lady of the Manor, Mrs. Jarrett.[25]

Problems and Accidents

In the early years of the century the miners in Camerton formed a welfare society known as the Camerton Club. In October 1809 Skinner confided in his diary that he had refused to preach to them at Whitsuntide because many of the colliers never set foot in the church on Sundays, and he considered it a mere mockery to do it by way of a parade at any other time. 'But if they would show themselves more regular in their attendance on me in future they might depend on my attendance on them, and giving them a sermon every year and doing all in my power to promote their Association.'[26]

Skinner was aware of the problems and accidents that all too frequently afflicted the miners. In July 1803 he told of one Robert Paine who received a stranger, a seaman named Holford, into his home. This man had taken refuge among the colliers to avoid being press-ganged, and so he worked with Paine in the pits and lodged with him in Wick Lane. He must have put everything into his new occupation, 'as he worked two tons a day' but unfortunately he was soon fatally ill with consumption. After his death it was found that he had been tricked by Paine who, while pretending to have taken Holford in from charity, had in fact, done so for his own selfish gain.[27]

Another miner, an Irishman named Macnab, had too much to drink one Saturday night and was drowned when he fell into the recently completed Coal Canal. About the same time, when a man called Cook was working at the bottom of the pit he was killed by some loose earth falling on him, despite the effort of his two sons to dig him out.[28]

> 'Aaron Horler, another collier, was killed in a very extraordinary manner. He had been drinking at the public house, whence … he walked to the Lower Pit, and it is supposed, endeavoured to slide down the rope, (by which the coal is hauled) to the bottom; but going too quick; not being able to retain his hold, he fell down many fathoms and was dashed to pieces, his hands being much burnt by the velocity with which the rope passed through them before he let go his hold. A person going down the pit about ten o'clock to feed the asses kept under-ground was presented with this horrid spectacle on his descent, and was so much frightened as not to recover himself for some time.'[29]

Not only were there accidents but also suicides. Somebody wilfully cut the winding rope so that it was almost severed in the hope that when it was their turn to descend it would give way. It would have carried some six men and boys to their death at the same time. Fortunately on this occasion it was discovered in time and a tragedy avoided.[30] About a year later the *Bath Journal* reported on an inquest into the death of a man, who in a state of intoxication, walked into the coal pit one Sunday night. The shafts must have been largely unprotected as it was recorded that the poor man had fallen 155 fathoms to his death.[31]

The danger to young boys employed underground was underlined by Skinner in his *Journal* when, in September 1805, he wrote:

> 'A little boy of the name of Cottle, son of the Schoolmistress, was killed in the coal pit by some loose ground falling upon him. He was only eight years old and had worked a year. Surely the parents and the proprietors of the works are to blame for permitting such little boys to work, who cannot possibly take care of themselves and must be ignorant of the dangers they are exposed to; but what is not sacrificed to the shrine of covetousness?'[32]

Early in 1806 there were two more accidents at the pit. William Britain was riding underground in a small coal cart drawn by an ass 'which vehicle is usually employed to convey the coal from different parts where it is dug to the large store below the mouth of the pit, but was then empty'. He did not notice the lowering roof and failing to bend his head 'his back was bent double by the sudden violence of the shock and his spine snapped.' James Edward of Carlingcott, whose business it was to see the coal brought to land at the Old Pit, reached over too far in order to steady the basket which was coming up the shaft. He lost his balance and fell to the bottom of the pit.[33]

Finally to return to the canal, Skinner's concern over the observation of the Sabbath may be noted in the following extract from his Journal. 'While walking in the Village ... I saw a boat laden with coal going down the Canal. On enquiring whose it was I found that it was under the direction of William Goold, junr, who carried coal for his brother, Joseph Goold. I told the boys who were with it how improper it was to be boating coal on a Sunday, and begged they would tell their master I should notice the impropriety of this behaviour. The name of the barge was *Vulcan No.7*. On Monday I went to Goold's, found he was with the boat, and was not expected home for a day or two. Friday he came up after breakfast, said he was very sorry for what he had done, but he was fearful he should not get his coal up into the country if he had not done as he did, as there was likely to be a stoppage on the canal.'[34]

The phrase 'up into the country' suggests that this load of coal may have been destined for somewhere in Wiltshire. The time for any journey along the canal would be increased considerably by that required to pass through the twenty-two locks at Combe Hay. It has been estimated that this may well have taken something in the order of six hours in either direction, and at this time of the year, August, there was the threat of stoppage due to lack of water in the canal. It is easy to understand Goold's concern to get his barge under way and down the canal.

Notes to Chapter Three

Fuller's Earth and the Failure of the Caisson

Neil Macmillen with Mike Chapman, *A History of The Fuller's Earth Mining Industry around Bath*, Lightmoor Press 2009.

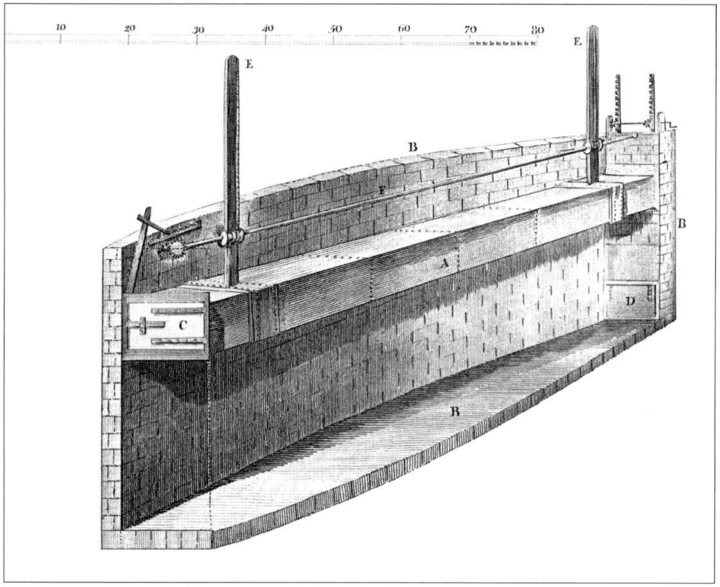

Diagram of the Caisson Lock, from John Billingsley's *General View of the County of Somerset*, 1797.

The Hydrostatic Caisson Lock System at Combe Hay

Three caisson locks were proposed to overcome the difference in level of about one hundred and thirty four feet. Each lock was to consist of a masonry chamber in which was suspended a wooden tube or caisson submerged below the water level at all times. The tube would be pressed against the inside of an opening at the top so as to give a watertight seal. When the doors at the end of the tube and in the aperture had been opened, a boat could be floated, with its crew, into the tube. The caisson would then be lowered by the addition of a small quantity of water until it would sink to align with a second aperture at the next lower canal level.

When the tube had been sealed against this lower aperture, doors could be opened to allow the boat to be floated through a tunnel and out into the lower canal pound. A similar process was used to raise the caisson, using a pump to eject water to lighten the tube.

Note to author from the late Ron Fullagar.

Note on the comparative costs for the transporting of coal from North Somerset to Bath.

This information is taken from an advertisement placed in the *Bath Journal* on 26 January 1807 by the Somersetshire Coal Canal Company.

Land Carriage	£	s.	d.
Price of coal at pits		12	0
Loading the waggon			1 ½
Turnpike 2 tons			9
Waggoner and expenses		1	6
Value of four horses and depreciation		7	6
	1	**1**	**10 ½**

Water Carriage	£	s.	d.
Prime Cost		12	0
From pits to the canal		11	
Tonnage		3	11
Freightage		1	6
		18	4
Expenses at wharf and carriage to consumer		1	8
	1	**0**	**0**

The Camerton Colliery Leat

This was an open channel, cut as soon as Old Pit was sunk in the 1780s, which ran from a weir near Radford nearly half a mile to the west. It is still shown on the Camerton tithe map in 1844 although by then some of it had become arched over to form a culvert. This would suggest that the water engines were still in use, but it is reasonably certain that they had already been supplemented at an earlier stage by the Cornish engine which later evidence indicates was at Old Pit. The last remnants of the open leat disappeared as a result of the re-alignment of Durcott Lane when the Camerton Branch railway from Hallatrow was built in 1880, the rest being already buried under Old Pit batch. Remains of the culverted section in Durcott Lane, recently uncovered at Bramley Cottage beneath the foundations of a garage, showed that the channel was about 6ft wide, with the arch of the stone-built culvert at least 4½ft high above the bed, the latter being much filled with gravel and silt.

A description of the canal in 1809

> 'Leaving the Kennet and Avon Canal to the left we follow the delightful course of the Somersetshire Coal Canal, which brings us to the vale of Midford ... Finding a scarcity of water, from leakage and other causes, the proprietors have erected two powerful steam-engines, one here (Combe Hay) and the other at Dunkerton. The latter of these is perpetually lifting the contents of a brook sixty feet in perpendicular height, which it discharges into the canal, and generally supplies the deficiency of water during a considerable part of the dry season; but it is at times found insufficient for the purpose, when recourse is had to the former, which raises the water from another source about one hundred and twenty feet.'

Wood and Cunningham, *The improved Bath guide, or picture of Bath and its environs*, c.1809.

The Hierarchy in Camerton Coal Works in the early 19th century

The land was owned by James Stephens, and following his death, by his daughter Anne Jarrett and later her two daughters. They would receive royalties (or 'freeshare') on all the coal that was sold and would maintain an interest in the colliery. The rights to mine under this land were then granted to the owners of the coal works who were the shareholders in the Camerton Coal Company. They owned the buildings and all other assets.

These coal owners, or proprietors, appointed Bailiffs to manage the day-to-day running of the business, assisted by book-keepers and accountants. They were answerable to the coal owners. The mine would have a foreman or bailiff in charge of all the work on the surface and responsible for raising and lowering the cages, and an engineer in charge of the boilers and all the machinery. Below ground there would be another foreman in charge of loading the trams into the cages and overseeing the safe winding of the coal and men to the surface.

John Skinner 1772-1834

Born in 1772 at the Old Hall at Claverton near Bath, where his mother (née Page) of Tottenham resided, and to Russell Skinner of Newtown House, Lymington and Claverton House. He attended school in Cheam, Surrey, followed by Trinity College, Oxford, where he graduated BA 1794 and MA 1797. Ordained deacon that year, when he was the curate of Richard Graves, Rector of Claverton 'who interested him in the study of antiquities'. He was ordained priest at Brent Knoll, Somerset, in 1799 and the next year his uncle purchased the living of Camerton for him.

Adapted from *Oxford Dictionary of National Biography* Vol.50 2004.

See also Lecture by H.J. Hunter M.D. 'Mr. Skinner of Camerton', *Bath Field Club* Vol. 2, 1873.

The Rev. John Skinner. *Radstock Museum Archive*

References to Chapter Three

1. Hugh Torrens, *Journal of the Bristol Industrial Archaeological Society* No.8, 1975, p.4-9; see also Bevis Thacker, *AIHCAM*, Summer 1985, Avon Industrial Buildings Trust, pp.28-31.
2. Clew, *op.cit.*, p.51.
3. *Ibid.*, p.48.
4. *Ibid.*, p.52.
5. *Ibid.*, p.57
6. *Ibid.*, p.57.
7. Robin Atthill, *The Curious Past*, The Wessex Press 1955, p.7f.
8. *Bath Journal*, 22 April, 1805.
9. Clew, *op.cit.*, p.64.
10. Wood and Cunningham (printers), *The Improved Bath Guide or Picture of Bath and its environs*, Bath c.1809, p.115f.
11. Clew, *op.cit.*, p.32.
12. R.K. Bluhm, article *op.cit.*, p.54.
13. *Bath Journal*, 26 January 1807.
14. *Ibid.*
15. *Op.cit.*, 2 March 1807.
16. *Ibid.*, and comment by R.K. Bluhm in his thesis 'A Bibliography of the Somerset Coalfield'.
17. *Bath Chronicle*, 30 August 1810.
18. N. Coombes & A.N. Bax (editors) *Journal of a Somerset Rector* 1803-1854: *John Skinner*, Oxford University Press 1984, p.xi.
19. Bulley, *op.cit.*, II, p.30f.
20. Bluhm, article *op.cit.*, p.59ff.
21. Wedlake, article *op.cit.*, p.33.
22. C. & J. Greenwood, *Somerset Delineated*, 1822. Reprinted; Alan Sutton Publications Ltd., 1980.
23. Down & Warrington, *op.cit.*, p.113.
24. Richard Lock, *Supplement to Collinson's History of Somersetshire*, Taunton 1939, p.108.
25. Skinner, *op.cit.*, p.182.
26. *Ibid.*, p.43.
27. *Ibid.*, p.11.
28. *Ibid.*, p.12f.
29. *Ibid.*, p.13.
30. *Ibid.*, p.13.
31. *Bath Journal*, 13 August 1804.
32. Skinner, *op.cit.*, p.25.
33. *Ibid.*, p.29.
34. *Ibid.*, p.41.

CHAPTER FOUR

COMPETITION AND CONSOLIDATION 1810-1820

The Roads

It has been suggested that the Turnpike Road network reached its peak about 1810 but in the years that followed improvements were always being considered particularly to tap some of the coal traffic, which the new canal was now carrying away from the Camerton-Timsbury area. In 1815 the Wells Trust, realising perhaps the hazards and difficulties of the Chilcompton-Radstock-Dunkerton section of the Great Western Road, had proposed a bold and entirely new route for a turnpike road to Bath. This route would have bypassed Radstock striking north and east from Old Down, passing the hamlets of Clapton, Radford and Tunley, and join the Fosse Way at the top of Dunkerton Hill.[1]

John McAdam was appointed General Surveyor of the Bristol Turnpike Trust in 1816, and the same year he was approached by the Bath Trust but was not engaged. A trustee, Benjamin Wingrove, succeeded in obtaining the post for himself and it was to be another ten years before McAdam replaced Wingrove. Wingrove has been described as an 'eminent and practical road surveyor' and an exponent of Telford's repair methods. He resigned in 1826 when criticised for the mismanagement of accounts on repairs.[2]

Some of these repairs would be caused by the extensive coal traffic. Skinner, speaking of the Priddy road, says it was 'rendered bad by farmers' carts going to Paulton from this part of the country for coal.'[3] These farmers would probably be fetching cart-loads of small coal to burn in their lime-kilns to make fertiliser. It has been estimated that a kiln might use fifteen quarters or one hundred and twenty bushels of refuse coal a week (about four tons).[4] About 1816 there had been an accident at the turnpike gate at Odd Down when Skinner's horse bolted, carrying off his daughter Laura and son Owen; 'although the distance was upward of half a mile and several coal carts were in the road, she neither screamed nor attempted to jump out, but sat quiet till the turnpike man put to the gate, which the mare attempted to leap and broke the upper bar ...'.[5]

An early watercolour sketch of a collier and his cart descending the steep Mendip slopes towards Glastonbury – using an unusual braking system. *Radstock Museum Archive*

The terminal basin of the main line of the canal at Timsbury in c.1870. The tramway from the collieries can be seen converging from the hillside above, with several wagons on the wharf waiting by the boats in the basin. Another tramway from Paulton approached by the bridge over the Cam Brook to the left. In the centre is the wharfinger's house, and to the far right the stables for the horses which towed the wagons back up to the pits. The large building between them with the hipped roof appears to have been a coal store.

An enlargement of the above illustration; two front-tipping wagons are waiting at the edge of the wharf on the right, another already tipped forward into the boat to the left. Behind them several empty wagons with their front doors still open stand under the trees waiting to be returned.

The Canal

Jeremiah Cruse, a colleague of William Smith, prepared a large-scale map of the whole Somersetshire Coal Canal and its related network of tramways in 1812. During this decade there were important developments with regard to the Radstock branch of the Coal Canal. It too had had to deal with similar differences in level between Midford and Twinhoe, and there were also problems obtaining sufficient water to fill this section. The difficulties were finally resolved in 1815 with the completion of a tramway along the entire route of this branch of the canal. The *Bath Chronicle* reported as follows:

An image of a tramway wagon which ran between the Timsbury collieries and the Coal Canal, depicted on a tombstone in Cameley churchyard. It commemorates the death of a young man as a result of an accident with one of these wagons in 1808.

> 'We cheerfully avail ourselves of the opportunity now afforded us, of conveying to the subscribers of this Canal and the public, the gratifying intelligence of the completion of the New Rail Road, from the village of Radstoke [*sic*] to the Canal near Midford, a distance of upwards of seven miles; by which means a certain and regular communication is now opened to the several great collieries of Radstoke, Welton, Clandown and Smallcombe, from which works a constant supply of the very best Somersetshire coal may now be depended upon to any extent.'[6]

There was still fierce competition between the two alternative methods for bringing coal into Bath. In March 1816 an advertisement in the *Bath Herald* announced a reduction in the price of coal. Six month later 'Canal Coal' was being offered at 11½d a hundredweight at the Sydney Wharf in Bath, 'All goods sold at R. Carpenter's wharf are weighed at Pulteney Engine by a sworn agent'. On the 12 October the merchants using land carriage reduced their prices to the same figure.[7]

This indicates that after some eleven years of operation there was little to choose between the two ways of transporting coal to Bath. It either made the long trip down the Coal Canal and along some six miles of the Kennet & Avon Canal to Bath, or it went over the hills by waggon and horse. The similar prices indicate the strong competition between the rival routes. The canal must certainly have helped to relieve the congestion on the roads as well as the wear and tear on the surfaces caused by so many carts and waggons. For the proprietors of the canal, the Bath market was a secondary one. Their main outlet for the sale of coal from Somerset were the towns to the east.

Coal owners and canal proprietors showed their opposition to coal from other regions being sold in Bath. The Canal Company opposed the Bath and Bristol Canal Act of 1811, when it was introduced in Parliament, since it feared the threat to its trade with the probable introduction of Welsh coal to the markets in Bath and places further east.[8] This canal would have linked Bristol to the Kennet & Avon Canal at Bath, thereby avoiding the difficulties of navigating the river Avon, but the project soon had to be abandoned as a result of a general depression in national trade.

A view of the Coal Canal at Tucking Mill in South Stoke. The buildings and wharf on the right were built by William Smith, where he established his sawing machinery for the export by canal of Bath ashlar stone.

The Somerset coal owners combined in a petition in 1818 against the threat of duty-free privileges being granted to the Severn ports, as again this would have given Welsh coal another decided advantage. The competitive nature of Welsh coal on this side of the Severn Estuary was noted in 1820 when Skinner paid a visit to Sea Mills. He found that Welsh coal was being sold at seven pence a bushel, 'as cheap as I purchase it at the Camerton pits, which must be a great advantage to the poor in the vicinity'.[9]

Gas from Somerset Coal

Coal was finding a new use around 1819 with the production of gas in the principal towns, such as Bristol, Bath and Taunton, for which the kinds of coal found in Somerset were especially suited. An advertisement in the local Bath papers of that year invited those who intended using gas lights to have their houses and shops fitted up with the proper pipes and lamps, as these had to be approved by the Inspector of the Bath Gas Light & Coke Company.[10] When Skinner visited Oxford at the end of the following year he found that a gas works there were using coal that had been brought from Bitton, near Bristol, and delivered at a guinea a ton. He remarked that the tar from the gas works in Bath was sold as paint for outdoor work.[11]

It was during this same visit to Oxford that Skinner met 'Mr. Buckland, Professor of Mineralogy [*sic*], who has visited our coal pits at Camerton and the vicinity. His opinion respecting the different beds of this vegetable matter is that it was done by a succession of deluges depositing these wood plants, etc., etc., of the country, the lightest parts being the uppermost, the sand and heavier clay subsiding; that the marine strata imbedded over the vegetable was a continuation of the same process to the tops of the highest hills.'[12]

A view of Bath Gas Light & Coke Company works behind Twerton Suspension Bridge in the 1830s, one of the first gas works to be opened in the country in 1819. It appears here much in its original form, and as the Rev.John Skinner would have seen it to witness various balloon ascents in the 1820s.

The Social Conditions in the Area

The work of William Smith had led to the informed exploitation of the coalfield in its early stages. The result was that the coal owners were becoming an increasingly prosperous and influential group, shaping the life of the local community as it became more dependent on coal. They could thwart competition from other coalfields, and with the canal system completed to the east, they were in a position to meet the rising demand for coal from there. Unfortunately, the increasing pressure of industrialisation on a village like Camerton also had its social consequences, of which Skinner was all too aware. The rough conditions that existed among the colliers and their families are revealed in his *Journal*. In 1811 there was an alleged rape case, committed in the mill house of the coal pit, by a collier named Aslip. The men at New Pit were so afraid of the mother of the victim that they refused to work in case she cut the rope and endangered their lives when going down the shaft. The rope to have been cut deliberately on previous occasions. 'I heard from Joseph Goold that the rope once was cut at the coal pit, by which a man of the name of Parfitt lost his life. Indeed I remember some years ago having heard two twists of the rope at the Lower Pit were found cut, but in time to prevent an accident. What a diabolical method of revenge. What a nefarious race.'[13]

Later in that year the Rector visited Hannah West of Red Hill who had been drunk when she fell off the horse on which she carried coal. Her skull was fractured and she was not expected to live. Hannah promised, that if she did, 'she would not swear or drink again, indeed she would sell her coal horse and not drive coal again to Bath, for that was the way she got into liquor, stopping at public houses by the wayside and falling into evil company'. It was a similar case with an old man called Evans from Tunley 'as not a day of his life passed without his returning drunk from Bath, after having sold his coal.' Sadly, neither Hannah nor Evans made amends. She was such a disturbance in the poor houses on Red Hill that the overseers threatened to turn her out, and Evans came to church for one Sunday and then stopped. 'I should not be surprised if he actually meets with his death by a fall from his horse some night on his return from Bath'.[14]

Tensions among the Miners

There was more friction over Sunday work in 1816. Skinner had complained to Goold, the bailiff at the colliery, on several occasions about the colliers working on Sundays. 'The bailiffs of the coal works without scruple employ it in repairing any accidents which may have occurred in the week, in cleansing out the boilers of the steam engine, etc.'[15] It was all to no avail, bailiffs, coal owners and the local squire had little time for the observation of the Sabbath, and did not encourage their employees to rest on that day.

Tension in the coalfield came to a head in the opening weeks of 1817 with a 10% reduction in the wages of the miners. The civil disturbance required the intervention of the Royal Lancers of the North Somerset Yeomanry to restore order.[16] It is not clear to what extent Camerton was involved in this event but the *Bristol Mirror* reported that some three thousand colliers had assembled in the vicinity of Paulton. It has been suggested that one of the main causes of the discontent in 1817 was the widespread unemployment of miners. This led them to find alternative work on the land, such as hay making and helping with the harvest.[17]

The Courier of London for the 6th March 1817 carried the following report:

> 'Rioting of Colliers at Paulton, Radstock etc. On February 28th a tumultuous and disorderly proceeding commenced this morning amongst the colliers at Paulton who, in consequence of an arrangement amounting to a reduction of one tenth of their wages, refused to work. This irregular step was but too readily followed by the miners in several of the neighbouring collieries who, being assembled in considerable numbers, were collectively and most impressively addressed by that active and vigilant magistrate, Sir J. Coxe Hippisley, Bart., but they did not seem disposed to separate until the Riot Act had been read, in consequence of which they dispersed and order seems completely restored. A reward of twenty guineas is offered for the discovery of the principal mover of this most ill-advised procedure.'

Apparently the situation worsened that evening and a party of the Royal Lancers, 'some of the brave and modest heroes of Waterloo', commanded by Captain Lewis, arrived from Bristol. The ringleaders were arrested during the following days and on the 4th March the miners returned to work. A letter from Sir John to *The Courier* explained that the cause was due to a few troublemakers among the 6,000 colliers in the district.[18]

Camerton Manor House, home of Mrs.Jarrett, depicted by the Rev.John Skinner. It was replaced by her son John Jarrett in 1838-40 by the present Camerton Court in Camerton Park, a Grade II listed building designed by Humphrey Repton's son, George. *Rev. D.E. Cooper*

A New Lady of the Manor

James Stephens, owner of the pits at Camerton, chairman of the Coal Canal Company through its formative years and local squire, died and was buried at St.Germans in France on the 1st July 1816.[19] A year later Skinner met the new lady of the manor, the widow of Herbert Newton Jarrett of Golden Grove, Jamaica, the daughter and heiress of Stephens. Anne Jarrett had been born in 1783 and was to live at Camerton until her death in 1830. There were to be many confrontations between Mrs Jarrett and the Rector during the following years.[20]

Two months after the death of James Stephens the *Bath Chronicle* carried the following notice:
Dated 20th September 1816: [21]

> Camerton Coal Works
> Mr.John Rennolds having this day resigned his situation as Clerk and Book-keeper to the Camerton Coal Company all persons indebted to the concern are requested not to pay the same to the said John Rennolds or to any person on his account. And all persons to whom the said Coal Company stand indebted, are desired to send their accounts to Mr.William Rennolds at the said works.
> Nathaniel Bayly Robert Haynes
> Eleazer Pickwick Peter Fry

Rennolds or Reynolds, was the bailiff at the coal works at the time of the case of rape referred to earlier. Skinner had also spoken to him with regard to work being done on Sunday at the pits.[22] More light is thrown on the notice of resignation by an entry in the *Journal* for the 18th July 1817 when Skinner was talking with Mrs. Jarrett who had arrived recently.

According to Skinner's account William's tenure was short-lived and both men were dead within a year. It appears that they were guilty of embezzling the Company's funds and using the proceeds to meet their debts in the ale-house. The bailiffs who followed were not much better. 'I told Mrs. Jarrett she herself must be aware that there was a system of rascality going on more especially in the Coal works, that there was Goold, then Reynolds and Soper who had all turned out to be great knaves... She said that was very true, there had been no honesty among the bailiffs ever since the Coal works had been established.'[23]

Notes to Chapter Four

Fertiliser from Limestone

Before the introduction of modern chemical fertilisers farmers were dependent on manure or marl until the introduction of quick lime produced by the burning of limestone in the 18th century. It was an advantage to use the small coal mixed with limestone to raise the temperature in the kilns to between 850° and 1000° C. There were several reasons for using quick lime; first, in areas where the soil was acidic, this was neutralised by the lime; second, on heavy, clay soil it helped to break up the soil and encourage better drainage; third, lime is essential for the healthy growth of most plants, as it acts as a food. Furthermore, acid soils tend to lock up other plant foods and the lime unlocks these by making them soluble and available to the roots of the plants.

The Gas Industry

The gas industry was to become an increasingly important consumer. It was to take 40% of the total saleable output by the late 1930s. This slightly reduced the seasonal fluctuations in demand, although short-time working in the summer months continued to be commonplace.
Note to the author from Penny Bonsall.
See also Dr. Harold Nabb, 'Gas and Coal', *Five Arches*, Issue 25, 1996.

Plateway wagons of the type used on the Radstock tramway, photographed c.1870 on the Hay & Kington railway in Wales, both built by the same engineer at about the same time. The structures behind the wagons belonged to the Kington Gas Works, opened in 1830.

The Radstock Tramway

The tramway was laid along the towpath of the canal to a gauge of approximately 3ft 4in. and horses drew eight to nine wagons, each holding around twenty-five hundredweight of coal, to the basin at Midford where it was loaded into boats for the onward journey to the Kennet & Avon Canal. The Tithe Apportionment Map of Wellow, dated 1839, shows passing-places every six hundred yards on the tramway from Radstock to Midford, together with the basin at Midford, with its three arms and loading wharves. The tramway overcame the problems of the canal being closed by prolonged drought in summer and in winter being frozen over for a considerable period. An advertisement would then appear in the local papers announcing that the canal was open again.

R.K. Bluhm, article, *op.cit.*, p.55.

Monktonian, Vol.XXVI, April 1954, No.2, p.108f.

Bath Herald, 5 March 1814.

Somerset Guardian, 22 March 1968, article by Robin Atthill, 'When thirty pits were working in Somerset and tramroads fed the coal canal'.

Jeremiah Cruse 1758-1819

Jeremiah Cruse was a fellow land surveyor and colleague of William Smith. After leaving the employment of the Canal Company in 1799, Smith went into partnership with Cruse from 1802-1804, taking a shop in Bath at No. 3 Trim Bridge to exhibit his fossils and, presumably, his maps. Cruse was already employed as Clerk and surveyor to the Marquis of Bath's estates, including Lord Weymouth's properties in Bath, but also produced parish maps independently, such as those of

Twerton, Hallatrow and Rode. Some of his work seems to have been derived from his association with Smith, for example in 1813 when he produced a map of the Cold Bath Farm Estate in Batheaston (site of Smith's unsuccessful exploration for coal there the previous year). The reference to Camerton shows that he was active in this region in 1807, possibly in connection with the Coal Canal, which would support the assumption that it was he who produced the large Company wall plan of the Canal, c.1809 (now preserved by the Bath Royal Literary and Scientific Institute), based on earlier drafts by Smith.

William Buckland 1784-1856
In 1819 he became the first University reader in geology at Oxford. He saw in the vestiges of the ice age striking proof of the Biblical story of the Flood. He was appointed Dean of Westminster in 1845.
The Oxford Dictionary of the Christian Church, F.L.Cross, 1961.

During 1824 Buckland and Coneybeare carried out their surveys above and below ground in Somerset and Gloucestershire and then published their findings. This was another major step forward in the understanding of the coalfield from that taken nearly twenty years earlier in the work of William Smith. W.Buckland and W.D.Coneybeare, 'Observations on the South Western Coal District of England', *Transactions of the Geological Society*, 2nd.series, Volume I, part 2, pp.210-366.

References to Chapter Four

1. R. Atthill, *Old Mendip*, p.137.
2. W. Albert, *op.cit.*, p.143.
3. J. Bulley, *op.cit.*, I, p.54.
4. J. Bulley, *ibid.*, I, p.61.
5. Skinner *op.cit.* p.135
6. *Bath Chronicle*, 20 July 1815.
7. *Bath Herald*, 16 March 1816, 14 September 1816, 12 October 1816 and *Bath Chronicle*, 19 September 1816.
8. Bulley, *op.cit.*, I, p.58.
9. Skinner, *op.cit.*, p.128.
10. *Bath Chronicle*, 3 June 1819.
11. Skinner, op.cit., p.152.
12. *Ibid.*, p.150.
13. *Ibid.*, p.61f.
14. *Ibid.*, p.70f.
15. *Ibid.*, p.99.
16. Down &Warrington, *op.cit.*, p.32.
17. Bulley, *op.cit.*, II, pp.33, 37, 44.
18. *Somerset Guardian*, 1 March 1940.
19. Clew, *op.cit.*, p.81.
20. Skinner, *op.cit.*, p.101f.
21. *Bath Chronicle*, 26 September 1816.
22. Skinner, *op.cit.*, p.99.
23. *Ibid.*, p.105; p.117f.

Sketch by the Rev. John Skinner of his home, Camerton Parsonage. *Rev. D.E. Cooper*

CHAPTER FIVE

SKINNER AND THE COLLIERS 1820-1830

Skinner and the Canal

The Somersetshire Coal Canal sometimes provided those who lived nearby with a means of relaxation and leisure. There was the happy occasion in June 1822 when Skinner had a coal barge prepared for an outing along the canal. An awning was spread to screen the guests from the sun, and tables and chairs placed under it. Fifteen people enjoyed the outing:

> 'My horse, under the direction of a man from the coal works, towed us along. We first visited the head of the canal at Paulton Basin, and returned thence through Camerton and Dunkerton to Combe Hay. Having explored the beautiful grounds we partook of our cold collation under the shade of the elm trees near the cascade, and in the cool of the evening proceeded homewards. Passing the 'Swan' at Dunkerton the Camerton band came on board and played marches and Scotch airs the whole way home. The music and the dressed-out coal barge attracted multitudes, who followed our course along the banks of the canal and lined the bridges under which we passed, which gave a novel appearance to the scenery and a pleasing termination to our rural fête. On quitting the water the ladies drank tea at Camerton, and I accompanied them to Radstock.'[1]

The former Swan Inn, now a private residence, by the Bath to Radstock Road. William Smith stayed here during the building of the canal which ran behind the inn, beside the houses in the background. The Camerton band would have joined the Rev. John Skinner's party at Dunkerton wharf a little further up the road.

'Sketch of the Camerton Valley, Canal & Coal Pits', by the Rev. John Skinner. To the right is New Pit, and beyond the trees to the left, Old Pit, the two joined by the Coal Canal. In the foreground is Colliers' Row, which still exists, as also the bailiff's house on the hill above and the Methodist Chapel at the summit. This view, taken from Camerton Park, is now obscured by later spoil-heaps and vegetation. *Rev. D.E. Cooper*

During the winter months when the canal was frozen over it was used for skating. Where the canal widened at Bengrove, Skinner taught his son Owen and 'young Jarrett, who for the first time put on skates'.[2] This was in 1821, and two years later another spell of severe weather brought the whole canal to a standstill. 'As it had frozen hard during the night and the boys wished me accompany them to skaite [*sic*], I walked with them to the Dundas Aqueduct in the Claverton Valley, and skaited for four hours on a fine piece of ice where the Combe Hay canal had not been broken. Some of the Catholic gentlemen from Downside passed us, and said they had come on the canal the whole way from Camerton.'[3]

Skinner also built a boat for his boys so that they could use it on the canal, but it had to be locked away in the cart-house when not in use 'as the colliers would destroy it in one week if it were left in the

A recent view of Collier's Row (New Pit Cottages). The coalworks stood on the rise just visible to the left. New Pit batch, now overgrown, can be seen top right.

canal'.[4] He himself enjoyed walks along the banks of the canal: '.. after dinner we walked to the canal, my sons wishing to sail in the boat, as the wind blew fresh; they amused themselves awhile. As Anna and myself were returning home by Colliers' Row [adjacent to New Pit] a stone was thrown at me from the end house, where Goold lives …'.[5]

A coal wagon outside the Cross Ways Inn (now closed) at the top of the hill from Dunkerton Wharf where the road from Camerton and Tunley met the main road to Bath. The trace horse shown here assisted the climb up the hill. The stable was opposite the inn.

Throughout the years a number of people lost their lives in the canal by accident or deliberately. It was not unknown for lock-keepers and bargemen to fall in and drown and some people used the canal as a convenient method of ending their lives. At times of heavy rain the canals could become dangerous. The *Bath Journal* reported in December 1821 that 'during the past week six barges laden with Bath coals have sunk in the Kennet & Avon Canal between Newbury and Reading. The river being overflowed from the recent rains has rendered the navigation very dangerous'.[6]

The amount of coal and coke being carried on the coal canal increased steadily during this period. A figure of 100,000 tons passing through Midford has been quoted for 1820,[7] and by 1828 this had risen to 113,000 tons valued at £15,000.[8] These figures would also include much of the coal from pits in the Radstock area which had been brought along the tramway of the southern branch as far as Midford and there transferred to boats on the coal canal. To this end, William Ashman of the Clandown Colliery designed and built a locomotive for the tramway between Radstock and Midford in 1827. It was intended to haul the coal wagons along the route but in the event proved to be too heavy for the track and eventually had to be abandoned.[9]

Between 1825 and 1850 the canal served twelve collieries and the tramway another twelve.[10] The large tonnage passing out into the Kennet & Avon Canal accounted for half the amount which that canal carried during its early years. By the end of 1830 it was being announced in the press that the Kennet & Avon had carried the highest tonnage in its history over the past six months, and that the receipts amounted to £28,000.[11]

About one third of the exports of the Somersetshire Coal Canal entered the Wilts & Berks and was distributed along its line, a quarter of this going as far as Abingdon for consumption in that town and for carriage onwards to Oxford and down towards Reading. As Charles Hadfield points out, 'the Kennet & Avon, the Wilts & Berks and the Somersetshire Coal Canal could call themselves successful, if success meant that they were of solid service to the districts they passed through. For thirty years they shared this service with the turnpike roads, and by the evidence of their revenues the wealth of the countryside and the collieries at least doubled in that time. Financially, only the coal canal gave a good average return to the investor … The local proprietors, usually landowners, obtained indirect benefits from the general development of the countryside and the cheapening of coal and other imports'.[12]

The Somersetshire Coal Canal was forced to charge higher tolls for its ten miles compared with those on the larger canal. These tolls would have been due largely to the additional charges imposed by the flight of locks at Combe Hay. At one stage it cost 23/3d for the coal canal as against 5/- for the seventy miles on the Kennet and Avon Canal as far as Reading.[13]

The Roads

The hilly route between Radstock and Bath continued to exercise the minds of the trustees of the Bath Turnpike Trust. On New Year's Day 1825 Skinner attended a meeting of the Trust in Bath to vote on the question of the road on Radstock Hill, but it seems that it was so short of funds that it could not seriously consider alterations or improvements.[14] In 1827 the Trust proposed a diversion of the main turnpike road through the villages of Dunkerton and Carlingcott to avoid traffic having to make the long climb up the southern part of Dunkerton Hill, but this was never implemented.[15]

A considerable quantity of coal was still finding its way to Bath along the roads from the pits south of the city. It has been suggested that while some did go by canal, the circuitous route and the high tolls meant that most of the trade stayed on the roads. A waggon drawn by four horses could manage to haul two tons, and carts pulled by two horses could pull a ton in winter and 25cwt in the summer months. Even the pack-ass trains were still to be seen during the 1820s bringing coal into the city.[16]

These coal hauliers worked on very small margins in a fiercely competitive trade. They were not known for kindness to their animals, and to make a living they had to work long hours. Some were known to have fallen off their waggons through tiredness, and to be crushed or injured by falling under the wheels of their own vehicles.[17] The *Bath Journal* complained in 1823 that the coal carts frequently broke down in Bath. They were considered to be inconvenient and badly constructed. 'The poor animal in the shafts has to sustain a load sufficient at times to dislocate his back.' It was also hard for the horse to keep his balance on the road surfaces. It was frequently 'almost bruised to death, by falling under the weight of an immoderate burthen ... the horse has to endure hardships and cruelties daily and most particularly so in this part of the kingdom'. Some years later the same newspaper contained a caution to drivers of donkeys who brought coal to Bath. This had been prompted when George Chivers was fined 10/- for cruelty to his donkey.[18]

In the same edition, the paper pointed out the unfairness of the toll system, following the increase in tolls which had been announced the previous week. 'A man who sends a waggon from Bath to Timsbury via Twerton and Marksbury [the 'Lower Wells Road'] will pay two full tolls ... while a waggon going through the Holloway gate [the 'Upper Wells Road'], and thence through the Tunley Road will pay but one full toll. The result of this will be the throwing open the coalpits at Camerton, and the immediate neighbourhood, to the serious injury of the parishes whose roads lead to the Timsbury pits.'[19]

Skinner and Education

There had been a School House in Camerton which had been built with voluntary subscriptions. Rather surprisingly, Stephens had it pulled down because it was too near his Manor House. He did not seem to have much time for 'instruction for persons who were to work hard for their bread'.[20] Soon after his arrival, Skinner had established a school 'under the idea of instructing the colliers' children' which he supported at his own expense, but by 1822 he complained that it was now defunct due to the interference of Mrs. Jarrett.[21] Later, he wrote 'we have no school to inculcate honest principles, the school of the Coal Pits is decidedly against everything which is in the least connected with them'.[22] The following year he wrote to Mr. Bailey, one of the proprietors of the Camerton coal works, to Mr. Purnell of Woodborough, and to Mrs. Jarrett respecting their contributions towards a parochial school in connection with the National Association.[23] A month later he had received no assistance from the coal company, but Mrs. Jarrett had reason to believe that they would give £5 a year towards the schoolmaster's salary and the same amount towards the building.[24] In July 1824 Skinner commented with respect to the Sunday School that the proprietors of the Coal Works were not particularly concerned about the spiritual education of the lower orders.[25]

Despite all these difficulties it has been pointed out that by 1828 the schools in Camerton had in fact a high proportion of children. In that year there was a school population of one hundred and sixty six out of a total population of twelve hundred. In addition, the Camerton Church Sunday School had fifty children enrolled. It should be noted, however, that the majority of the pupils were girls, in the ratio of ten to three.[26] The population of the village had increased by two hundred since 1822.[27]

The Colliers

Skinner was often called to see the victim of some accident at the pits or to comfort their dependants. In March 1822 a miner named Job Cromwell was killed by the rope of the gug-wheel winding round his body. The *Bath Journal* carried a report of the inquest and also the case of John Bull, whose back had been broken by a stone of two tons falling on him in the Camerton pit.[28] The following January Garratt of Wick Lane was brought home in a 'most deplorable state, the spine having been put out below the shoulder by a mass of coal falling on him. This is the third instance within these last two years of the same accidents having occurred'.[29] Garratt was attended by Curtis, the doctor of the Camerton Club, which existed for the welfare of the miners. The next year a young man called Tyler died when a stone fell on him underground. This may well have been a fossilised tree stump which fell out of the roof of the workings, and being of great weight would crush everything under it.[30] Robert Payne was killed when 'his candle went out in the pit last night, and in stepping forwards, thinking he was on solid ground, he fell down and was dashed to pieces'.[31]

The colliers at Camerton were fortunate in that at least they had their Camerton Club. It would have been one of the earliest welfare clubs in the area. The doctor who was engaged by the club attended the sick and injured miners in their homes,[32] and the club was also prepared to help the wife of an injured miner if the parish was unable to provide sufficiently for her.[33] Meetings of the Club were evidently open to others who were not miners, as Skinner noted on one occasion that; 'The masons, and my servant Heal, deserted to attend the Camerton Club'.[34]

The Camerton miners' annual parade was the high point in the life of the Club. In 1821 the miners walked to the church through Skinner's grounds. He would have preached to them but their conduct was bad; 'they are incorrigible'.[35] In June 1829 some fourteen hundred people took part in the parade and as they passed the parsonage their band played the National Anthem.[36] The parade, which also took in the surrounding villages, was held on the 11th of June every year. The 'Club Days' continued to be a feature of mining culture until well into the 20th century. Among the miners, 'tight breath' or miner's asthma was common; today it is known as pneumoconiosis. When a miner was burned, his injuries were bathed with hot cow's milk and ointment provided by the coal owners.[37]

It was not unknown for the miners to be on a four-day week which reduced their earnings and added to their hard times. On some occasions Skinner offered the miners a little work in helping him with his

Camerton Rectory.

archaeological digs and in hay-making in his glebe.[38] He recorded in 1828 that some colliers came to mow the Rectory grass, for which he paid them £3.15.0 and also provided them with food and beer.[39]

> 'In an age when even the introduction of machinery had not persuaded the employer that a reduction of working hours was a desirable and practicable reformation of the industrial system, and when the public conscience was still not fully aroused to demand such a limitation, it is hardly surprising that excessive hours of labour did not appear to be such an economic evil as short time and irregularity of employment. This was especially true of times of depression. The Camerton miners in 1830 complained of having to work a four-day week, and Moses Horler recalled the times in the 1820s and 1830s when the hewer brought home a paypacket of about 8/- because he had been limited to a four-turn week.'[40]

During a period of very bad weather in January 1830, when there was a heavy fall of snow, Skinner wrote; 'that the poor are much distressed, and will be more so if this weather continues ... I tell the cook always to have a quantity of soup in the boiler, that we may be able to assist those who are really in absolute want; but as our Collieries are in full work we shall not be so much pinched here as in other places'.[41] The balance between too much work and too little to support a wife and family must have been a fine one. It appears that some men were expected to work excessive hours; 'The mason told me he had been working all night in Radford coal-pit ... he told me that his brother, who attended the engine, for one whole week only slept four hours, as he was engaged night and day for that period in the engine house. I hardly think this is true and indeed, if it be, it argues great want of foresight and humanity in the masters of the works'.[42]

Early in 1822, according to the *Bath Journal*, 'There is at Camerton, a heap of earth, which has been on fire many months. In consequence of burning coke on the ground instead of kilns; and it has been found very difficult to extinguish it'.[43] This method of burning coal in the open to produce coke would have been very unpleasant for all the villagers who lived nearby. Coke made in the open air was 'firmer and better for drying malt than that burnt in the oven, but the latter method is the most profitable to the coal maker as the coaks burnt this way measure as much as new coal'.[44]

Disagreements and Disputes

Throughout much of his time in Camerton Skinner had great trouble in collecting the tithes he was due. He wrote in 1821 'Clarke, the Schoolmaster, in whom I had given the tithe of the gardens as his salary, called to say that Mr. Feare [Bailiff of the Coal Works], had forbidden the colliers to pay their accustomed composition for the tithe of the grounds they occupied, under the pleas that they were included in the composition of £30 paid by the Coal Company. I went immediately to Feare's house and showed him my tithe book as drawn out by [Jeremiah] Cruse, the surveyor, in 1807, wherein the gardens are reckoned separately from the other grounds occupied by the Coal Company, and as such had paid tithes for several years past'.[45]

The result of this dispute was a visit to the magistrate later in which the case went in Skinner's favour. He felt that the Bailiff had intended to set the colliers against him. 'I had always been very careful to advise this body of men to be obedient to the agents employed to superintend them, and that I well knew the evil of stirring up sedition among so numerous a class of men, and that even when they made their just complaints against some of the late bailiffs who had defrauded them I still recommended their obedience for the general benefit of society.'[46]

Skinner appears to have done his best to exert his influence for moderation during times of industrial unrest. In 1820 there had been strikes over unfair dismissals and wages.[47] At the end of April 1828 there was some sort of civil disturbance and he complained that 'The whole collieries are put into excitement, and the pockets of their families picked, because we have no proper person to control the turbulence of the people'.[48]

On the 18th April 1830 there was a more serious situation at Camerton. On that day Skinner called at the Manor House to see Mrs. Jarrett about the intended opposition of the miners to their employers. She attempted to dismiss the whole matter as being over some £80 and that it was all connected with the man who raised the steam. She offered to pay his wages in the meantime. Skinner countered by saying that the real issue was the threatened reduction in wages: 'What authority Mrs. Jarrett had to interfere with the management of the works is another question. She has only a free share, but this politic lady has one thing which gives her the fullest power over the men, and which, if the Proprietors ever come to open conflict with her, they find to their cost, renders her power absolute. She has authority over the residences of the colliers, who are only weekly tenants, and may be dismissed *ad libitum*.'[49]

The following day Skinner went into the centre of the village as he understood that the colliers had in fact struck, not because of the steam man being taken away; 'but because some of them were lowered 3s a week in their pay, which they said they could not afford, as most of them had to pay £5 or guineas for the hire of their houses, and sometimes they did not work above four days in the week. I said I was sure if this was properly represented to the Proprietors by two or three of the men, and if on examination they found it true, they would not persevere in the measure; that it was not in their interest to have the men work for sums on which they could not live; that I should recommend their deputing three of the most intelligent men to see the Proprietors before they came on Wednesday to Camerton ... They said it would be difficult to find any to go on the mission, as the masters had determined, they said, to turn the people out who would venture to speak to them on anything of the kind, and would first be dismissed from their works. I know there are some artful, ill-disposed fellows among the colliers, but there are others who will suffer beyond bearing if the three shillings a week are taken from their scanty pay'.[50]

There was more trouble in the area at the end of the year:

> 'While writing in my study I saw numbers of men, at least fifty, cross the Park in front of my windows to go down to the pits at Camerton. I had learnt that the colliers meant to make a rise. Soon after, I saw this mob proceeding to our pits. I then walked to Clan Down [Common], having heard that there had been a mob of the colliers assembled there yesterday, and that the Riot Act was read by Mr. James, accompanied by other magistrates; indeed, they told me that some of the Camerton people had joined them, and meant to be there again today. I saw all was quiet on the Down, and the Steam Engine [at Clandown Colliery] working, as I approached the pit. I walked thither, and found that the Radstock Rioters, for I can call them by no other name, had gone on to Paulton. The people at the pit said they were well satisfied with their wages, but that these fellows from Radstock had ordered them to stop work. I counselled them against cutting the ropes of the pits and the damaging of the machinery, etc., and advised them to return to their duty: that there were barges then waiting for their loads. The men said they would load the barges, and should not stop work: that they had nothing to complain of, only that they thought the small coal landed ought to be paid for as well as the large coal, since they procured one as well as the other. I said that this ought to be a consideration with their masters.'[51]

The miners were certainly justified in their grievances when they saw that the small coal was being sold to the farmers for making lime. The *Bath Journal* of the 20th December 1830 commented on the situation as follows:

> 'For some time past, a considerable feeling of dissatisfaction has existed among the colliers of Radstock, in consequence of a regulation which prevails in the Pits, by which they are paid only for the large or round coal which is hauled up, and are allowed nothing for the small, which is mixed in a very considerable quantity with the other. Last week they struck for wages upon this sort of coal at several Pits including Camerton but a proper representation of their grievances being made to the proprietors and magistrates, an arrangement was entered into, and the men on Friday last went back to work.'[52]

It was estimated at this time there were about two thousand miners in the Paulton, Camerton and Timsbury pits and that as a result of this settlement the men would have earned another eighteen pence a week.[53] Commenting on this period as seen through the eyes of Skinner, Coysh wrote that his notes reveal a picture of change and unrest, poverty, illness and drunkenness. The colliers started to organise themselves, but 'These spontaneous uprisings seldom produced any useful results'.[54]

Celebrations

Occasionally there were happier events, as in July 1822. There was a great deal of shouting at the coal works, with people singing and music playing. When Skinner asked the reason, he was told that 'the Proprietors of the Coal Works were present at the Bailiff's, and had distributed money, on account of the discovery of a fresh vein of coal which promised to be very advantageous. This, I think, is indeed good news for the parish, as it regards the future prospects of so many who depend on the prosperity of the mines'. Unfortunately by the next day Skinner was complaining of the drunkenness and uproar; 'No work done at the Pits, and the people are more brutified than ever'.[55]

There were celebrations for a different reason in July 1823. It was the coming of age of John Jarrett, the eldest son of Mrs. Jarrett, when the Camerton mines passed to him under the terms of James Stephens' will.[56] The bells were rung, and cannon fired. The Camerton Band played all day long. 'On a lofty elm near the coal works was erected a platform on which was a chair for the oldest collier, he was called the 'King of Camerton'.' Ox and sheep were roasted and the day ended with a grand ball at the Manor house in the evening.[57]

From Skinner's Journal one gains the impression that there were almost separate celebrations and festivities for the miners and their families and for the agricultural workers, who were on even lower incomes and whose lives were every bit as hard; 'Great preparations having been made for this important event by the killing of an ox and the purchase of ten hogsheads of cyder, besides strong beer, spirits, etc., etc., with seven sacks of potatoes and a waggon load of bread'.[58]

In 1828 the Somerset coalmasters again showed their influence when they combined to oppose the bill before Parliament proposing the Tramway from the Gloucestershire coalfield to the river Avon at Bitton.[59] Bluhm has pointed out that most of the collieries in the area were quite small affairs at this time but that those at Camerton and Timsbury were larger than most. No colliery would have produced more than twenty thousand tons in a year. 'A typical colliery at this time was a single small diameter shaft, little wider than a well shaft.'[60] He also mentions that the shaft at Camerton extended to 840 feet, which would have been quite difficult to operate without a proper ventilation system.

Notes to Chapter Five

The Radstock and Midford Tramway

The tramway, like the canal, had its other uses: 'On Saturday, the "tubs" were well brushed out and boards placed across them from side to side and used as passenger vehicles to convey folks from Midford, Wellow and Single Hill to and from the Radstock Market, so here again we find the first tramway service in the country...'.[15]

Article by S. Lloyd Harvey in the *Somerset Guardian*, 2 August 1925.

A Tramway from Coalpit Heath in the east Bristol coal mining district to the River Avon

Ross Barber, *The Dramway*, Avon Industrial Buildings Trust, 1986

Skinner on Education

His reference to the National Association may be an error on his part. It is possible that he was referring to the National Society which was an Anglican organisation established in 1811 by the Rev. Dr. Andrew Bell. Its full name was the National Society for Promoting the Education of the Poor in the Principals of the Established Church throughout England and Wales. Bell cooperated with the Quaker Joseph Lancaster who led the non-conformist British and Foreign Schools Society. The two men were the originators of the monitorial system whereby the older children taught the younger ones. These two societies were at their peak by 1816. In 1833 Parliament granted £20,000 to assist the two societies with the building of schools, viz. National Schools.

W.A.C. Stewart & W.P. McCann, *The Educational Innovators* 1750-1880, Macmillan 1967.

Robert Raikes 1735-1811

Raikes was a native of Gloucester and a journalist who owned the *Gloucester Journal*. Stimulated by the neglected condition of the local children and their behaviour on Sundays, he was led to assist in the

establishment of a Sunday School in a nearby parish. In 1780 he started a little school in Sooty Alley which was open on weekdays and Sundays for the teaching of Scripture, reading and other elementary subjects. In 1783 he felt that his school was sufficiently established to draw attention to it in his own paper. Before his death, Raikes combined all the efforts into one great movement and as a result of his endeavours, the National Sunday School Union was founded in 1803. His methods were soon followed by Hannah More.
Adapted from F.L. Cross in *The Oxford Dictionary of the Christian Church*, 1961.

Hannah More 1745-1833
She was educated at her sisters' school in Bristol. When she visited the Mendips with William Wilberforce in 1789, both were struck by the ignorance in the country and lack of religious provision. Under Wilberforce's influence she established schools at Cheddar and neighbouring villages. At this time schemes of popular education were almost unprecedented. Her system of schools was finally commended by R. Beadon, Bishop of Bath and Wells, 1802-24. The schools taught religious education and the girls were taught spinning which was designed to relieve poverty.
F.L. Cross in *The Oxford Dictionary of the Christian Church*, 1961.

References to Chapter Five

1. Skinner, *op.cit.*, p.190.
2. *Ibid.*, p.158.
3. *Ibid.*, p.232.
4. *Ibid.*, p.302.
5. *Ibid.*, p.409.
6. *Bath Journal*, 10 December 1821.
7. Michael Arlett, *The Railways of Midford*, Somerset & Dorset Railway Trust, 1983.
8. Coysh, *op.cit.*, p.211.
9. K. Clew, *The Somersetshire Coal Canal, op.cit.*, p.85.
10. Bulley, *op.cit.*, I, p.55f.
11. *Bath Journal*, 20 December 1830.
12. Charles Hadfield, *The Canals of Southern England*, Phoenix 1955, p.161; p.171
13. Kenneth Clew, *The Kennet and Avon Canal*, Revised Edition, David and Charles 1985, pp.82, 94.
14. Skinner, *op.cit.*, p.276.
15. R. Atthill, *Old Mendip*, p.133.
16. R.K. Bluhm, article, *op.cit.*, p.55.
17. *Ibid.*, p.55f.
18. *Bath Journal*, 29 September 1823. The Royal Society for the Prevention of Cruelty to Animals was founded on 16 June 1824 following an Act of Parliament in 1822.
19. *Bath Journal*, 18 May 1829.
20. W.J. Wedlake, 'Tithe Disputes at Camerton, Somerset, 1800-1839', *A Second North Somerset Miscellany, op.cit.*, p.37
21. Skinner, *op.cit.*, p.182.

22. *Ibid.*, p.226.
23. *Ibid.*, p.244.
24. *Ibid.*, p.246
25. *Ibid.*, p.264
26. Bulley, *op.cit.*, II, p.49.
27. Greenwood, *op.cit.*
28. Skinner, *op.cit.*, p.186; Bath Journal, 1 April 1822.
29. Skinner, *op.cit.*, p.229.
30. *Ibid.*, p.267.
31. *Ibid.*, p.302.
32. Bulley, *op.cit.*, II, p.39f.
33. Skinner, *op.cit.*, p.302.
34. *Ibid.*, p.336.
35. *Ibid.*, p.164.
36. *Ibid.*, p.388.
37. Bulley, *op.cit.*, I, p.69.
38. *Ibid.*, II, p.37.
39. Skinner, *op.cit.*, p.367.
40. Bulley, *op.cit.*, p.37.
41. Skinner, *op.cit.*, p.394.
42. *Ibid.*, p.332.
43. *Bath Journal*, 1 April 1822.
44. Bulley *op.cit.* I p.62.
45. Skinner, *op.cit.*, p.177.
46. *Ibid.*, p. 178.
47. Coysh, *op.cit.*, p.212.
48. Skinner, *op.cit.*, p.330.
49. *Ibid.*, p.406f.
50. *Ibid.*, p.407.
51. *Ibid.*, p.424.
52. *Bath Journal*, 20 December, 1830.
53. *Ibid.*
54. Coysh, *op.cit.*, 209.
55. Skinner, *op.cit.*, p.198.
56. Down & Warrington, *op.cit.*, p.113. (They have nephew instead of son).
57. *Bath Journal*, 14 July1823.
58. Skinner, *op.cit.*, p.238.
59. Bulley, *op.cit.*, I, p.58.
60. Bluhm, article, *op.cit.*, p.56.

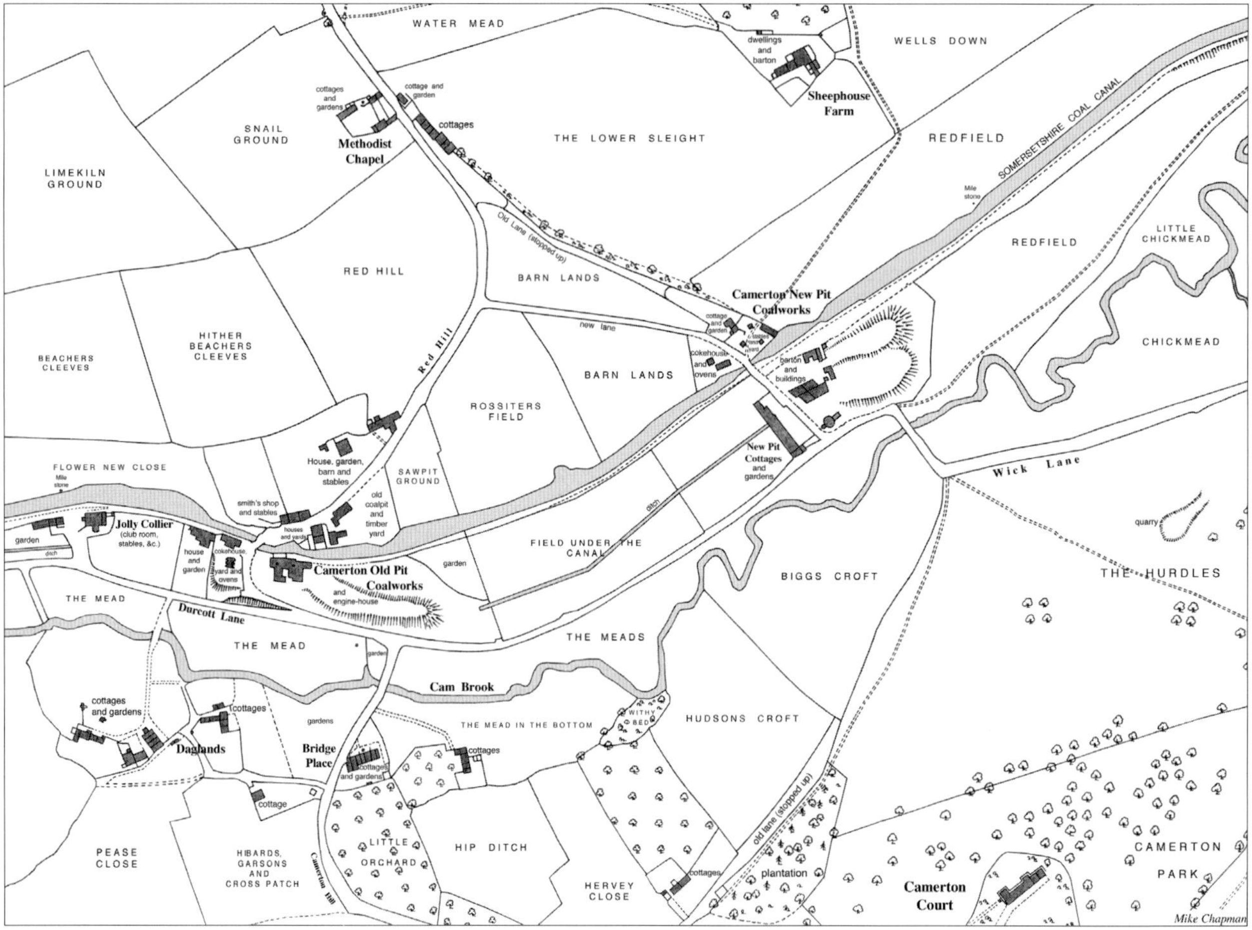

The area of Camerton collieries based on the 1844 tithe map. By this time cokehouses and ovens have appeared at both pits. At New Pit, the old lane from the north has been completely stopped up, with a rank of cottages built on it at the top of hill, opposite the Methodist Chapel.

CHAPTER SIX

A TIME OF IMPROVEMENTS 1830-1860

The hectic pace of development of the previous forty years slowed to a more leisurely one during this period. The pits were now being worked more efficiently, and the methods of transport had been developed and improved. Dunning says that the development of the Somerset coalfields after 1840 in the Radstock area gave rise to an expansion in the population in that part of the county.[1] In his *Rambles about Bath* published in 1847, Tunstall said of Camerton that it was celebrated for its coal and that the population now stood at 1,501.[2] By 1851 this had risen to 1,543 and may well have been due to the stability of employment provided by the Jarrett family. It was to continue to rise throughout the century.[3]

Frances, Countess Waldegrave.

Future Prospects for the Mines

In 1833 a Mr. T.Y. Hall was using large iron tubs holding up to one and a half tons of coal at South Hetton in the vale of Houghton near Durham, but the following year he invented the 'cage' to carry the trams from the pit bottom. The next development was that of steel wire, shoes and guide rods in the shafts. These improvements resulted in the doubling of coal output.[4]

Radstock was the scene of important improvements in the middle of the century, when Frances, Dowager Countess Waldegrave, asserted an active proprietorship over the four mines of the Radstock coal works and had a new pit sunk at Tyning. Under her direction and the management of James McMurtrie, shafts were widened, new machinery installed, and steam power increased. McMurtrie investigated methods of systematically exploiting the thin seams of the area. The Waldegrave enterprise represented an extension of the general pattern of small-scale mining operations, financed by local capital from landowners and businessmen, working usually through small partnerships.[5]

James McMurtrie. *Radstock Museum Archive*

There were other improvements which not only reduced the risk of accidents but also increased the productivity of the pits. On the surface the early condensing steam engines were being replaced by those using steam at high pressure. About 1854 the hemp ropes which had been known to fray, or be cut deliberately, were replaced with wire ropes. Iron 'hudges' replaced the old wreath carts or baskets, so enabling a larger amount of coal to be raised with each winding. As this period came to a close, cages, guides and wheeled coal-tubs were rapidly being introduced into the Somerset coalfield in place of hudges. The introduction of wheeled-tubs was a significant step forward. Once the coal had been brought out from the face it was dragged to the main roadways in the putts and there loaded into tubs. These were taken to the pit-bottom and wheeled into the cage. This method reduced handling and with it there was less breakage of the friable coal so that a higher proportion of large coal was raised, which fetched a better price than the small coal.

View of Hepburn Colliery in the north of England, before the changes in appearance of structures for winding brought about by the introduction of cages and tubs. Compare with the much simpler arrangement at the two Camerton pits shown in Skinner's sketch.

A three-deck cage at Writhlington Colliery in the 20th century. *John Cornwell collection*

There was a further Act in 1855 to strengthen the law with regard to inspection and notification of accidents. The first Code of General Rules required 'the provision of adequate ventilation (but did not define it), also the fencing and lining of shafts, means of signalling up and down the shaft, and the provision of an indicator for the winding engineman of the position of the cage in the shaft, chiefly to prevent the terribly frequent accident of overwinding. Without this device the cage, when wound up against the pulley wheel, is broken off and falls to the bottom of the shaft, instantly killing the occupants'.[6]

Camerton was in the news early in 1842. 'On the morning of Tuesday week between 2 and 3 a.m. a fire broke out at the Coal Pit Engine House which owing to the timbers being saturated with oil soon destroyed all the woodwork of the building leaving the engine wholly exposed. It was first discovered by one of the men employed on the coal boats of Messrs Spencer and Co. and the fire was extinguished in a couple of hours.' They were afraid that some of the smoke might go into the mouth of the Old Pit and suffocate the men coming up. It was thought that the fire might have been caused by the woodwork smouldering for some hours before it was discovered.[7]

An Outbreak of Cholera

The first major outbreak of Asiatic Cholera in Britain occurred during 1832. The disease was prevalent in Bristol, Bath and through out the area, eventually reaching Camerton at the end of that year. Skinner received a letter with the news:

> 'After breakfast I received a letter from Mr. uton, the bailiff of the coal works, announcing the breaking out of the cholera at Camerton. I immediately walked to his house, taking with me some camphor and aromatic

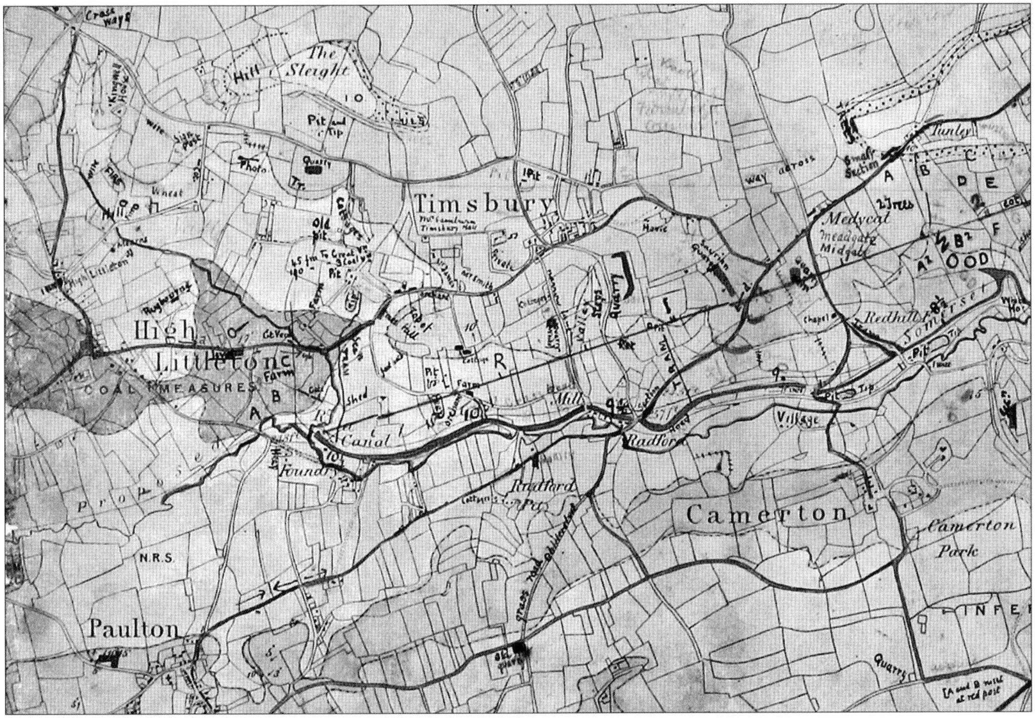

The Camerton area based on William Sander's geological survey of the North Somerset Coalfield, later annotated by a geologist to show quarries, coal pits, and other relevant topographical detail.

> vinegar to give him. This being pay day with the colliers it occurred to me that if the infection be among them he must take every precaution to avoid it … I immediately wrote to Curtis, the apothecary, desiring him to come to Camerton.
>
> The Post brought me a letter from Mr. John Jarrett who is staying in Suffolk, enclosing £20 draft in Tufnell's Bank, Bath, and desiring me to lay it out in remunerating the sufferers who burnt their bedding on account of the Cholera. It will be of great service providing other things besides … In the course of my walk this morning I visited Harris of Dagland, Edward Luton, Moon and Cook of Collier's Row, and old Mrs.Harding of Cridlingcott. Luton, the Bailiff of the Coal Works has been, I find, very kind to the people during their affliction and has distributed money and bed-linen among them.
>
> Memoranda of monies disbursed on Mr. Jarrett's account to the Colliers' families who have suffered from the Cholera at Camerton. I had supposed that ten pounds would settle the whole of the Colliers' disimbursements on account of the Cholera and so I mentioned in my letter to him, and the other £10 I said I would lay out on clothes for the little boys who are not yet able to work in the Pits, as some of them are nearly naked.'[8]

Unfortunately Skinner's Journal, which has been so useful in providing a picture of life in Camerton, ends in 1834 although he was to live for another five years until his death in the village in 1839. It was around this time that the two Jarrett sisters were born. Anna Mary Jarrett, born on the 25th January 1838, was to become the landowner. Her sister, Emily Elizabeth, who was later to take control of the pits, was born on the 4th December 1840.

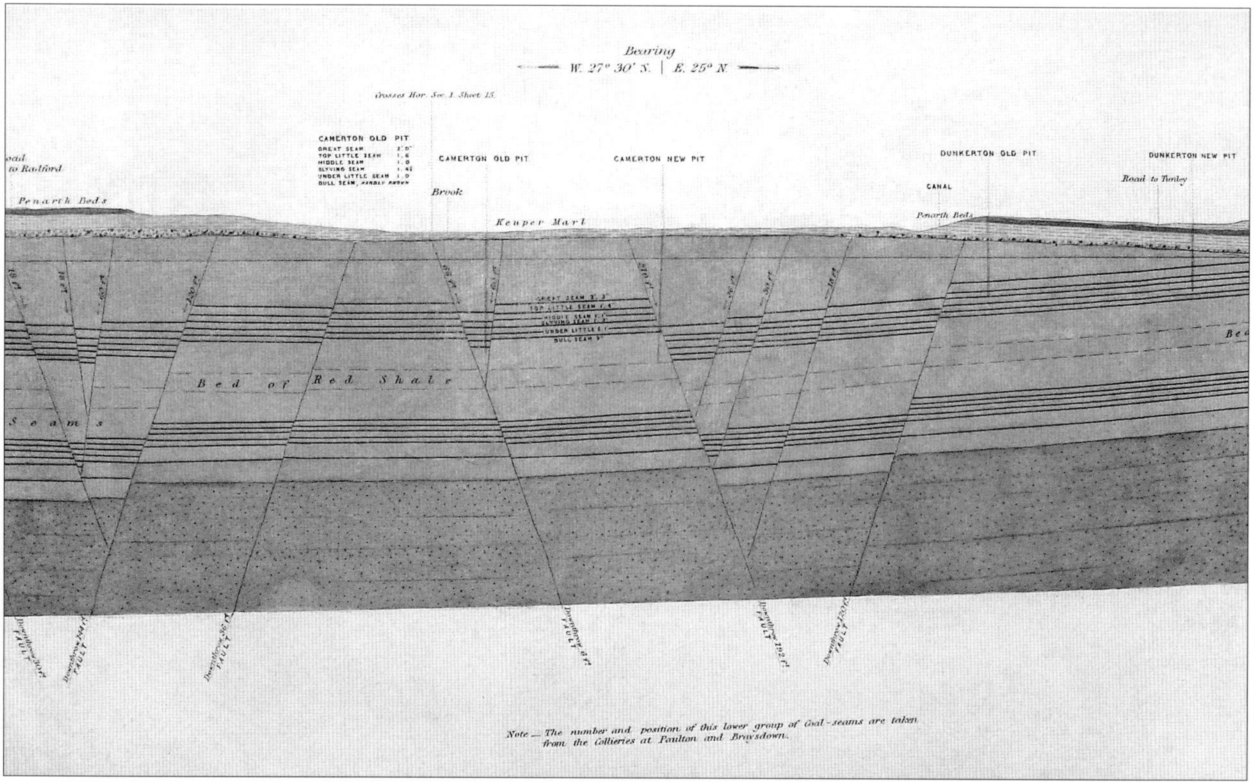

An early geological section of the coal measures through Camerton. *Radstock Museum Archive*

Statistics and Profit

Further scientific study of the coalfield was ensured with the formation of the Geological Branch of the Ordnance Survey in 1832. This was to lead to the production of geological maps, including North Somerset, by William Sanders in the years that followed.[9] Then in 1854 Robert Hunt, of the Geological Survey, began to collect and publish statistics of the coal industry.

At the beginning of the century it had been estimated that the output of the Somerset coalfield was considerably less than 200,000 tons per annum. In the 1830s a railway prospectus for a line, which was not intended to cover the whole of the coalfield, gave a figure of 300,000 tons, which may well be inflated. By 1840 it is believed that 400,000 tons were produced for the first time. The first official figure for the output of this area of Somerset, given by Hunt's Mineral Statistics for 1860, is 400,000 tons.[10] It may well have stood at this level during the previous twenty years. The figures for the Camerton Pits were 30,540 tons landed for the year from May 1844 to May 1845.[11]

It was reported in 1843 that the 'prospects at Old Pit are discouraging. It is not advisable to sink pits to the second series of coal seams but I believe they prove under the Pits'.[12] This was a reference to the deeper Farrington series. In order to help the collieries become more profitable, John Jarrett reduced his freeshare to 1/10 in 1833, but in 1843, when asked to accept a further reduction to 1/12 he refused, and lessees of the pits promptly closed one seam and sacked a number of men.[13] However, 'Financially the pits were in a good state in the early 1800s. Between 1830 and 1843, profits totalled £16,761 against losses of £1,741; £11,576 was disbursed as dividends'.[14]

In 1847 there was an application by Robert W. Carpenter on behalf of Horatio Davis and Major William Eleazer Pickwick (colliery owners) to Edwin Lovell (acting for John Jarrett) for permission to enlarge the area of operation of Old Pit at Camerton under land on the north side of Tunley Road because the coal in this pit was nearly worked out. It was expected to last for only another five years. According to the records, it had the 'best engine' compared with New Pit, and coal from the latter pit was 'more tender' and 'would not bear land carriage'. 'The Water carriage of that Pit would be affected by any new Company working Tunley Farm, as they would run their coal to Bengrove and thereby become the first in the market for the Water Trade ... Camerton Company is now the first in Land and Water.'[15] This well illustrates the anxiety of nearby competition felt by every coal owner.

There was a court case in London in 1852 involving the Coal Company. It concerned one of the original shareholders, a Mr. Brickdale, who had become bankrupt but had not received the dividends on his shares since 1831 which amounted to £2,432. These were eventually paid to him despite objections from the company, which complained that Mr. Brickdale had made no application to receive the dividends in the intervening years.[16]

In November 1853 the neighbouring pit at Radford was in the news when all the machinery there was put up for sale. This appears to have been as a result of the exhaustion of its coal reserves, a feature of other early pits further west in the Cam Valley. There was to be a sale by auction 'comprising a valuable, powerful and nearly new double acting steam engine, for winding, 31" cylinder with suitable air pump, condenser and two boilers attached to the same. The engine considered to be the best and most efficient in the neighbourhood. One powerful engine for pumping with a cylinder 10 feet long, 44" diameter, round and flat ropes, iron hudges, cranes and chains, 10 iron and 6 wood tram waggons, tramplate, timber - oak, ash, elm. Two powerful cart horses'.[17]

Accidents in Mines

In 1835 a Select Committee of the House of Commons was appointed 'to enquire into the nature, cause, and extent of the lamentable catastrophes which have occurred in the mines of Great Britain, with the view of ascertaining and suggesting means of preventing the recurrence of similar fatal accidents'. The Committee made a number of suggestions dealing with ventilation, safety lamps, complete and accurate plans of the collieries, better education of miners, appointment of competent and trustworthy officials and enforcement of discipline in the industry. 'At the instance of Lord Shaftesbury, a Royal Commission was appointed in 1840 to enquire into the employment of children and young persons in mines and quarries, and it proved that children of five years old and upwards were employed underground and constantly being injured ... The revolting revelations of the Report were a great shock to the public, and led to the immediate passing of the Act of 1842, which wholly prohibited the employment of women and girls underground, and of boys under ten years old. Other safety provisions in this, the first of the more important Mines Acts, were the limitation of the apprenticeship periods to eight years, the prohibition of persons under fifteen years old being left in charge of winding engines, and the appointment of inspectors'.[18]

It had been common practice to employ boys of six and seven in the mines of Somerset for a number of years where they were used to open and shut the underground doors, or brattices, which controlled the currents of air providing ventilation.[19] As carting boys, at the coal face, they loaded their small putts with lumps of coal dug out by the hewer or breaker at the seam. They also pushed along the tubs of coal and turned the 'gugg-wheel' which wound these up the inclines to the main roadways.

Enquiries made by the Child Employment Commission of 1842 revealed more about the conditions under which children worked.[20] Its Report concluded that these were better in Somerset than the national average. Here at least no women or girls were employed in the pits, as happened in other parts of the country. In 1844 the *Bath Herald* reported that a boy of thirteen worked at Camerton Pit from 8 p.m. to 4 a.m. for five nights a week and later in the same year it commented that a third of the miners in Somerset were under twenty years of age.[21]

Coal Traffic on the Roads and the Canal

Coal was still being hauled to the local markets by road, sometimes with little regard to the welfare of the animals involved. The *Bath Chronicle* reported in January 1841: 'On Thursday Will Parfit, a coal carrier of Camerton was fined 40/- for cruelty to his horse, as the animal was labouring to pull a load up Dunkerton Hill. John Coney, a County Magistrate, was passing at the time, and having remonstrated with the man for barbarity towards the poor dumb creature in beating it with a bludgeon of the thickness of a man's wrist, Parfit answered with great insolence, and continued to beat the animal as before. Mr. Coney resolved to summon the offender before the Magistrates at Chandos House [in Westgate Buildings] in Bath.'[22]

Both the Bath and Wells Turnpike Trusts each had over 40 miles of road by 1837. The Bath Trust managed 51 miles and its financial condition was reported to be in a satisfactory state.[23] Such was the pressure on the roads that new routes were forever being sought to convey the coal from the mines to Bath. In 1853 the Commissioners of the Radstock Turnpike wanted to apply to Parliament 'for a new Act to extend the powers of the Trustees in making additional means for carrying the produce of the coal mines to the city of Bath and its neighbourhood.' This prompted a requisition to the Trustees 'from a clergyman, churchwardens and others, inhabitants of Dunkerton … requesting that a clause might be introduced in the New Act to convert a lane leading to Tunley which is chiefly traversed by coal

A typical 19th century Bath coal waggon.

The Saw Close in Bath, the city's coal market. In the centre is a typical city coal wagon standing by an octagonal weigh-office, with weigh-bridge visible in the road surface on the left side. This 'weighing engine' was installed by the Corporation 'for weighing hay, straw, coals and other things' in 1763, presumably based on the compound lever weighing machine invented in the 1740s by John Wyatt of Birmingham. *Paul De'Ath collection*

waggons, into a Turnpike Road and which lane is most constantly out of repair ...'. However, the Trustees said that this was too distant from Radstock and recommended that the applicants join the Bath Trust.[24]

As late as 1858 a man was still being employed by the Radstock collieries to help the coal carts of the Bath traders up the hill at Dunkerton. These hauliers would have been carrying good house coal while the farmers took the small coal for their lime kilns.[25] Somerset coal, however, did not have a monopoly of the Bath market. In 1853, for example, Joseph Lansdown advertised coal for sale in Bath from Wigan, which he claimed was 'ideal for the Drawing Room, because of the pure flame, no smoke or smell, no stirring required' and gave a very cheerful fire.[26] All coal brought by horse traffic from the pits went to the central depot at the Sawclose, opposite the Theatre Royal where there was a weigh engine and the coal was sold in sacks at 6d for small coal and 7d to 9d for the best hard coal.[27]

Meanwhile there were three depots for coal boats, at Bathwick Hill, at the bottom of Widcombe Hill, and the third on Broad Quay. There was a weigh house of a different kind on the Somersetshire Coal Canal by 1831. This was situated at Midford to the east of the junction of the two branches of the canal. It survived into the early years of the 20th century:[28] 'The loaded barges were floated by means of a side cut to within this temple-like edifice, which was furnished with a cradle apparatus, on which they were suspended and their weight recorded, when sufficient water to cause them to 'ground' on the bed of the cradle had been let off through a sluice.' They were refloated by admitting more water and they then went on down the canal. The maximum size of craft was 72ft with a width of 7ft 2ins and draught of 3ft, in effect, what was later known as a 'narrowboat'. The maximum headroom was eight feet.[29]

In 1849 a new boiler was required for the Dunkerton Pumping Station on the canal. An advertisement was addressed to Ironmasters and Boiler Makers for erecting an engine boiler and for supplying fifteen foot lengths of tram plates and chairs.[30] Three years later steam power appeared in a different form on the canal when the Rev. C.R. Davey of Combe Hay launched his thirty-foot long pleasure boat *Fairy* with a 1 h.p. steam engine on the canal. It was restricted to a maximum of four m.p.h. so that it did not damage the banks of the canal.[31]

Clew pointed out that the late 1830s were the golden years of the three canals and it is understandable that some of the proprietors of the Coal Canal, who were probably also coal owners,

The Somerset Coal Canal Wharf in Bath, at the head of the Kennet & Avon Canal Lock Flight in Bathwick.

The Somersetshire Coal Canal Weighhouse at Midford, erected in 1831.

were initially against the Bath and Weymouth Railway when it was being canvassed in 1836. The tonnage being carried on the Coal Canal was 138,000 tons in 1838 and in the previous year the Wiltshire & Berkshire Canal had carried 43,600 tons of which 10,700 tons were handled at the Abingdon Wharf. When it is recalled that two thirds of the tonnage on this canal was coal traffic it shows the importance of that trade.[32] Later they came round to the idea of this railway 'with branches to the collieries at and in the neighbourhood of Radstock and Timsbury'. It was to be another nine years before this project received permission to proceed as the Wiltshire, Somerset and Weymouth Railway.[33]

Railways are suggested to carry the coal

In 1845 both the Kennet & Avon Canal and the Somersetshire Coal Canal considered changing over to railways. The more far-sighted coal owners and canal proprietors could see that the days of the canal monopoly were already numbered, but it was to be many years before the canals were finally replaced by railways.[34] 'For some years the Somersetshire Coal Canal was the most prosperous in the whole of southern England and the shareholders received a comfortable dividend. The first serious threat was in August 1844 when the directors of the Great Western Railway decided to promote an eight-mile long broad gauge line from Frome to Radstock. This was begun in June 1845 but abandoned because of lack of funds. It was restarted in 1850 and by 1854 it was completed as far as Radstock as a mineral railway.[35]

Warnock says that when George Greenwell was appointed in 1853 as manager of the Countess Waldegrave's pits in Radstock, he decided to send all the coal on the new railway and not along the tramway to Midford.[36] The result was a large drop in this revenue to the Coal Canal Company, although it did not affect the tonnage being carried by the Canal overall due to the general increase in the coal trade.[37] In 1858 Mr. Feare of Camerton and others proposed to construct a private railway line from Radstock to Timsbury but this scheme was never carried out.[38] It was to be one of many ideas that were to be proposed before the Cam Valley was eventually linked with the surrounding railway network.

Notes to Chapter Six

Cholera

Irene Burchill, 'Cholera in the Somerset Coalfield [1832]', *Five Arches*, Issue 50, 2004.

Profits made at Camerton Pits

The records show the profits which were made at the Camerton Pits between 1829 and 1842. 'The annual dividend, spread out evenly over the fourteen year period came to about £800 per annum; and if the original division of shares held good at this time it meant that the largest shareholder received about £35 per annum. Receipts for the sale of coal at Camerton in 1842 were £17,966.' The units of capital invested are not known, so it is not possible to give an accurate assessment of these profits as a percentage of capital. 'However, in the light of what is known about neighbouring concerns at corresponding times it is likely that the yield at Camerton was between 5 and 10 per cent.'
Bulley, *op.cit.*, II, p.30f.

Tonnage on the Canal

The Radstock to Frome railway seems to have had little immediate impact upon the tonnage carried by the canal, where trade had again increased during the last decade. Receipts however did not keep pace and had fallen to two thirds of those received for the comparative period.

Year	Tonnage	Revenue	Dividend
1848	131,001	£12,921	£10,650
1858	165,740	£ 8,558	£ 4,613

Clew, *op.cit.*, p.96 and p.100.

Lord Shaftesbury 1801-1885

A.A. Cooper, 7th Earl of Shaftesbury, was largely responsible for the Act of 1842. Later he was at the heart of the struggle to work for the Ten Hours Act in 1847 which limited the working day of women and young people. The statue of Eros in Piccadilly Circus is a memorial to him.

William Sanders, F.R.S., F.G.S. 1799-1875

Sanders was a native of Bristol, and for upwards of forty years his life was intimately associated with the most distinguished names that have enriched geological science. He devoted his life to the study of the physical structure of the Bristol area, and early in his scientific career was the friend and companion of Professor Phillips in his Geological Survey of North Devon and Cornwall, which occupied some years.

His chief labour, however, and that by which his name will ever be remembered, was the preparation and construction of an elaborate geological map of the area comprised within the Gloucestershire and Somersetshire Coal field. The scale of this map is four inches to the mile (four times the scale of the then available Ordnance Maps), and the detailed geological structure of the entire area was conscientiously and carefully worked out. The labour devoted to this map by Mr. Sanders extended over fifteen years, and the work occupies nineteen folio sheets geologically coloured, and with the physical details added. He was active as a citizen and as a member of local scientific societies, especially in developing the Bristol museum, of which he was honorary curator for many years.
From his obituary in the *Bristol Press* 1875

George C. Greenwell 1821-1900

In November 1900, the *Somerset Guardian* reported the death of one of the most distinguished mining engineers in the Somerset coalfield. George C. Greenwell was born in Newcastle on the 25th July 1821, and after studying at Edinburgh University had started work in the West Auckland collieries in 1844. Between 1853 and 1863 he had practised as a mining and civil engineer in Radstock before moving to similar work in the Cheshire mines. He was succeeded at Radstock by James McMurtrie. About 1879 he resigned to become a consultant and finally in 1882 settled in Duffield in Derbyshire. He had been a close associate of James McMurtrie, and together they had written works on mining in this region.
Somerset Guardian, 24 November 1900.

James McMurtrie 1839-1914

James McMurtrie was born in 1839 at Dalquharran near Dailly, some five miles north east of Girvan, in Ayrshire. He left Scotland about 1856 to become a mining student near Newcastle-upon-Tyne and it was from the north east of England that he came to Somerset in 1862 to assist George Greenwell in the mines around Radstock (Coleford, McIntosh and Newbury pits). He succeeded Greenwell as Lady Waldegrave's manager, a post which he held for some forty years until his retirement in 1903. During this period he became one of the most knowledgeable mining engineers of the Radstock and district coalfield, publishing many of his findings and observations. It was McMurtrie who replaced the asses, which had been used in the Camerton mines from the time of Skinner, with pit ponies between 1863 and 1893.

From the lengthy obituary that appeared in the *Somerset Guardian* in 1914 a fuller picture emerges of the life and work of this devoted engineer. He had taken an active part in establishing the Conciliation Board in the Radstock area. He was a director of the Bath Stone Firms Ltd, and manager of the Waldegrave Collieries at Radstock.

Politically McMurtrie was a Liberal who had seceded on the question of Home Rule for Ireland and had then become a Liberal Unionist. Throughout his time in the coalfield McMurtrie had worked for more economical exploration and development of the resources underground. He had introduced ponies to haul the coal to the pit bottom, the up and down air shafts and pit props. His fine personal collection of fossilised plants was donated to the British Museum. On his retirement he was succeeded by his eldest son, George.

Somerset Guardian, 6 February 1914
H. Stanley Jevons, *The British Coal Trade (1915)*, David and Charles 1969, p.376.
Dennis Chedgy, 'James McMurtrie, Victorian Manager of Radstock Collieries', *Five Arches*, Issue 10, 1990.

Lady Waldegrave 1821-1879

Frances Elizabeth Ann Waldegrave had four husbands. After the death of the first, John Waldegrave of Essex in 1840, she married the seventh Earl Waldegrave, but he died in 1846 leaving her as Dowager Countess. She then married George Granvill Harcourt, and it was possibly at his suggestion that legal proceedings were successfully brought about in 1847 which removed the lessees from her pits, leaving full ownership in her hands. From hereon the Waldegrave collieries traded together under the title 'Radstock Coal Co.', although the style of 'The Radstock Coalworks' was adopted about 1863. After Harcourt died, Lady Waldegrave took a fourth husband, Chichester, Lord Carlingford in 1871, and by 1873 the title of the concern had changed again to 'Frances, Countess Waldegrave, Radstock Collieries'. These titles were designed to prevent confusion with William Beachim's business which also operated under the name of 'Radstock Coal Co'., but it was only after legal proceedings that the matter was finally settled in her favour in 1878, the year before her death. Her memorial, with a record of her life, is in Chewton Mendip Church, Somerset.

Acts of Parliament

1. An Act to Prohibit the Working of Women and Girls in Mines and Collieries, &c, 1842. Its aim was to prevent the working of women and girls underground, the securing of better conditions of work for boys, and the general safety of mines. It also provided for the appointment of Inspectors of Mines.
   Robert Peel, *Coal Mining*, Blackie & Son 1893 Appendix A.
2. By an Act of 1850 adult males were also protected by a Mines Inspectorate, and step by step, the provision of safety in Mines became the care of the State.
   G.M. Trevelyan, *English Social History*, 1946, p.544.
3. An Act To Amend the Law for the Inspection of Coal Mines in Britain was passed in 1855.
   Robert Peel, *Coal Mining*, Blackie & Son 1893 Appendix A.

References to Chapter Six

1. Dunning, *op.cit.*, p.92.
2. James Tunstall, *Rambles about Bath*, 1847.
3. Down & Warrington, *op.cit.*, p.37.
4. R.L. Galloway, *A History of Coal Mining in Great Britain*, David and Charles 1969, p.211.
5. Buchanan and Cossons, *op.cit.*, p.85.
6. H. Stanley Jevons, *The British Coal Trade (1915)*, David and Charles 1969, p.380.
7. *Bath Chronicle*, 27 January 1842.
8. Skinner, *op.cit.*, all information on the epidemic from this source, p.452 and pp.470, 472, 473.
9. W.J. Williams, *op.cit.*, p.3.
10. Bluhm Article, *op.cit.*, p.54.
11. Bluhm Bibliography, *op.cit.*, p.170.
12. Down & Warrington, *op.cit.*, p.113.
13. *Ibid.*, p.113.
14. *Ibid.*, p.113.

15. Somerset Record Office, DD/BR/tsk 19.
16. *Bath Chronicle*, 25 November 1853.
17. *Bath Chronicle*, 10 November 1853.
18. Jevons, *op.cit.*, pp.376-7
19. *Victoria History of Counties of England, op.cit.*, p.382f.
20. *Ibid.*, p.382f.
21. *Bath Herald*, 6 January 1844; 30 November 1844.
22. *Bath Chronicle*, 28 January 1841.
23. W. Albert, *op.cit.*, p.244.
24. *Bath Chronicle*, 27 October 1853.
25. Bulley, *op.cit.*, I, p.61.
26. *Bath Chronicle*, 27 October 1853.
27. *Somerset Guardian*, 9 July 1926.
28. Clew, *op.cit.*, p.86.
29. *The Engineer*, Vol.103, 27 May 1907.
30. *Bath Chronicle*, 11 January 1849.
31. *Ibid.*, 8 July 1852.
32. *Clew*, *op.cit.*, p.87.
33. *Ibid.*, p.88.
34. *Ibid.*, p.93.
35. D. Warnock, *The Bristol and North Somerset Railway 1863-1884*, Temple Cloud, 1978.
36. *Warnock*, *op.cit.*
37. Colin G. Maggs and Gerry Beale, *The Camerton Branc*h, Wild Swan Publications 1985, p.8.
38. G. Greenwell and J. McMurtrie, *The Radstock Coalfield*, 1864, p.15.

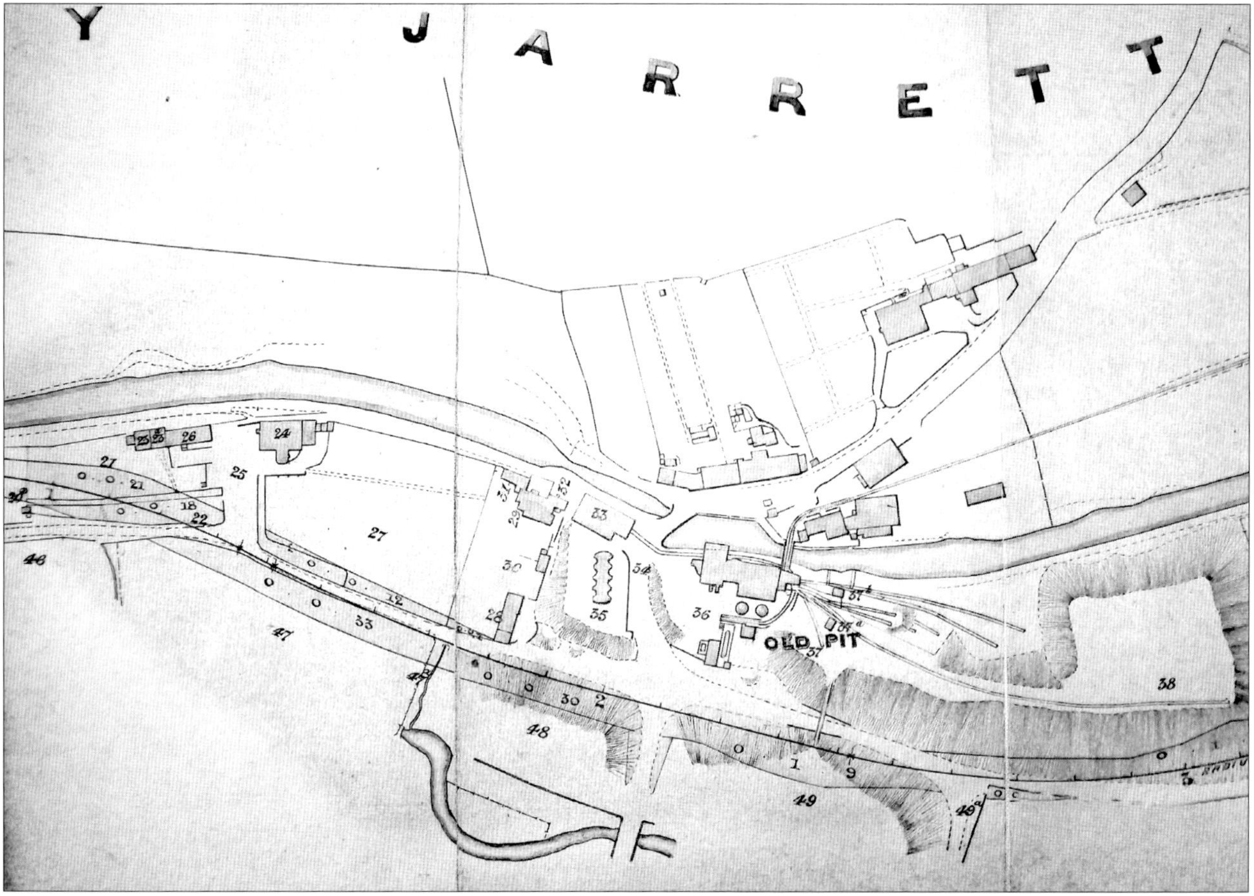

Plan of the intended railway to Camerton. The line followed the route of Durcott Lane which had to be moved further south towards the Cam Brook and reconnected to Old Pit by a bridge over the railway. Below this is shown a new road bridge over the Brook leading to Camerton village. *Somerset Record Office*

CHAPTER SEVEN

RAILWAYS, UNIONS AND SAFETY 1860-1890

Railway Schemes

A number of plans were put forward to link the main areas of the coalfield by rail with the surrounding markets during the 1860s. Among the schemes rejected was that of the North Somerset Railway in 1860 from Bristol, across the Mendips to Wells, with branches from Hallatrow to Camerton and to Radstock. Another, in 1861, was for a line from Keynsham to Radstock via Clutton, again with a branch from Hallatrow to Camerton. A third plan in 1862 by the Somerset Coal Railway was for a line from Wincanton to Hayeswood [Timsbury] with a tunnel between Clandown and Radford.[1]

The first successful scheme after the Frome to Radstock coal line opened in 1854 was the standard gauge line, promoted by the Bristol & North Somerset Railway, from Radstock to Bristol via Hallatrow. Again it was envisaged that there would be a branch from that station to Camerton. The plan included

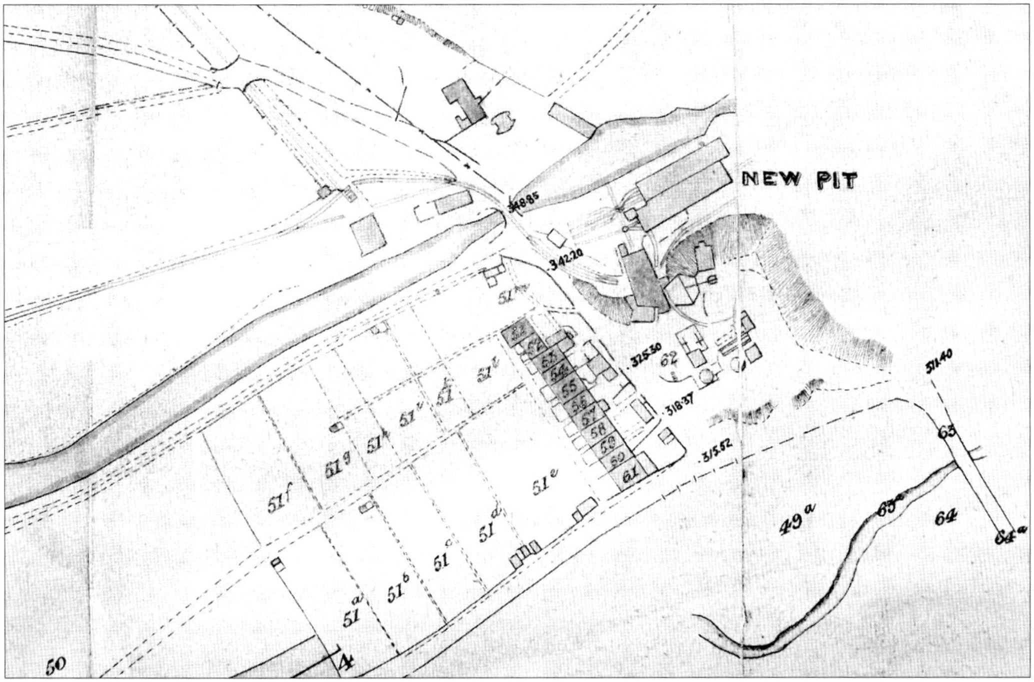

Camerton New Pit shown on the same plan, but with only a railway siding by Wick Lane. By this time the works here have been considerably enlarged, including the inclined plane or 'gugg' up to the top of Red Hill, and the tramway between the pits.
Somerset Record Office

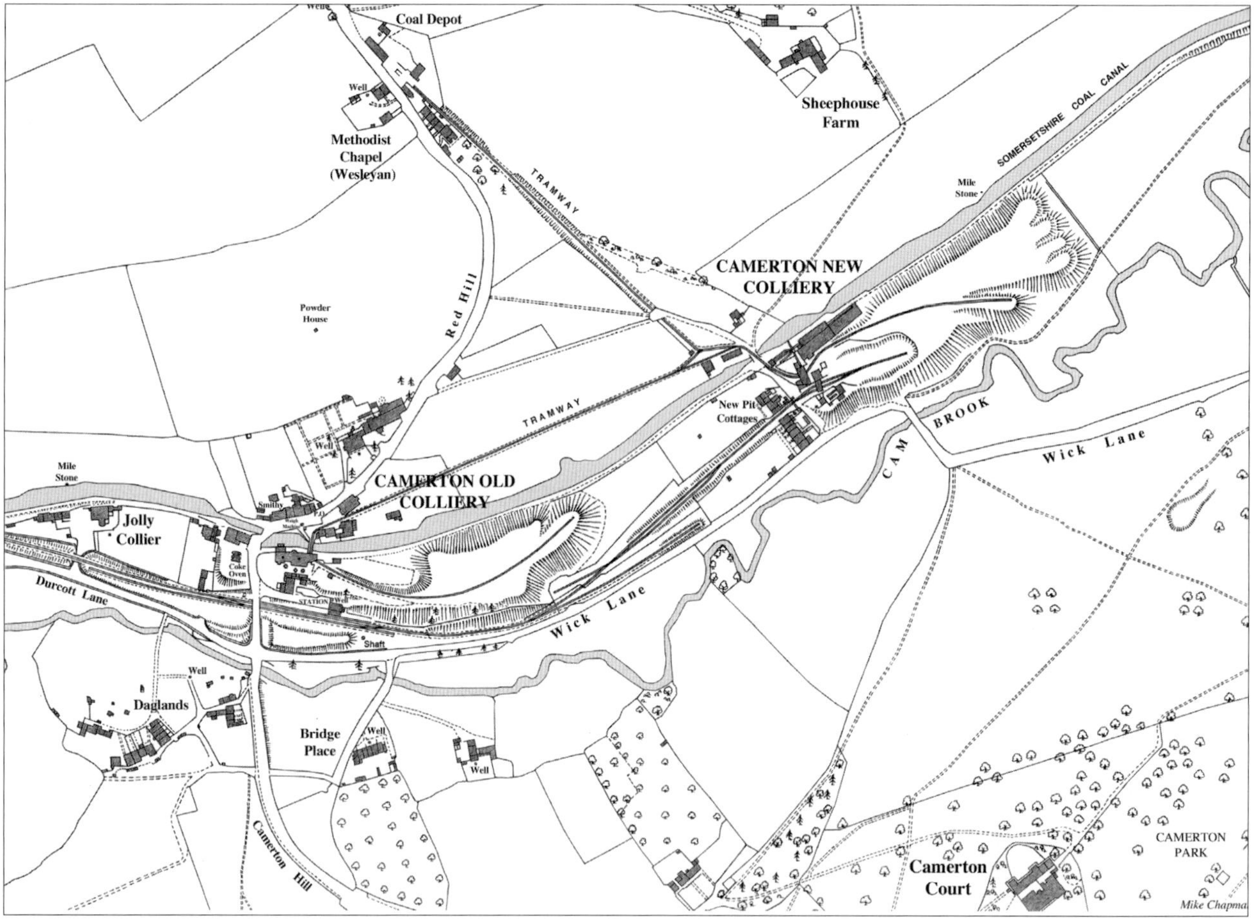

The area of the Camerton Collieries in 1884, compiled from the OS 25-inch maps. The new railway is shown complete with station and New Pit sidings leading up the bank through the middle of Colliers' Row to the screens, as are the new roads and bridges below Old Pit.

making the section between Radstock and Frome into mixed gauge. The proposal received the Royal Assent in July 1863 and work started in October.[2]

The *Bath Chronicle* reported in September 1863: 'We are given to understand that the directors of the Bristol & North Somerset Railway seriously contemplate the extension of their branch, which now terminates at Camerton [in their plan] to this city, and that the requisite application will be made to Parliament in the ensuing session. This timely measure will put Bath in immediate communication with the surrounding colliery district, thus materially cheapening the cost of fuel in our city and by means of the proposed extension to their system southward will give immediate and unbroken access to the narrow gauge railways of the West and South of England ...'.[3] Here 'narrow gauge' refers to what became known later as 'standard gauge', to distinguish it from the broad gauge which was then prevalent on the Great Western Railway.

However, the Bristol & North Somerset Railway encountered a number of difficulties, both financial and physical, with the result that the construction of the line made very little progress before

1870. 'This line is now in course of construction, and at the present rate of progress may be completed during the next century.'[4] It was eventually opened in 1873, but still with a change of gauge at Radstock. This was remedied the following year, and an Act was applied for, to build a branch line from Hallatrow to Camerton.[5]

The Somersetshire Coal Canal Company itself proposed a broad gauge line from Radstock to Limpley Stoke in 1864. It was to be along the course of its tramway to Midford. This scheme was withdrawn.[6] The same year a Camerton to Bath railway failed because of the opposition of local landowners.[7] Meanwhile the Midland Railway had reached Bath from the north of England in 1869, and the following year the Somerset & Dorset Joint Railway announced its plan to extend its system north from Evercreech to Radstock and Bath. The Radstock tramway of the Canal Company had been losing tonnage ever since the Frome to Radstock coal line had opened and more losses were envisaged when the Bristol and North Somerset Railway was completed. The Canal Company really had no option but to sell off their southern tramway to the Somerset & Dorset Railway and in 1871 it was sold for £20,000 and the new railway opened in 1874.[8]

The Railways reach Camerton

It was not until 1878 that the Hallatrow to Camerton branch, which had been talked about for so many years, was actually started, and although ready by 1880, it had to be inspected again in 1881 because there were a number of deficiencies. Also, strangely, no railway access had been provided to the collieries themselves at Camerton. All was put right, and in 1882 the long awaited branch was opened and in use, with a colliery siding at Camerton being agreed with Anna Jarrett. The result was that some 75,000 tons of coal were diverted from the Coal Canal to the new railway. When the line opened in March 1882 there were passenger, mixed and goods trains in both directions but as the years passed there was very little passenger traffic. Two years later the Bristol & North Somerset Railway became part of the Great Western Railway.[9]

A poem appeared in April 1882 to mark the occasion of the railway reaching Camerton:

And now our Railway is complete,
We wish success to every train.
With others now we will compete
And never more complain.

Our coal trade will now soon revive
There's better times for us in store
Whilst trains continually arrive
Close to our very door.

'Tis true that Camerton hitherto
Hath been considered years behind.
Now passenger and traffic too
Facilities will find.

There's prospect now for Camerton folk
For over fifty years to come
And Camerton trucks of coal and coke
Will comfort many a home.

Anon.[10]

The growth of railways throughout the country meant that coal from the Somerset coalfield now had to compete with that brought from the North and Midlands. There was a further threat to local producers when the Severn Railway tunnel opened in 1886 allowing a greater influx of coal from the pits of South Wales.

Camerton Station in its original form just before alterations in the early 20th century. The large chimney belonging to Old Pit in the background was reduced in height soon after this photograph was taken.

The Impact of the Railways on the Canal

The rise of the railways also marked the beginning of the decline in the fortunes of the Somersetshire Coal Canal. James Hewitt who entered the service of the Canal Company in November 1880 recalled that the coal merchants owned their own barges and that all the coal from Timsbury and Camerton went away from the pits by road or canal until the railway came in from Hallatrow. This considerably reduced the water traffic and the bed of the canal began to silt up. Boats that once carried forty to fifty tons of coal had difficulty in getting seventeen tons aboard, which was too little to pay the expenses involved.[11]

By 1884 the state of maintenance had fallen to such a degree that the Timsbury Coal Company

A Camerton Collieries railway wagon made by Gloucester Railway Carriage & Wagon Company Ltd in July 1898. *Gloucestershire Archives*

View up the railway bank through the middle of Colliers' Row (visible left) to New Pit screens. *Radstock Museum Archive*

instructed its manager '... to write to the Somersetshire Coal Canal Co. drawing their attention to the bad state of the canal which in its present condition is disastrous to trade ...'.[12] Four years later the section of the canal between Radford and Paulton was out of use, all the pits, except Lower Conygre in Timsbury having closed. The tollgates had disappeared from the turnpikes in 1870 and the increase in heavy coal traffic on the roads round Bath was noted in the *Bath Journal* in 1895.[13]

Matters were not helped when, in 1889, there was a strike for higher pay that lasted from June to September. During this period no coal moved along the canal.[14] There were new expenses, a new boiler had to be bought for the Dunkerton Pumping Station in 1887 and in 1890 a new water course was constructed at Dunkerton to supply more water to the canal.[15] The Canal Company made its last profit in 1889.[16] Time was running out for the Somersetshire Coal Canal which had played such an important part in the development of this coalfield.

The Geology of the Mines

There was now a better understanding of the geology of the area. As a result of their experience as mining engineers, Greenwell and McMurtrie published their monograph *The Radstock Coalfield* in 1864.[17] This was followed by a wider view in Brice's *The Coalfield of North Somerset* in 1867.[18] A survey of the Bristol coalfields together with maps was made by William Sanders in 1866. In his map of the Camerton area he shows the coal deposits overlaid with Inferior Oolite. It is also interesting to note that, according to his map, the proposed railway from Hallatrow was to run north of the canal to a large basin at Hopyard, to the east of Camerton.[19]

A view of the screen canopy at New Pit, with timber yard and hoist in the foreground. *Radstock Museum Archive*

Perhaps the most important geological work was done by John Anstie, who between the years 1866 and 1871 assisted in the deliberations of the Royal Commission into the Coalfields of Gloucestershire and Somerset. He worked initially under Joseph Prestwich who had been piecing together and classifying the existing information to give a clearer statement of the rock sequence which formed the basis of all later classifications.[20] Prestwich's work was published in the Report of 1871,[21] but Anstie wrote a less formal book, published in 1873. It is still considered to be one of the most important books on the North Somerset coalfield.[22] It contained the first comprehensive survey of coal resources in the county.[23]

This better understanding of the disposition of the coal-bearing rocks, along with the steady extension of the railway network, led to increasing output from the mines in this area of Somerset. Even in 1875, coal from the 'Great Vein' at Camerton continued to find a sale at a higher price than coal from the Midlands, which could now reach Bath via Mangotsfield on the Midland Railway. At the same time, inferior coal came down in price as it could not compete so successfully.[24]

Although the demand for coal was rising nationally it is not clear how far this was met by a rising production in the Somerset coalfield. Bluhm maintained that the output of the area was pretty static between 1880 and 1900.[25] Jevons has pointed out that while something like half a million tons was produced annually in 1870 and had risen to a million tons by 1912, yet that was only equivalent to the output of a single large colliery in South Wales or Durham.[26] 'In the period from 1888 to 1900 coal landings [at Camerton] had doubled to over 70,000 tons pa, receipts rising from £17,000 to £40,000 pa.'[27]

Improvements in Mining Methods

During this period there were a number of improvements in mining techniques which helped to increase productivity and to improve safety.

McMurtrie reported these improvements in the mechanisation of the pits in 1864:

1) There were wider shafts and these had two cages.
2) High pressure steam engines had replaced the condensing engines of a previous age.
3) Tubs which could hold up to eleven hundredweight of coal were being used instead of putts.
4) Coal was being hauled underground using engine power instead of horses.
5) Better methods of pumping using water tanks were being employed.[28]

Another improvement that dates from this time was in shot-firing. Until 1886 this had followed the practice of the lead miners, but in that year the first ratchet-boring machine was introduced at the nearby pit of Braysdown.[29]

The National Demand for More Coal

The *Royal Commission on Coal Supplies* 1871 had been asked to investigate how long supplies of coal would last. They estimated the reserves for mining and excluded seams less than one foot thick.[30] A year later the *Bath Chronicle* commented that the price of coal was rising and there was the danger of a 'Famine of Coal'. The newspaper went on to advocate 'extended application of capital and labour in order to raise the necessary supplies' and that greater depths of working could be considered.[31]

At Camerton this national drive to extract more coal may be reflected in the fact that there was an assessment of the reserves in the Great Vein at New Pit in December 1870 and possible improvements were suggested which would allow more coal to be raised. The present winding engine could be used for underground haulage with the ropes and drums etc. A new ventilation furnace was required 'at the top of the coal hole' and an engine and boiler were to be erected at Old Pit. Early in February 1871 alterations were proposed for New Pit, with a view to increasing production, cheapening transit, providing better ventilation, and security against a possible influx of water from the old Dunkerton workings.[32]

The Camerton powder house in the field overlooking the Old Pit.

Such was the desire among colliery owners in the area to raise as much coal as possible that it led to the 'Braysdown Trespass' on Camerton Manor workings between 1886 and 1888. It was claimed that 3,514 tons had been taken illegally. The claim was for £728.[33] The next year it was reported that there was only 18 months coal remaining at Old Pit and that the pit would then become uneconomical.

It may have been as a result of this demand for more coal in a time of shortage that the decision was made at Camerton to sink the down cast to the Farrington seams. This was done some time before 1886, the shaft then reaching a depth of 1,818 feet having penetrated the bed of barren red shales that separate the Radstock from the Farrington series. Exploratory cross measure drifts were driven from the pit bottom and the first coal was produced in the latter part of 1913, but it did not prove to be a profitable venture.[34]

The Colliers become more organized

As in previous generations the balance between shortage of work and shortage of coal was a fine one. In 1862 the newspapers carried the following report:

> 'There was general distress in the North Somerset collieries especially High Littleton and Timsbury in consequence of the men having been for a considerable period working on short time, and more particularly in consequence of Heywood Pit [*sic*] (Hayeswood Pit) being completely stopped. The local people complain of the failure of the recent South Western Railway scheme, which if it had been carried would have greatly improved the prospects of the district, they alleged.'[35]

Two years later in 1864 the general unrest in the coalfield was revealed in a long article in the *Bath Chronicle* about the situation in some of the local mines. There had been trouble at Foxcote, Braysdown and Writhlington because the managers had reduced the men's wages on the basis that of every six hundredweight worked only five and a half hundredweight was actually saleable coal.

Consolidation among the miners moved a step forward when a large meeting was held at Radstock the same year attended by two thousand miners and their wives. After opening with singing and a prayer, the chairman of the meeting said that the men only wanted a fair wage for a fair day's work, that the inspectors of mines were no use because they always gave notice in advance of their intended visits, so that any defects could be put right, and that, finally, the only answer was a union to support one another and to stop being down-trodden and abused. A collier from Mangotsfield said that he thought that the Somerset miners were worse off than those in South Wales, Yorkshire and the north east of England. The real dispute, according to him, was about weighing. Why would the managers not weigh all that came up and pay the men fairly? The result of this meeting was that it was unanimously resolved that 'a union be formed in connection with the South Wales Miners' Association to be called the No.1 Lodge, East Somerset'. The meeting ended with the doxology,[36] an ascription of glory to the Trinity. The period of increasing unrest among the miners continued, however, as they pressed for better conditions and higher wages.

On the 15th June 1870 'the first meeting of men and boys employed in the Somerset collieries was held which formed the Somerset Miners' Union. .... The meeting took place on the Downs at Clandown, and was well attended', with Joseph and William Robbins as representatives from Camerton. In 1870 'standard wages in Somerset averaged 2s.4d per day for eight hours. A man would sometimes put in eight to nine turns per week, to be able to make an existence. An unmarried carting lad in those days received 1s.10d per day, and when he got married he was advanced to 2s. per day'. In 1872 wages were increased by 40% but not for long.[37]

The *Bath Chronicle* reported in June 1872 on another gathering. 'A large meeting of colliers of the district was held at Clandown on Monday night. Delegates from the Colliers' Union were present. About four hundred men connected with nearby pits [which included Camerton], joined the union, whose object is to raise the standard of wages and alter the system of payment. Delegates to form a central committee were appointed.'[38] This led to the formation of the Somerset Miners' Association with organisational help from the Midlands Association of Miners. The motto of the new Association was 'For Union and for right'.[39]

The *Somerset Guardian*, in its obituary of McMurtrie in 1914, referred to the 1871-1872 'coal famine' and commented that the wages question assumed a serious aspect throughout the Somerset coalfield and that the Miners' Association, hitherto unknown in the district, became a powerful organisation. Wages and prices rose at a rate that had not been known before, nor were to be exceeded for another forty years. Although serious difficulties arose between the owners and men from this time, things seemed to improve after McMurtrie became the honorary secretary of the Coal Owners' Association with the result that between the years 1874 and 1888 a sliding scale was applied. This promoted a better atmosphere in the industry.[40] The Association of Coal Owners in East Somerset was formed in 1888.[41] Prior to that the Somerset Colliery Association had been formed about 1872.[42]

There had been strikes in 1874 but it was the much more serious strike of 1889 that swept away all the improvements in working relations that had been achieved. The strike lasted for nine weeks and it was responsible for one of the two miners' songs that are known. It was sung to the tune of 'Onward Christian Soldiers':

Onward ye brave miners, forward as to war,
Battles are not fought without an honest scar,
Tyrants must be punished, blacklegs made to run,
The future's bright before us, if firmly we press on.

Chorus
Forward be our watchword, let us all unite,
And bravely fight for Whitehouse; for Union and for Right.

Whitehouse was the miners' agent.[43]

Another devastating dispute followed in 1893 in which the men at Camerton were not involved. This was a lockout to force down wages. It lasted for seventeen weeks and caused much loss to the owners and a great deal of suffering to the miners and their families.[44]

New Laws concerning Safety

There was more legislation during this period to improve safety in coalmining, affecting the Camerton area as elsewhere. Another Act for the Regulation and Inspection of Mines was passed in 1860. This limited the age of boy labour to twelve years and above, except in the case of boys between the ages of ten and twelve who had obtained a certificate in competency in reading and writing or of school attendance. The qualifying age of persons controlling steam was raised from 15 to 18 years of age, and

A late 19th century photograph of the Camerton carting boys standing under the canopy of the New Pit screens. All wear candles in their caps, the lads in front carrying their 'tommy bags' under their jackets. Several are holding tea cans and wear the 'guss' around their waist.
Radstock Museum Archive

there were new provisions which required the drilling of bore holes in advance of a heading which was near old workings. This was to avoid the sudden flooding of a pit by accumulated water. The Act also sanctioned the appointment of check-weighers by the workmen themselves. Practice did not always follow legislation. For example check-weighmen in many instances continued to be employed by the Company rather than paid by the men.[45]

An Act of 1862 prohibited the working of coal mines without two outlets from each seam, so that if an explosion wrecked one shaft the uninjured men would still have a means of escape. This Act was passed in the same year as the disastrous accident at Hartley in the north of England where there was heavy loss of life. It was for this reason that the shaft of the Old Pit was kept open for many years after coal was no longer wound there.

Jevons wrote of the Coal Mine Regulation Act: 'The Act of 1872 is of great importance, as it may be said to be the foundation of modern legislation to secure safety in mines. It embodied most of the fundamental principles which subsequent Acts have elaborated and enforced more adequately. The outstanding reform of 1872 is the certification of managers. Henceforward no incompetent man was to be allowed to have charge of the working of a mine, and competency was to be certified by a board of examiners appointed by the Home Secretary.'[46] The Act also provided for the daily inspection of the whole mine by officials who were recognised for the purpose. There were now strict regulations for the use of explosives used for blasting underground. Refuge holes had to be provided in the walls of roadways where coal was being drawn by mechanical traction and there were further safeguards for check-weighers. Jevons has pointed out that although Workmen Examiners were appointed under this Act it was not until 1911 that they were in a strong and independent position.[47]

As a result of a number of explosions in the following years a Royal Commission was appointed in 1879. This led eventually to the passing of the Coal Mines Regulations Act in 1887 which strengthened much of the earlier legislation. The age of engineers was raised to twenty two and those in charge of machinery had to be over eighteen. Eight new General Rules were prescribed and these had to be posted at the pithead.[48]

Although no information is given with this photograph, it appears to have been taken about the same time as the one preceding, but on the higher level around the pit head. Except for two men on the left wearing candles in their caps, the rest are presumably surface workers [the little boy on the extreme right is probably only a guest]. *Radstock Museum Archive*

Notes to Chapter Seven

Railways
Chris Handley, 'Transport and Industrial Development in the Somerset Coalfield', *Five Arches*, Special Issue, 2006.

The Geology of the Coalfield
In 1873 James McMurtrie published a diagram of the Somerset coalfield, a copy of which may be seen in the Bristol District of the Geological Museum at South Kensington. In March of the following year the *Bath Chronicle* published a long article in three parts entitled 'How the Study of Stratigraphical Geology commenced near Bath', based on the research by W. Stephen Mitchell LLB FGS into William Smith's discoveries during his employment in the building of the Somersetshire Coal Canal. The second of the articles told the history of the canal up to that date.
Alan Bentley, 'How Geology shaped our Mines', *Five Arches*, Part 1, Issue 72, 2011; Part 2, Issue 73, 2012.
See also J. McMurtrie, *Faults and Contortions of Somersetshire Coal Field*, Bath Field Club Vol. 1.
J. McMurtrie, *The Geographical Position of the Carboniferous Formation in Somersetshire*, Bath Field Club Vol. 2.

Single Shafts
'Not withstanding the oft-repeated condemnation of the system of working collieries by means of a single bratticed shaft, no steps had yet been taken to put an end to the practice. In January, 1862, however, the long list of calamities arising from this defective arrangement culminated in the great catastrophe at Hartley Colliery, [six miles north of North Shields] in Northumberland, when two hundred and four persons lost their lives by half of the beam of the pumping-engine breaking off and falling down the pit, wrecking the brattice, and destroying the ventilation, and cutting off all communication with the surface. This, at length, led to the passing of a short Act of Parliament prohibiting collieries from being worked unless provided with at least two means of exit, separated by not less than ten feet of natural strata.'
R.L. Galloway, *A History of Coal Mining in Great Britain*, David and Charles 1969, p.244.

Camerton Reserves 1870
Estimated quantity of Great Vein Coal unwrought, Camerton Old Pit
December 31 1870. Radstock Museum Archives RMA RRB33.34

Estimated quantity of Great Vein Coal unwrought, Camerton New Pit
with similar estimates for Middle Vein and Little Vein.
December 31 1870. RMA RRB33.34

At Camerton New Pit the quantity of unwrought Great Vein Coal had been estimated at 506,000 tons, with a further 742,800 tons and 446,400 tons (from the other seams).

Future Plans 1870-1 and 1889
Memoranda of Proposed New Work at Camerton Collieries
17 December 1870 RMA RRB33.32

Estimated Cost of Alterations proposed to be executed at New Pit Camerton Collieries with a view to increasing production etc.
February 1871 RMA RRB33.33a

Report and Estimates of Costs of Proposed Work at Camerton Old Pit, giving eighteen months coal here.
1889 RMA RRB33.

The Braysdown Trespass 1888
Miss Jarrett and the Braysdown Coal Company. Proposal for Settlement of the Trespass
1888 RMA RRB33

Copy of Claim sent to the Braysdown Colliery Company
signed by J. McMurtrie.
Includes *Claim for damages against the Braysdown Company Colliery in respect of the Trespass committed on the Great Vein with in the Manor of Camerton, the property of Miss Jarrett.*
February 23rd 1888 RMA RRB33

Report on the Braysdown Trespass on the Great Vein at Camerton by J. McMurtrie. Also plans showing the Trespass by the Braysdown Colliery.
Includes *Letter to Miss Jarrett re the Braysdown Trespass*
February 2nd 1888 RMA RRB33

Meeting at Bath re the Braysdown Colliery Trespass
Present from Camerton Messrs McKaye, McMurtrie etc. and from Braysdown.
Wednesday March 14th 1888 RMA RRB33

Miners' Unions
The Radstock branch of the Amalgamated Association of Miners was recognised as a representative body in 1874. This was a rival federation of miners' unions which started in north west England in 1869. It gained great strength in South Wales between 1870 and 1873 but later declined. The Miners' Federation was formed in 1888 and ten years later the South Wales Miners' Federation joined the Miners' Federation of Great Britain.
Coysh, *op.cit.*, p.216.
Jevons, *op.cit.*, pp.457, 463, 468.

'Onward Christian Soldiers'.
The hymn was written by S. Baring Gould in 1864. The tune, *St. Gertrude*, first appeared in 1871. It was composed by Sir Arthur Sullivan (1842-1900).

S.H. Whitehouse.
Radstock Museum Archive

S. H. Whitehouse 1849-1919

'In 1888 Somerset miners invited an experienced trade unionist from the Black Country, S.H.Whitehouse, to become their agent [of the Somerset Miners' Association, on the 28th February 1888, after eighteen years without a permanent agent]. Samuel Henry Whitehouse, the son of a miner, was born at Swan village, Staffordshire, in February 1849. He went into the pit at an early age, was a checkweighman for many years, held office in the Amalgamated Association of Miners and, later, in the National Miners' Union ... He served as agent to the Somerset Miners' Association for thirty years ...'.
Penny Bonsall, Dissertation, *Masters and Men: a study of trade unionism, class and politics in the Somerset Coalfield 1890-1914*, Bath College of Higher Education 1984.
Report of the funeral of S. H. Whitehouse *Somerset Guardian* 2 January 1920

Acts of Parliament

1. An Act for the Regulation and Inspection of Mines 1860
   'No boy under twelve years of age to be employed in mines unless he can read and write, or otherwise he must attend school for three hours on two days in every week.' Winding engines, for winding men in shafts, not to be in charge of persons under eighteen years old.
   Robert Peel, Coal Mining, Blackie & Son 1912.

2. Coal Mines Act 1872
   This was enacted 'to consolidate and amend the law relating to the regulation and inspection of coal mines ...'. All the chief features of the previous Acts were continued in this Act.
   Robert Peel, *op.cit.*

3. Coal Mines Regulation Act 1887
   This Act repealed all former Acts. Its wide ranging provisions included the hours of employment of boys underground and above ground, women on the surface, certification of managers and under-managers, and the appointment of checkweighers. The Special Rules were drawn up for the duties and responsibilities of deputies, firemen, coal-getters and those dealing with machinery, timbering, explosives etc., etc.
   Robert Peel, *op.cit.*

References to Chapter Seven

1. Maggs and Beale, *op.cit.*, p.8.
2. *Ibid.*, p.8.
3. *Bath Chronicle*, 24 September, 1863.
4. G.C. Greenwell and J. McMurtrie, *The Radstock Portion of the Somersetshire Coalfield*, 1864, p.15.
5. Maggs and Beale, *op.cit.*, p.9.
6. *Ibid.*, p.9.
7. Warnock, *op.cit.*
8. Maggs and Beale, *op.cit.*, p.10.
9. *Ibid.*, p.14.

10. C. Howell, *Round here in them days*, Fosseway Press 1980.
11. *Somerset Guardian*, 11 January, 1946.
12. Clew, *op.cit.*, p.111.
13. *Bath Journal*, 16 January, 1895.
14. Clew, *op.cit.*, p.112.
15. *Ibid.*, p.111.
16. *Ibid.*, p.112.
17. Greenwell and McMurtrie, *op.cit.*
18. S.W. Brice, *The Coalfield of North Somersetshire*, Bemrose and Lothian 1867.
19. Howell, *op.cit.*, endpapers.
20. Coysh, *op.cit.*, p.217.
21. Royal Commission on Coal Supplies, 1871; Reports, 3 volumes.
22. Williams, *op.cit.*, pp.1, 3.
23. Coysh, *op.cit.*, p.217.
24. R.K. Bluhm, *Bibliography, op.cit.*
25. Bluhm, *op.cit.*
26. Jevons, *op.cit.*, p.79.
27. Down & Warrington, *op.cit.*, p.114.
28. Victoria County History, *op.cit.*, p.382ff.
29. Bulley *op. cit.* I. p.67.
30. Jevons, *op.cit.*, p.722-731.
31. *Bath Chronicle*, 25 July 1872.
32. See Camerton Reserves and Future Plans in this Chapter's Notes.
33. See Braysdown Trespass in this Chapter's Notes.
34. Down & Warrington, *op.cit.*, p.115.
35. *Bath Chronicle*, 10 July 1862.
36. *Bath Chronicle*, 23 June 1864.
37. Comment by 'Onlooker' in local press 15 June 1920. Radstock Museum Archives
38. *Bath Chronicle*, 13 June 1872.
39. A.J. Parfitt, *My Life as a Somerset Miner*, 1930.
40. *Somerset Guardian*, 6 February 1914.
41. Williams, *op.cit.*, p.24.
42. Somerset Record Office, DD/BR/tsk 19.
43. Down & Warrington, *op.cit.*, p.35.
44. *Somerset Guardian*, 6 February 1914.
45. Jevons, *op.cit.*, p.381.
46. *Ibid.*, p.383.
47. *Ibid.*, pp.383, 408-409.
48. *Ibid.*, p.384.

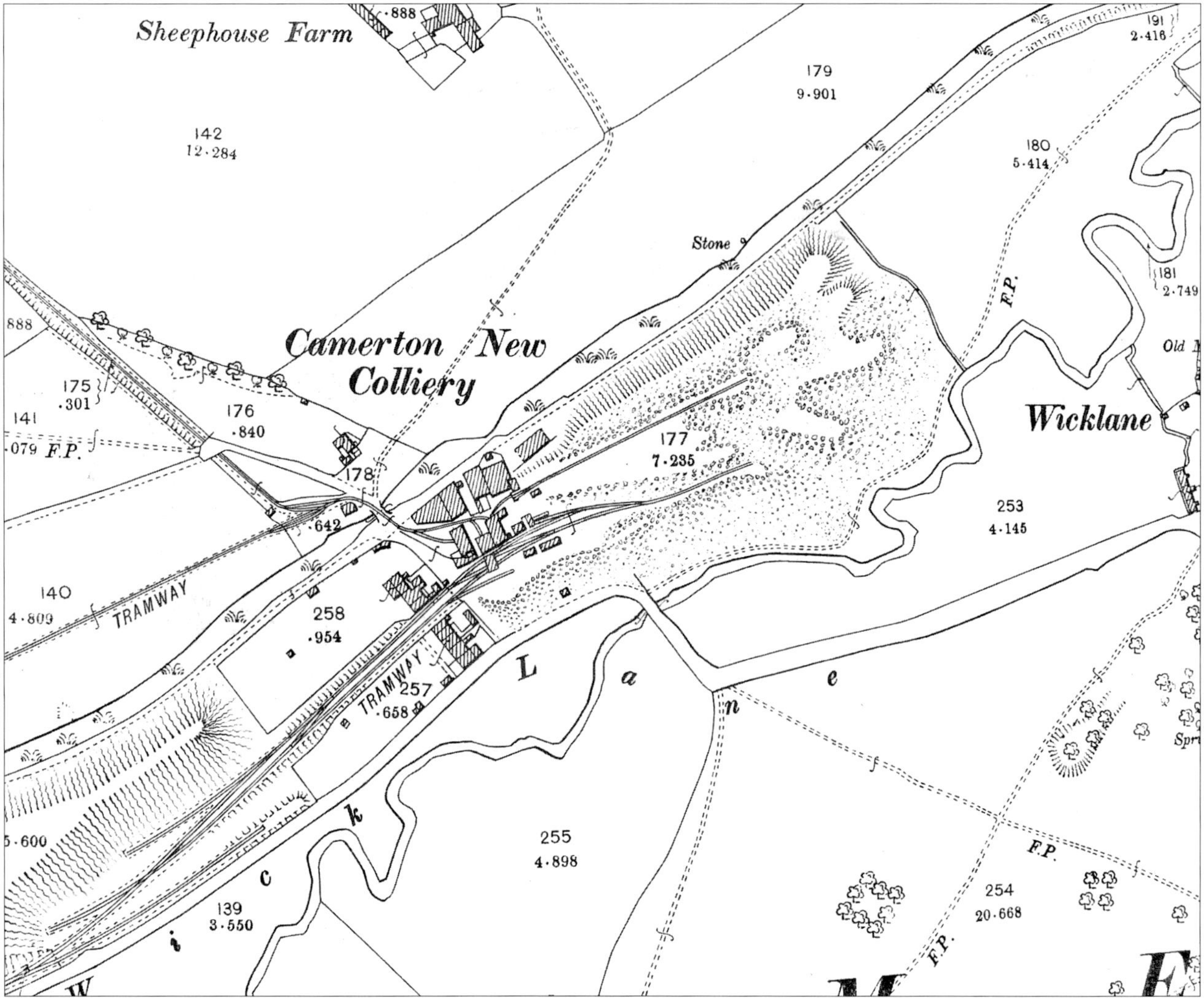

The New Pit area from the Ordnance Survey 25-inch map of 1904, just before the building of the Limpley Stoke extension, showing the new layout of the colliery next to the overgrown and abandoned canal.

CHAPTER EIGHT

THE END OF THE CANAL AND AN EXPLOSION 1890-1910

Mining the Coal

One of the best pictures of underground working is provided by A.J. Parfitt in his *My Life as a Somerset Miner* which was first published in 1930. He described how the miner may not only have a long early morning walk from his home in Timsbury, Carlingcott or Paulton, but that underground he could also have another lengthy walk to the face. He carried his tommy bag, containing his food, a bottle of water or cold tea, and candles in his candle box for his shift. He was not paid for this distance to the face, yet it could take up to forty minutes. This distance had exceeded six hundred yards at Camerton by 1830.[1]

When Parfitt began, a carting boy had to provide his own piece of inch-thick rope with which to make the girdle of the guss. The chain was called the 'tugger'. The crook would be made in the blacksmith's shop at the pithead. The putt which he hauled was based on the earlier corves although by this time hazel rods were no longer used to form the sides. It was described as being a sledge-like box about 2ft 9in. long, by 2ft wide and with a depth of 6in., which was mounted on iron runners. It could hold between one and a half and one and three quarter hundredweight of coal and was pulled and pushed by the carting boys. The guss and crook enabled him to pull the putt to the tramroads or to use it as a brake when descending an incline. At the tramroad the load of coal was tipped onto a flat metal sheet or boarded area six feet square prior to being loaded onto the trams for the journey to the pit bottom and into the cage. Parfitt described pulling a loaded cart like crawling under a chair.[2] The carting boys sometimes wore padded basin-shaped hats of thick material because of the danger of rocks falling from the roof of the roadways, and a candle was stuck on the brim of the hat.[3]

An original photograph entitled 'William Frank Whittock of Peasedown wearing a guss & crook. Worked at Dunkerton Middle Pit and Ludlows. Later landlord of Prince of Wales, Peasedown.' Another inscription on different copy of same image says: 'Landlord of Jolly Collier, Camerton.' *Radstock Museum Archive*

A miner's cap with attachment for various methods of lighting; for a candle holder (below), an oil lamp (right), and a carbide lamp introduced in the early 20th century (left). *Radstock Museum Archive*

At the coal face there would usually be two miners, lying on their sides, working the coal loose with pick and wedges. The carting boys would then load the coal onto their putts, taking great care to stack the coal so that it did not get damaged as there was only a limited market for small coal. It was the big lumps that the customer wanted and the coal owners would pay for.[4]

Writing of Camerton in 1894 Stuart said:

> '... until recent years, shovels were not allowed in the coal faces, and only hand-picked coal was filled into the trams. Shovels are now used but the rule remains that no small coal is to be sent out. As part of the system to enforce care in excavating the coal, one end of the tram is left open, with simple tie-chains to keep the sides in their normal positions; the lumps which are of cubical structure, are built as a wall in this end, and properly speaking there should be no small coal except that made by attrition in conveyance, so that some small coal in the trams is inevitable.' [5]

If the coal was being 'mined to the rise' the loaded putt would be let down a self-acting rope-worked incline known as a 'gugg' or a 'topple' to the main roadway for loading onto the trams. Conversely, if the coal was being 'mined to the dip', the putt had to be mounted on a four-wheeled carriage and pushed up the 'dipple' to the tramway. When sufficient loaded trams were ready, they were assembled into a train of about eight trams and hauled by a pony, or later by the endless rope system known as the 'main and tail', to the bottom of the shaft.

> 'The puttways which connected with the coal face, if very steep, would be fitted with static ropes, anchored at both ends, and then called 'topples'. It was a dangerous and skilled job to work the putts when fully loaded down a topple, using the crook and the static rope as a braking system, and on a dipple it would require two boys to work a putt on its carriage up a dipple, one pulling with his guss and crook and the other pushing with his head! In both cases the dangers arose if the boy slipped and the loaded putt careered down the slope out of control.'[6]

The topples and dipples were only about three or four feet high so that it meant that the carting boys had to work on all fours, hands and knees taking heavy punishment and the chain between their legs pulling on the rope girdle as they dragged the heavy putt along the dark roadway.[7]

Greenwell and McMurtrie, writing in 1864 about the Radstock coalfield, which included Camerton, said: 'Where the seams dip much, the roads are commonly about forty yards apart, and the carting boys are expected to haul the coal on the putts from thirty yards on the high side of the road and ten yards on the deep side. Where the seams are nearly level, the roads branch off right and left and they are commonly driven from fifty yards to sixty yards apart, the coal being hauled about thirty yards each way to the horses'.[8]

In this area the roof was allowed to break down behind the workers. The space left underground after the coal had been taken out was known as the 'gob' or 'goaf' (sometimes the 'heads') and into it was stowed the shale from the rippings of the roof.[9] The roads were kept open through the gob by means of packwalls, made from rubbish from the roof.[10] This helped to support the surface above ground because for every ten feet of coal extracted there was a fall of one inch at the surface.[11] This packing of the gob provided support in addition to the timbers being used. The gobs would not always hold all the rubbish so the excess had to be sent up the shaft. The timber itself could be a problem, either it was not available or it was in six to eight foot lengths, and a foot or more in diameter. In some pits the men had to cut their own timber using handsaws before they went below ground, and at times there was a lack of pit-props available, thus increasing the hazards of working underground at the coal face. 'I class the best man to be the one who well timbers his place, sends up clean coal and as large as possible.'[12] The large amount of timber required in Somerset pits could take up to 15% of the total expenditure on materials at a colliery.[13] Miners were required to leave forty four yards of unworked ground between one mine and the neighbouring property. This was known as 'the Barrier'.[14]

Particular names were given to the surface roadways at Camerton. The Old and New Pit, linked by the 'Drammyway', was a tramway until 1910. The 'Gugg' was the incline which led from New Pit to the land-sales depot halfway up Red Hill. This was a rail track, passing under a small footbridge, along which the coal was hauled up to the depot, using an engine-driven endless rope. The 'Slope' was the name for the short, steep pathway leading from Wick Lane to the top of the heapstead at Camerton New Pit.[15]

The Last Days of the Canal

The life of the Somersetshire Coal Canal finally came to an end during this period, replaced by the Camerton and Limpley Stoke Railway. The tonnage carried on the canal had been declining steadily for a number of years, a situation not helped by the state into which the canal had fallen.

George Tucker, who went to work in Camerton Colliery as a carting boy about 1897, recalled that at that time boats were still coming up the canal from Devizes and Trowbridge. He remembered how, in winter, the boats would sometimes become frozen in the canal for days at a time. They would then bring up an iron boat, pulled by a team of horses, while those on board would rock from side to side to break the ice. Tucker said that while most of the boats were pulled by horses or mules, a certain

The canal bridge at the bottom of Red Hill (Old Pit is out of view to the right). Although this photograph was taken soon after the abandonment of the canal, the parapet walls remain standing, one of which, on the left, still survives as a garden wall. To the left are newly-built pit offices (formerly a smithy) next to the Post Office, and to the right a large colliery building replaced in 1911 by the new Church Rooms. *Radstock Museum Archive*

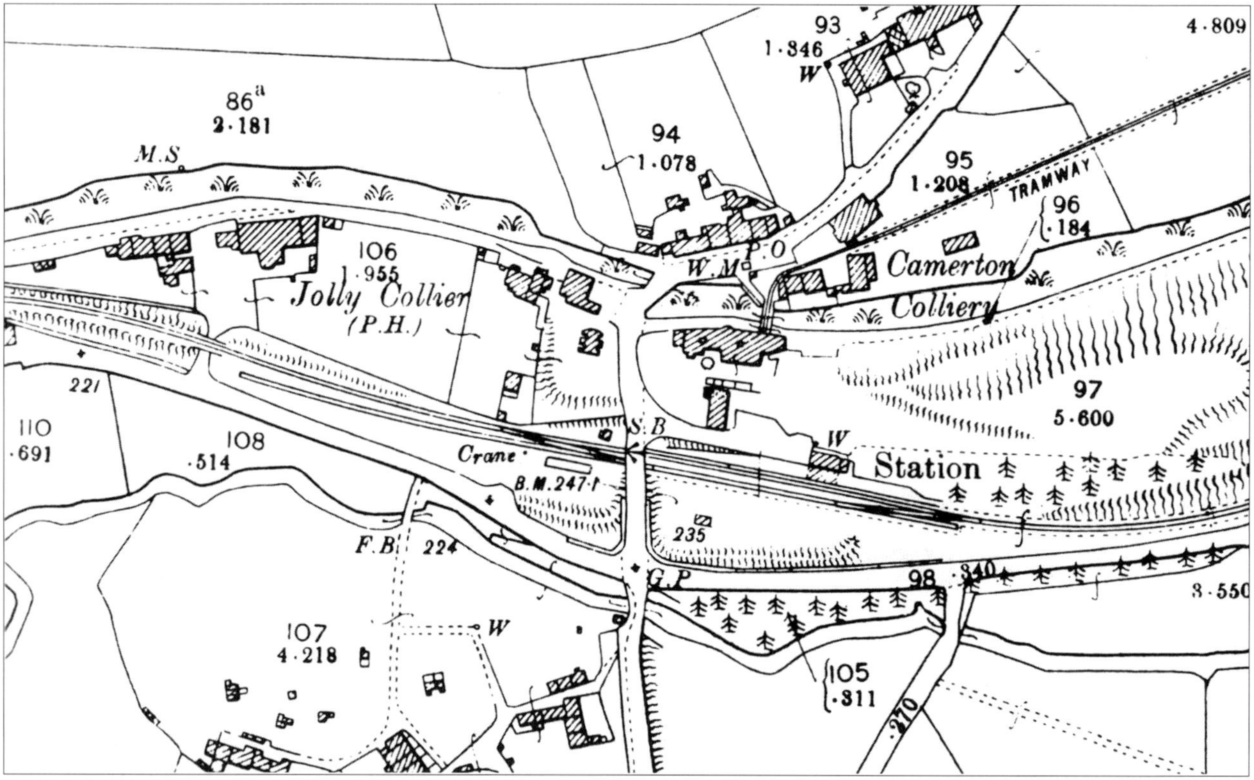

Detail of the Old Pit area from the OS 25-inch map of 1904. The canal is still shown in existence, but abandoned and overgrown.

Jimmie Mayo used to pull his own boat! He was a large man who called for a quart of beer at a time when in the public house.[16] Fortunately there were a number of such hostelries along or near the banks of the canal, such as the Hope & Anchor at Midford, or the Jolly Collier (formerly the New Inn) at Camerton.

The coal then being carried down the canal would have come only from Lower Conygre in Timsbury, the section between Radford and Paulton now being defunct. Camerton's output was either by land-sales or by the railway to Hallatrow. The boats would sometimes be used on the return voyage to carry timber for pit-props,[17] and it was the output from Timsbury of some 17,000 tons a year which would have kept the canal working. However, that coal company was becoming increasingly dissatisfied with the state of the canal.[18] For instance, it had been the custom for both the Camerton pits and the canal to close down for a week every year at Whitsun for essential maintenance to be carried out. Some of the miners found employment during this time in removing the rubbish from the canal. Mr. Thatcher, a blacksmith at Camerton, told of the rubbish being stacked beside the canal and then thrown back in again at night, so ensuring that the canal would need clearing out the next year.[19]

In 1893 the canal finally passed into liquidation, the tonnage carried having fallen to 11,000 tons, and the following year the Timsbury Coal Company opened negotiations with the Great Western Railway with a view to constructing a coal siding near Camerton Station, but nothing came of this scheme.[20] During that same year the canal was put up for sale by auction at Tokenhouse Yard in the City of London, but it failed to find a purchaser.[21]

The canal was offered to the Somerset & Dorset Railway in 1895 but it had no interest. Furthermore, the Wiltshire &Berkshire Canal, which had played such an important part in earlier years in distributing coal that had passed through the coal canal, was finally abandoned in 1897. The following year marked the end of the working life of the coal canal when on the 11th November 1898 pumping ceased at Dunkerton,[22] and from thereon all coal from Timsbury and Camerton had to travel by road or rail. It was almost exactly a hundred years since the first coal boat had moved along the canal.

Railway Schemes

From 1902 several light railway schemes were proposed along part of the canal from Midford to Clutton or Priston, but this was opposed by the Great Western Railway because it would have competed with the Hallatrow to Camerton Railway. In 1903 Mr. E.L. Heppel, the general manager of the Camerton Colliery, organised a petition signed by 688 people, asking that the Great Western Railway extend their railway from Hallatrow through to Limpley Stoke.[23] The severe gradient between Camerton and Hallatrow limited the trains to some fourteen wagons, which then followed a circuitous route through Bristol and Bath to markets in the east such as Southampton Docks where a good steam raising quality of coal was required for bunkering. Furthermore the pits of North Somerset produced a high quality gas coal which enjoyed a wider market than just Bath, Bristol and West Wiltshire, and it was therefore felt that a connection with the line through Salisbury would be a strategic move. A further incentive to completing this railway link was the new pit planned at Dunkerton in 1898 and fully operational in 1906. It was to become the largest in Somerset during its short life.[24] The way was now open for the Great Western Railway Company to make their own proposal.

In July 1903 the Board of Trade held an Inquiry in Bath into the abandonment of the coal canal, which was allowed under the Act of 1888 because part of the canal had been derelict for three years. The Inquiry recognised that the canal was becoming a public health hazard and a nuisance because of the stagnant water, the upper level being the most offensive. The main concern, however, was the maintenance of the banks and aqueducts in order to avert the danger of flooding, and to this end two men were employed to look after the banks. This was rapidly exhausting the Canal Company's remaining funds.[25]

It was at this point that the Great Western Railway put forward its plans for the railway link-up which, they maintained, would mean reduced rates for the Camerton Collieries, and for which they were prepared to offer the liquidator £2,000. The water rights would not be required, and would be restored to the original channels. At the end of the Inquiry all agreed to the proposal to vest the site of the canal in the Great Western Railway, and the Board of Trade would make a decision in due course.[26]

An Extension to the Camerton Railway

The result was the Camerton to Limpley Stoke Act of August 1904 which authorised the extension of the railway to the east of Camerton. Tipping in the canal had already started at New Pit about 1902 when the batch there started to spill over into the canal.[27] The final act was to drain the canal and this took place in 1906.[28] The water rights to many of the springs were sold to Mr. E.H. Bayldon, a prospective purchaser of the canal, to supplement the supply to the Combe Down High Level Water

A steam navvy at work on a cutting near Midford for the new extension of the Camerton Branch railway to Limpley Stoke. In the background, the top of a bridge belonging to the abandoned coal canal can just be seen on the extreme right.

Works Company which he owned. In 1907 the Dunkerton Pumping Station, which had been in charge of a Mr. Alfred Bampfylde, was sold to the new coal company there, the boilers for use at the pit head, and the remaining buildings and cottages demolished.[29]

The course of new line was marked out in March 1905 and work started at Camerton in July 1906. The *Somerset Guardian* reported that the main object was to meet the requirements of the coal traffic, especially that from Dunkerton.[30] In September the newspaper commented that the work was going ahead very quickly at Camerton and there were a hundred men at work on the site, who found it difficult to get accommodation in Camerton with the result that some of them lived rough. The contractors for the construction of the line were Messrs Pauling & Co. of Westminster, London.

At this stage the work was mainly of a preliminary nature, laying temporary railways, diverting the Cam brook in two places by cutting long lengths of trenches several feet deep to obviate 'the erection of several bridges over the hitherto winding course of the stream, and the erection of machinery'. A steam navvy was used for filling wagons with colliery waste from the tip at Camerton, for making an embankment. It was also used to excavate a cutting some fifty four chains (1,188 yards) in length and twenty two feet deep through the red soil half a mile east of Camerton, over seventy thousand cubic

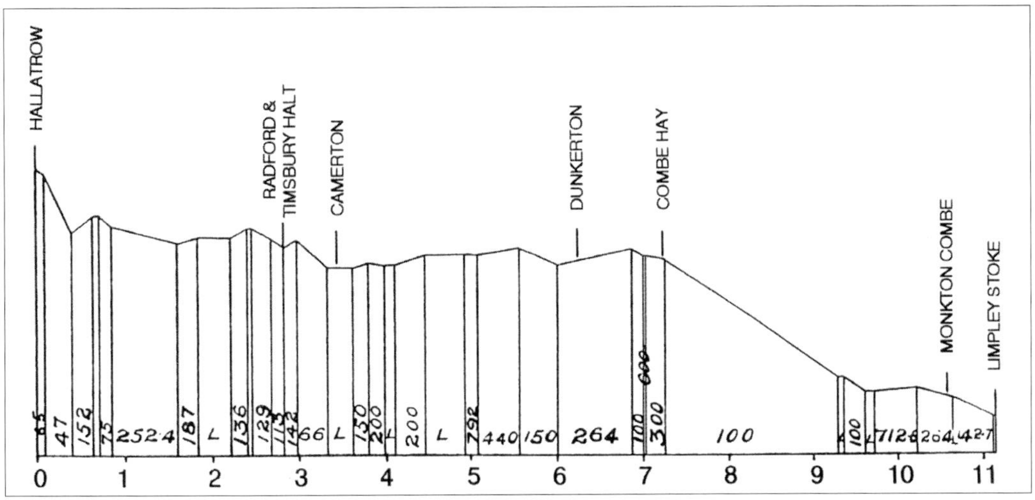

A similar view to the previous photograph, looking along the new line toward the Somerset & Dorset railway viaduct at Midford.

A diagram of the gradients along the complete line of the railway between Hallatrow and Limpley Stoke.

One of the first 'motor trains' from Hallatrow to Limpley Stoke at Camerton Station, c.1910. The pit-head gear of Old Pit can be seen in the background, with two pit-wheels, chimney, and the roof of the pump-engine house. *Radstock Museum Archive*

This photograph of station staff, taken somewhat later, shows the two pit-wheels of Old Pit protruding through the roof of the colliery. *Colin Maggs*

yards of material being removed in the process.[31] The section of the line between Camerton and Dunkerton was opened in August 1907, enabling coal from Dunkerton to leave the colliery by way of Camerton and Hallatrow.[32]

The railway was finally opened throughout its length to Limpley Stoke on the 9th May 1910. The *Somerset Guardian*, anticipating the event, said they expected to open the Cam Valley Railway 'and reap the fruits of the enormous expenditure and years of toil in overcoming the considerable engineering difficulties expended'. With the opening of the line 'the still developing coalfields of North Somerset and a chain of villages will be linked with Wiltshire and the main line'. Although the line was seen primarily as being for coal from Camerton, Priston (Tunley) and Dunkerton, the Great Western Railway was prepared to start a passenger service and it hoped to have enough traffic to justify five motor trains a day.[33] With the completion of the railway network in the area the

Another view of Camerton Station after the opening of the Limpley Stoke extension, taken from the road bridge looking eastward. New additions to the station included the passing loop and siding on the right. On the left is the spoil heap or 'batch' of Old Pit, with footpath leading up to the pit-head.

stage was set for bringing the collieries into a closer relationship with each other in the years ahead.

When the newspaper next appeared, after the line had actually opened, it commented that this would be good for Miss Jarrett. Trains of fifty wagons instead of fourteen could now leave the colliery. The ruling gradient was 1 in 100 downhill towards Dunkerton although the line subsequently climbed to Combe Hay tunnel and then fell to Midford. The newspaper pointed out that very little coal would now leave the area through Hallatrow and passengers would be able to see the 'celebrated flight of twenty locks - their passage must have been a tedious business. These locks remain, and so stout is the masonry that they are likely to endure, perhaps until in a remote generation antiquarians will be having controversy concerning their original use'.[34]

An Underground Explosion

Events below ground during this period were no less significant than those occurring on the canal and railway. Camerton received wide publicity following an explosion underground on the night of 13th–14th November 1893 in the New Pit, the cause of which was eventually traced to coal dust:

'The Radstock series of seams were worked at Camerton, and no fire damp had been found in them at Camerton or elsewhere. After the explosion, exhaustive tests were carried out by Prof. Clowes with his

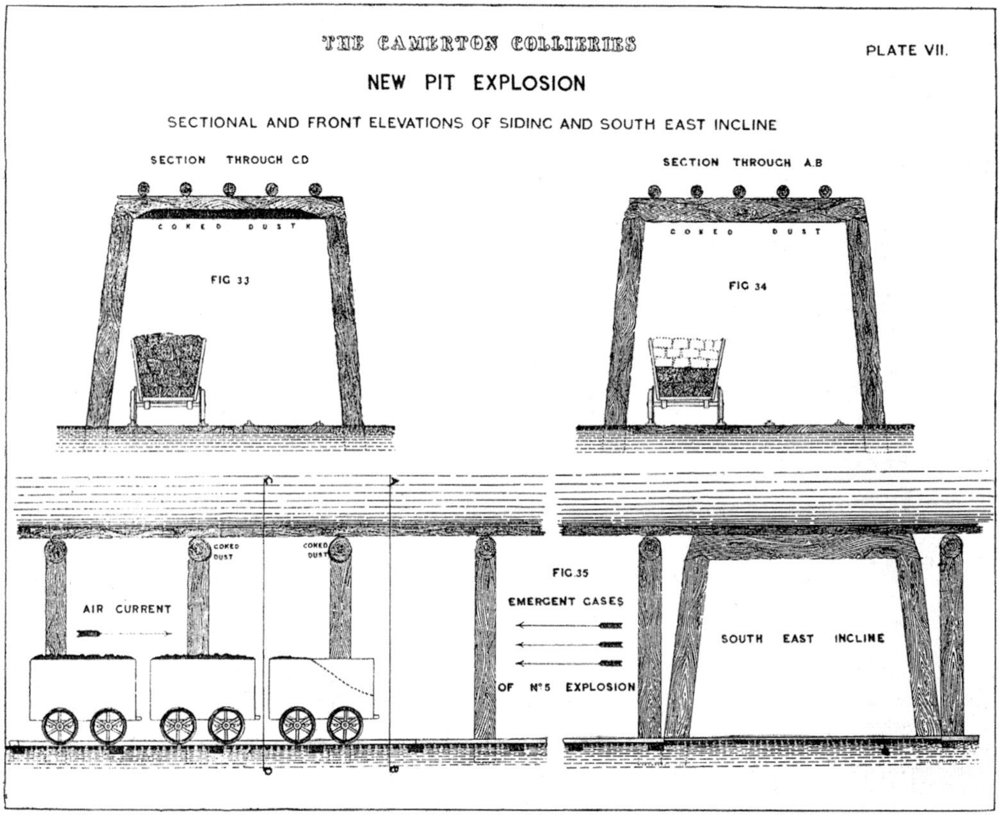

A diagram illustrating the cause of the coal-dust explosion at Camerton, from *Coal Dust, an Explosive Agent*, by Donald D. Stuart. *Bath Central Library*

hydrogen lamp, and by Mr. Stokes with his alcohol lamp. The explosion originated in a 'gugg' a self-acting incline where the roof was being ripped down, and it caused the death of a man and a boy, who were the only persons employed in the district at the time. The explosive they were using was powder, and there was evidence that the deceased had fired a shot in the roof, and had taken refuge in a manhole. When found the bodies were badly burned, and appearances pointed to their having endeavoured to escape when overcome. Examination of the dust under a microscope, revealed it to have been in a state of incandescence. There were indications of force both inwards and outwards for a distance of a hundred yards on each side of the shot, and practically ceased at points where the dust ended. About eleven hundred yards of roadway was wrecked by the explosion. The shot had done part of its work, and it seems almost certain that being over-charged it disturbed the dust on the floor under it, which on rising in a fine dust, was ignited by the flame from the powder and thus initiated the flame and force of the explosion, which was afterwards fed by the dust alone.'[35]

The *Bath Chronicle* reported the accident a few days later. At a depth of 750 feet the roof had been blown down and the air in the workings was very bad when the rescue party entered. One of the victims was Mr. W. Hawkins from Tunley who had five children, the other, a lad of seventeen named Tarrant from the Red Post at Peasedown. Miss Emily Jarrett visited the pit and 'made enquiries and spread sympathy as did the Rector the Rev. Richard Lawson'. The paper continued, 'The Camerton Pits have been working through the whole summer and a short time ago the men's wages were increased by 7½%'.[36] This was a reference to the fact that there had been a period of industrial unrest in the neighbouring mines but on this occasion Camerton had continued to work because the miners had had a wage rise, although in December the men were asked to give it up.[37]

The Inquest was held at the Jolly Collier on Friday the 24th November. It was reported to the Government Inspector of Mines that the first fall had occurred 750 yards from the shaft; there was a pungent vapour in the pit and the bodies were found 2,100 yards from the shaft in the south east workings. The men had been shot firing to rip out the roof and to make the roadways higher. The roads in this part were small due to the pressure from above and needed frequent enlarging by these methods. It was also reported that a new furnace for ventilation had been installed in the previous February.[38]

The previous week the newspaper reported on the funerals of the two men. Two hundred miners were in the cortège at Mr. Hawkins' funeral at Camerton and also the Sunday School class of which he was the teacher. The collection raised £8.7s.0d and the Jury at the Inquest also gave their fees to the families of the deceased. Mr. G. Tarrant, also known as Stock, was buried at Peasedown St. John with his sister, who died about the same time. Due to the large amount of debris still in the pit, mining in that area of the workings had not been resumed since the explosion.[39]

In 1891, two years before the Camerton explosion, a Royal Commission on Coal Dust had been set up 'to inquire into the effect of coal dust in originating and extending explosions in mines, whether by itself or in conjunction with firedamp; and also to enquire whether there are any practicable means of preventing or mitigating any dangers that may arise from the presence of coal dust in mines'. The Commission did not report until 1894 and two years later 'the Secretary of State was empowered to revise and modify the special rules in use with respect to the use and storage of explosives ... the prevalence of gas or coal dust in mines etc'.[40]

Coal dust was to cause two further accidents in the mines in Somerset. In February 1895 seven men were killed at the Timsbury Upper Conygre Pit, when shot-firing using a straw filled with gunpowder, even though much safer explosives were available by then. According to Penny Bonsall 'The conservative, traditional Somerset miners clung fiercely to 'customary practice' and were often suspicious of innovation'. In 1908 ten miners were killed at Norton Hill because the dust had not been sufficiently dampened down beforehand.[41]

It was not until the Act of 1911 that precautions were specified with regard to coal dust. To prevent its distribution in a mine, the Act required 'that screens for tipping or sorting the coal must be 80 yards at least from the mouth of the intake shaft, that within five years all trams (or tubs) shall be so constructed as to prevent coal dust escaping, and that the floor, roof and sides of the roads shall be systematically cleared of accumulation of dust, and roads watered where practicable'.[42] Fuller's earth was used in some pits to damp down the dust. This could be obtained locally from the fuller's earth mines at Odd Down and South Stoke near Bath.[43]

Accidents Underground

Camerton had its share of other accidents, sometimes caused by the low standard of safety that was prevalent in the pits at that time. These were reported through the pages of the *Somerset Guardian*, which had been founded in 1893, and was very much the newspaper of the mining region of Somerset.

At the inquest in November 1902 into the death of an eighteen year old, George Harding, who had died three months after being hit on the head by a post at Camerton, it was revealed that the post weighed about one hundredweight and was six feet long. This 'post' was evidently what was called by the miners a 'bell mould', the fossilised remains of a tree trunk which still remained in the rock above the roadway, and sometimes slid out without warning. He was found to have died of a brain tumour which might have been accelerated by the blow to the head, so the verdict was death from natural causes.[44] In the spring of 1903 Frank Wooley was found dead under an empty coal cart. Although only twenty eight years of age he was judged to have died of heart disease.[45] The inquest in 1905 into the death of Herbert Tucker, a twenty-year old underground pony driver, was held at the Jolly Collier. It was attended by Heppel, James Sellars, the under manager, and Francis Heal, the colliery bailiff. Tucker had been kicked below the eye and had died three days later. He had been driving horses for the last year and was known to be careful and kind to the horses.[46]

There was another inquest following an accident on the 20th October 1910, when Frank Young, a breaker at Camerton died at his home after having been hit by a stone weighing several hundredweights and measuring some three feet by one foot, which fell from the side of the roof as he was making an air course off one of the roads in the side of the Great Vein. The stone had been sounded in the morning by Heal, 'it gave a good ring' when he marked the spot. At the inquest he said that James Holvey, Young's mate, had pulled out a tight wall under the stone and that this could have caused the fall.[47] There had been an incident underground earlier that autumn which resulted in a court case. It appears that Thomas Barnes of Timsbury and Will Willcox of Meadgate were brought to court in Weston 'for refusing to stand back from the shaft', which was a breach of the Coal Mines Regulations of 1887 and 1908. These laid down that 'only ten men in a cage at a time, five in the top and five in the bottom'. It was alleged that these two men had got under the chain which restricted entrance at the bottom of the shaft. The danger was that they could have fallen into the sump at the bottom of the shaft. This had not been an isolated case, there was often overcrowding at the bottom, as men wanted to get up the shaft as soon as possible. Arthur Fairchild and Henry Blacker were the 'hitchers-on', and it was imperative that they could see the men and the wagons into the cage. Both these men had worked in the pits for around ten years and they knew the regulations. Fairchild had ordered the two accused to get back behind the chain. Many of the witnesses said that Barnes and Willcox were not ordered out by name. Both these men were fined £1 to cover costs and it was stated that the rules were for the safety of miners and that they had to be obeyed.[48]

Changes at the Pithead

Towards the end of the century there were changes at Camerton New Pit which more or less coincided with the end of winding at Old Pit. In 1895 the first winding engine at New Pit was replaced by a new horizontal engine, having two cylinders of 26in. x 54in., made by the Leeds Engineering Company.[49] Camerton Pit was in the news again towards the end of 1904. For several weeks it had been observed that a subsidence was in progress in the ground on which the boiler chimney and the engine works were erected. There were cracks in the engine house wall, and the boilers had shifted. The management had tried to discover the reason some six weeks previously, when they excavated and found that the ground beneath the boiler chimney was on fire. A bed of concrete was put into the excavation but the problem became worse so it was decided to stop work at the colliery.

Sketch of the pit-head structures of Camerton Old Pit about 1900, based on an old postcard view. Two opposing pit-wheels were used here, and the domed object in the foreground appears to have been a 'haystack' boiler.

New Pit viewed from the north in the early years of the 20th century, after re-development. *Radstock Museum Archive*

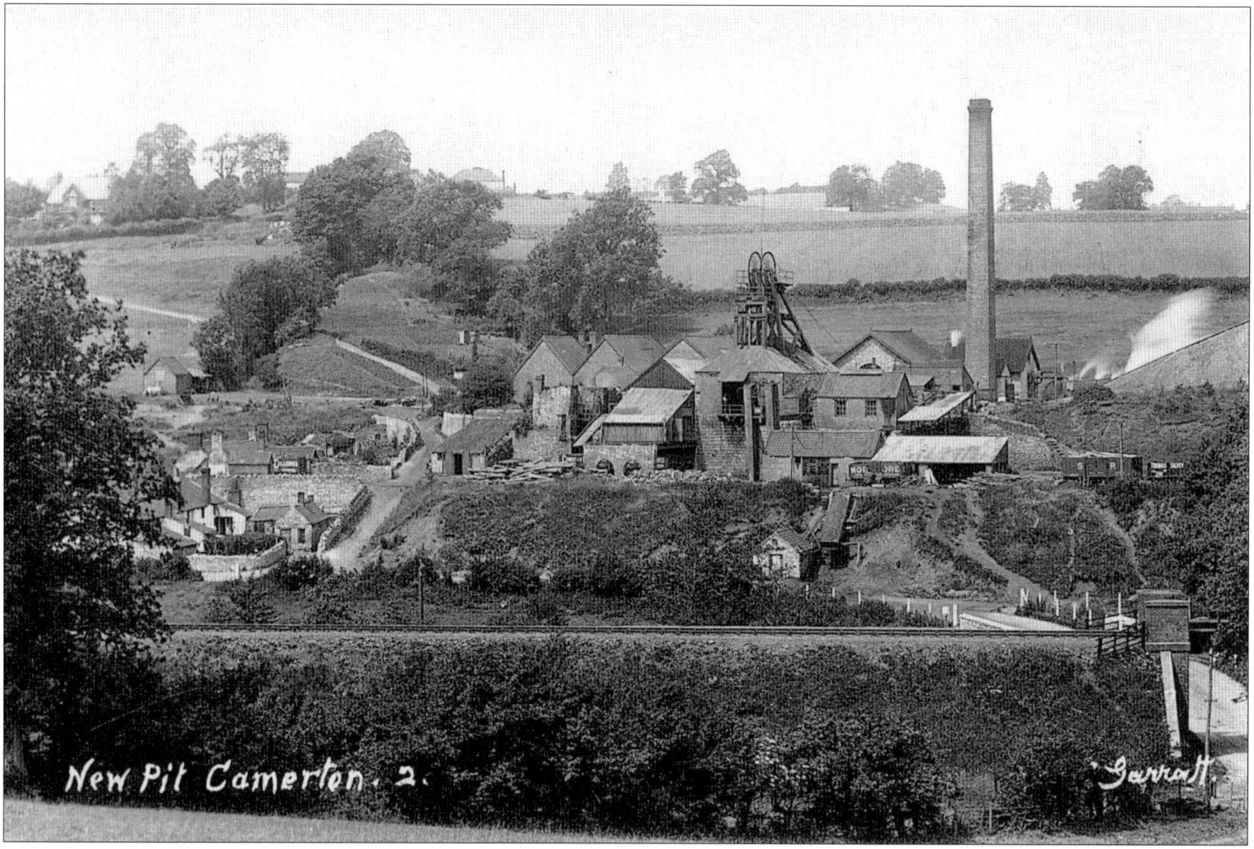

A view of New Pit from the south, not long after the building of the railway extension to Limpley Stoke which can be seen in the foreground on an embankment and bridge over Wick Lane. *Radstock Museum Archive*

The *Somerset Guardian* pointed out that all the buildings affected had only been built some ten years previously and that the boiler chimney had been erected on ground which consisted of small coal and rubbish. It was now believed that heat from the flues had cracked the concrete foundations and ignited the coal deposit beneath so that it was now a smouldering mass. One of the boilers was removed, with the possible necessity of moving the other two, and also the winding engine. Mr. Heppel, the manager, and Miss Jarrett did not want anybody idle so they decided to re-open the Old Pit shaft and to get the roadways in order as soon as possible.[50] When the newspaper returned to the saga in December, it reported that the mischief was far reaching. The boilers and the boiler chimney would have to be shifted, a new engine house built and the winding engine moved and re-erected. The chimney itself had not been affected nor the ground at the mouth of the shaft upon which the heavy angles and the wheels rested. It was estimated that it would cost some hundreds of pounds to remedy the trouble.[51]

The following March the newspaper's report was more optimistic. New Pit was now fully working again, the shaft having been idle since the fourteenth of November, following the fire in the foundations. During that time the winding engine and the boilers had been moved further back

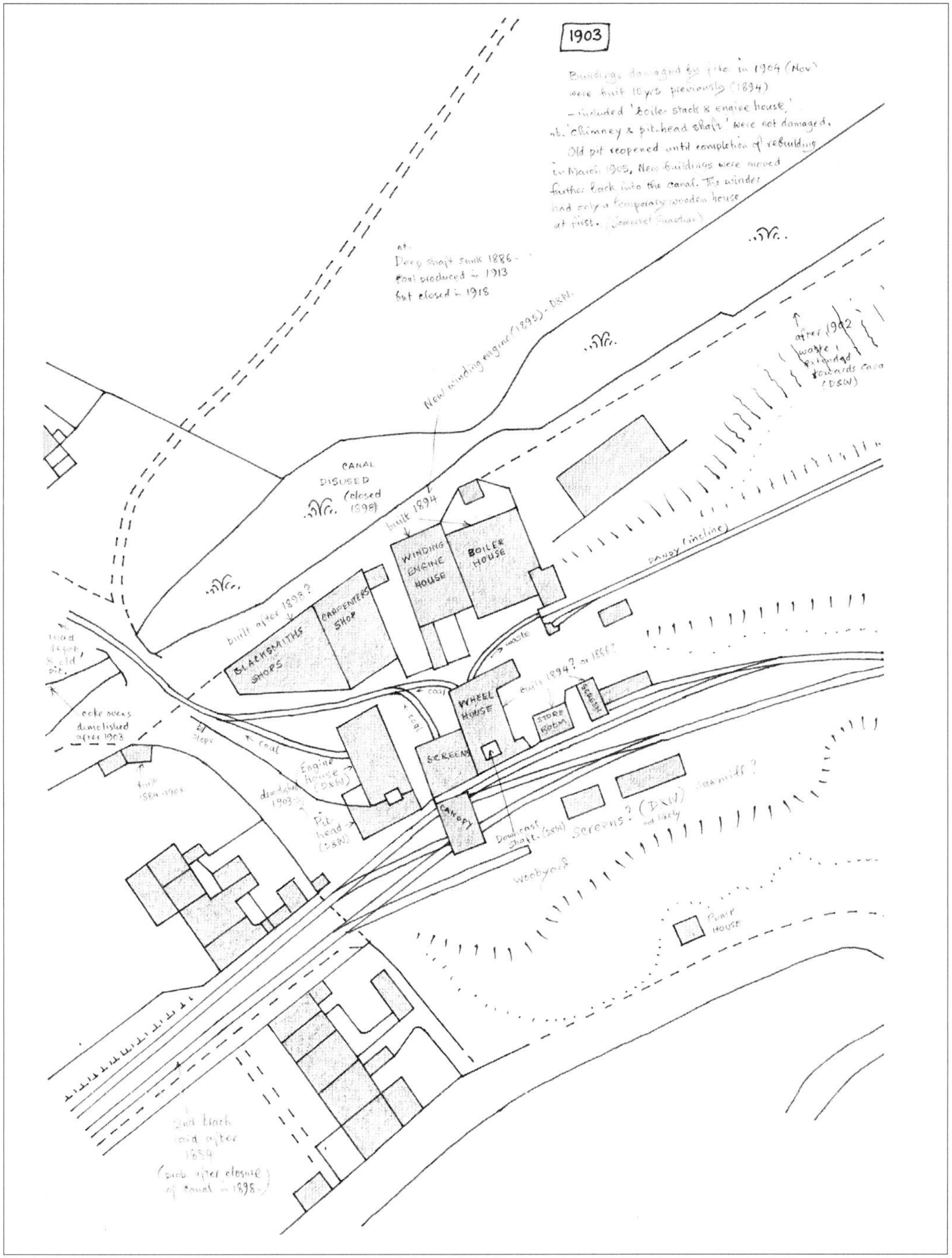

Notes on the possible layout of Camerton New Pit layout in c1903, taken from the interviews with the miners in the 1980s.

towards the canal, now disused, and despite the extensive nature of the work, it had been achieved in a comparatively short time. 'A wooden structure has been erected round the winding engine and the building of a stone engine house will be proceeded with at leisure while the engine is being worked. During the past months the seams have been worked from the old engine pit, but can now be safely resumed at new pit.' The local people were pleased that the men were kept in employment and in 'effecting so speedy a renewal of work at the new collieries'.[52]

The Old Pit had been closed for the winding of coal in 1898 but the trouble at New Pit showed its continued usefulness. It was to remain open as an airway and escape shaft for a number of years. In 1910 the tramway, laid to a gauge of 2ft 4in., that linked the two pits on the surface was removed and made into the present lane. The tramway or 'Gugg' which served the land-sales depôt at Meadgate by means of an incline was powered by a 50 h.p. motor which drove an endless rope.[53]

Best Years of Production

The late 1800s were the best years of production at Camerton. During the period 1888-1900 the coal landings had doubled to over 70,000 tons per annum and the maximum output was reached in 1903 when 76,827 tons were brought to the surface.[54] It has been estimated that this would require about twenty five wagon loads a day, equivalent to two trains, because of the gradient to the east of Hallatrow. The amount of coal transported by the railways in the years 1886-1899 was between 340,000 and 474,000 tons per annum, except in 1893 when the prolonged strike cause it to drop to 225,000 tons. Yet this was only one third of the total output, and since none was now being carried by the Somersetshire Coal Canal it meant that two thirds of the production went by road.[55] The output per man in 1940 was actually lower than it had been in the 1890s.[56]

In a Report in 1903 on minerals remaining unworked at Camerton, it was stated that '589 acres of Great Vein (2ft) and Top Little (18in.) are estimated to yield 1,213,800 tons of coal and 3,200 acres of Middle, Slyving and Under Little to yield 3,840,000 tons. When the top two are worked out it will be quite impossible to work the three thin seams (12in.)'.[57] There was an increase of 31% in production in this area of the coalfield in the years 1903-1914. When some of the mines did close it was not uncommon for the ex-miners to find alternative employment in the nearby Mendip road stone quarries.[58] By 1903 over six thousand miners were employed in the Somerset coalfield and the output was recorded as being 1.1 million tons by 1908. It was around this time that Camerton was considered as being in the list of the eighteen top collieries in Somerset as measured by production.[59]

Somerset Miners' Association

As the century ended miners were taking a greater interest in their working conditions. A meeting was held in January 1897 in the Lodge Room at the Meadgate Inn at Camerton with George Greenwell, the colliery bailiff and son of George C. Greenwell in the chair. It had been called to support the miners at the Malago Vale Pit in Bristol where the men had resisted a reduction in their wages. The meeting wanted an increase in wages and this was supported in the speech made by Mr. Whitehouse, the Somerset Miners' agent, who pointed out that the coal owners could afford to pay more. Before the meeting closed, the men decided that the Camerton representatives at the Somerset Miners' Association would vote in favour of seeking an advance in wages at the council meeting.[60]

At a similar meeting in the same place the following summer there was a report from the deputation of miners which had met with the manager of the Camerton Collieries to discuss the Workmen's

Compensation Act, to decide amicably the claims for death and injury. A committee of workmen and the agent, Mr. Whitehouse, were appointed to meet the manager again as the Act was due to come into force on the first of July 1898.[61]

A dinner for the Camerton colliers was held at the end of December 1900 in the Lodge Room there, at which forty miners met to honour Mr. W. J. Bird, the miners' secretary at the colliery, who was also the finance secretary of the Somerset Miners' Association. It was pointed out that in the 1880s this kind of meeting would have been impossible because of the low wages. There had been some improvement in wages and the conditions of work and living. The newspaper report of the meeting also commented that the Compensation Act of 1897 had been interpreted smoothly and without friction at Camerton, although many other employers opposed it, causing considerable conflict with the Union. The trade unions had improved mining for the employers as well as for the miners. There were now better roadways and ventilation in the pits than there had been a few years earlier.[62]

In its first edition of the new year 1901, the *Somerset Guardian* took the opportunity of reviewing mining events during the previous year. Wages had improved, Somerset miners had received a rise of 6d a day on the standard wage of the district which now was up to 3/- a day:

> 'Coal getting and other work is generally done on a piece work, the faulty nature of the seams make it impossible for the men and boys to earn a living at the prices fixed and it is the custom in the district under the circumstances to pay for the work done on a fixed standard, when the working places are not 'taleable', as it is locally called, with the current rate of percentage added, and a very large proportion of the men and boys are thus paid. The former standard was 2/6d for coal breakers with varying standards for other classes of labour, and the 6d per day on a coal breakers' standard has been added, thus making a standard of 3/- for this class of work and a pro rata amount on the other classes of work.'

The newspaper pointed out that a year ago the Eight Hour Bill had again been defeated in the House of Commons by twenty four votes, but the Workmen's Compensation Act had worked fairly well in the Somerset coalfields, the owners generally recognised that it was better to pay the injured person than to invoke the law.

In March 1900 a national deputation had gone to see the Home Secretary because they wanted a Bill to amend the Miners' Regulation Act of 1887 which was intended to deal with a number of important matters. These included using unskilled labour in the mines, the appointment and payment of checkweighers, and deductions from wages for rubbish in the coal. On a broader front the miners wanted a department in the Home Office for mining matters, the appointment of a Minister of Mines and corrections to the weaknesses in the Compensation Act. According to the newspaper, little had been done about most of these issues during the past year.[63]

When the Somerset coalfield was compared with others, at the time of the Royal Commission on Coal Supplies in 1904, it was found that the level of wages was low in comparison with elsewhere. This proved to be one of the stumbling blocks to the Miners' Federation of Great Britain when they were trying to get a minimum wage, i.e. a national minimum for hewers in all the coalfields. There were loud protests from Somerset, the miners fearing that their employers were right in saying that many of the mines would have to close down if the wages were raised to such an extent. The cause of low wages in this area may have been due to the coalfield being in an agricultural district with 'a surplus of youthful labourers, that Bristol is not growing fast as an industrial centre, and thus is not creating a great demand for coal or for men's labour in other employments, and that the mining has so far been mainly at shallow depths, the hewers requiring less skill, and intelligence than in most deep mines!'[64]

There were two major strikes during the period. The first in 1893 lasted over four months in which the men at Camerton were not involved. A short time before they had received a 7½% increase in their wages, but in December the men were asked to give up the rise. The second strike lasted from July to September in 1904, during which the men received support from other trade unions in different parts of the country.[65] The Miners' Association was now firmly established in Somerset and able to present the men's position, although not always successfully.

Notes to Chapter Eight

Dunkerton Pumping Station

Alfred Bampfylde was given a very good reference in 1898 when he ceased to be in charge of the Dunkerton Pumping Station. He was then employed as a maintenance engineer with the Fuller's Earth Union, at the fullers earth works nearby at Odd Down. Later he worked for thirty years with Jacob Long, building contractors.
Len Bamfylde, RMA ID9006.0115 009 88115

The Combe Hay Locks

The 'remote antiquarian interest' in these locks (actually twenty-two in number) conjectured in the 1910 newspaper report came about sooner than imagined. After only seventy years of their abandonment, increasing curiosity about these structures and the canal in general led to the formation of a Somersetshire Coal Canal Society in 1993 with the aim of preserving them. Having fallen into ruins, much work has been carried out since then, so that they now provide a picturesque and interesting ornament to the surrounding landscape.

New Civil Engineering Work on the Railway

The Cam Brook was particularly noted for its winding course, hence its name, derived from the Celtic *Cam*, 'crooked or bent'. The river was diverted by cutting long lengths of trenches. A steam navvy was used for filling wagons with the colliery waste from the tip at Camerton and using it to make an embankment for the railway. The work had involved the displacement of over half a million cubic yards of material, the stream had been diverted in five places and it had involved the erection of a 5-arched viaduct at Dunkerton, the alteration of the Combe Hay tunnel and three costly bridges at Midford including a further six overbridges and eleven underbridges: 'only an enterprising company would have sunk so much capital in an undertaking of this kind, but it is to be hoped that the company will reap of the benefits accruing from the expected development in the North Somerset coalfield'.
Somerset Guardian, 8 September 1907 and 6 May 1910.

Coal Dust and Shot-Firing

Dust was known to ignite in flour mills if the stones ran too fast, producing sparks, and coal dust was first suggested as the cause of explosions in coal mines as far back as 1803 at Wallsend Colliery on Tyneside which had fatal results. Only a very small amount of coal dust was required to cause an explosion. 'The Royal Commission [1879] appointed to enquire into Accidents in Mines....in their final report say: "The occurrence of a blown-out shot in working-places where very highly inflammable coal-dust exists in great abundance may, possibly give rise to violent explosions".'

'There is not any mention of coal-dust in the Coal Mines Acts until, as an outcome of the investigations and reports of the Royal Commission, rules were inserted in the act of 1887 referring to the firing of shots in mines where dry coal-dust exists.' The Act of 1896 'also contains regulations concerning .....the prohibition of coal-dust for stemming explosive charges'.
Robert Peel, *Coal Mining*, Blackie & Son 1912, pp.338f and p.362

Explosions due to Coal Dust

A thorough investigation into the Camerton explosion was carried out by Donald M.D.Stuart and published in 1894 under the title *Coal Dust, an Explosive Agent*. The book gives a good picture of the mine at the end of the century.

> 'The roofs are all of a strong character and have to be broken down with explosives to make height for the trams.....the portion excavated in this way often exceeding the thickness of the coal. This debris and other waste from benching, exceeds the capacity of the groves. Waste to coal is sent up in ratio 1:4. Small particles dropping from the trams and coal fallen between the rails gets trodden into fine dust by the ponies. The dust and debris in the newly made road is argillaceous (clayey) and incombustible matter.
>
> The ventilation of the mine is by a furnace and it was enlarged about eight months before the explosion by the erection of a new furnace which considerably increased the air in circulation. The result of this was a greater wind-speed through the workings which would take more fine particles from the trams, as well as greater evaporation of moisture from the walls of the airways.'

D.M.D. Stuart, 'Coal Dust, an Explosive Agent', *The Colliery Manager*, 1894, pp.1-10.

In a second book published in 1895 Stuart concluded that the explosion at Camerton had been caused by the oxidation of hydrogen gas obtained from the destructive distillation of coal dust. The amount of coal dust that was needed to cause this was quite small, as little as two ounces per square foot of floor surface. He concluded that when the shots were fired they released great quantities of heat and that when that heat came into contact with the coal dust it caused the latter to swell up, to become intumescent. It then released volatile matter in a gaseous state which exploded. The result was coked coal dust left behind in the workings, as had indeed been found at Camerton. The new ventilation system ensured that there was a good supply of air to the workings and this would probably have contributed to the extent of the explosion.
D.M.D. Stuart, *The Origin and Rationale of Colliery Explosions*, 1895,
John Wright & Co. Bristol.

Acts of Parliament

COAL MINES (CHECKWEIGHERS) ACT 1894

The checkweigher is appointed and paid by the coal-getters to checkweigh the weighings of the weigher appointed by the mine-owner of all tubs of coal sent out of the mine by the coal -getters. This Act makes it a penal offence to improperly interfere with the appointment of checkweighers.

Coal Mines Regulation Act 1896
This was a supplement to the Act of 1887. It dealt with explosives, safety lamps, the making of plans of mines and the prohibition of coal-dust for stemming explosive charges.

Workmen's Compensation Act 1906
The Act was to consolidate and amend the law with respect to compensation to workmen for injuries suffered in the course of their employment. The employer became liable under this Act to pay compensation if the workman sustained an injury at work which disabled him for a full week or more.

Coal Mines Regulation Act 1908
This Act amended the Acts from 1887 to 1905 "for the purpose of limiting hours of work underground." It limited the hours of work underground to eight and thus it was generally known as "Eight Hour Act".

Mines Accidents (Rescue and Aid) Act 1910
Its purpose was to make provision for the organisation of rescue and aid in the case of accidents in the mines.

'The Mines Rescue Service', *Five Arches*, Issue 17, 1993.
Julie Dexter and Dennis Chedgy, 'Mines, Safety and Rescue in the Somerset Coalfield', *Five Arches*, Special Issue, 2002.

References to Chapter Eight

1. Bulley, *op.cit.*, I, p.67.
2. Parfitt, *op.cit.*, p.10.
3. Bulley, *op.cit.*, 1, p.74.
4 Parfitt, *op.cit.*, p.10f.
5. D.M.D. Stuart, 'Coal Dust, an Explosive Agent', *The Colliery Manager*, 1894, pp.1-10.
6. Down &Warrington, *op.cit.*, p.49.
7. Parfitt, *op.cit.*, pp.10-12.
8. Greenwell & McMurtrie, *op.cit.*, pp.12-13.
9. Williams, *op.cit.*, p.20.
10. Brice, *op.cit.*, p.20.
11. Lecture by Alec Hann, November 1986.
12. Parfitt, *op.cit.*, pp.18, 26, 30, 40.
13. Down & Warrington, *op.cit.*, p.47.
14. Parfitt, *op.cit.*, p.38.
15. Conversation with Ken Taylor, August 1986.
16. *Somerset Guardian*, 26 April 1968; Reminiscences of Mr. and Mrs. G. Tucker on their 60th wedding anniversary, on life in the villages 62 years ago.

17. Clew, *op.cit.*, p.117.
18. Richard Kelham, *British Railway Journal*, No. 9, Autumn 1985, pp.339-341.
19. Clew, *op.cit.*, p.114.
20. Ibid., p.119.
21. *Ibid.*, p.117.
22. *Ibid.*, p.121.
23. Clew, *op.cit.*, p.122; see also Maggs & Beale, *op.cit.*, p.21.
24. Maggs & Beale, *op.cit.*, p. 21.
25. *Bath Herald*, 14 July 1903.
26. *Bath Herald*, 5 August 1903.
27. Down & Warrington, *op.cit.*, p.114.
28. M. Arlett, *The Railways of Midford*, Somerset & Dorset Railway Trust 1983.
29. Clew, *op.cit.*, p.130.
30. *Somerset Guardian*, 21 July 1906.
31. Clew, *op.cit.*, p.131.
32. *Somerset Guardian*, 21 September 1907.
33. *Somerset Guardian*, 6 May 1910.
34. *Somerset Guardian*, 13 May 1910; also *The Engineer*, Vol.107, 5 February 1909.
35. Memorandum to author from Mr. Alfred Church, taken from an official report on the circumstances attending the Camerton Colliery Explosion.
36. *Bath Chronicle*, 16 November 1893.
37. Down & Warrington, *op.cit.*, p.114.
38. *Bath Chronicle*, 30 November 1893.
39. *Bath Chronicle*, 23 November 1893.
40. Jevons, *op.cit.*, pp.384-385.
41. Down & Warrington, *op.cit.*, p.107 & 218.
42. Jevons, *op.cit.*, p.422.
43. Neil Macmillen with Mike Chapman, *A History of The Fuller's Earth Mining Industry around Bath*, Lightmoor Press 2009, p.129.
44. *Somerset Guardian*, 15 & 22 November 1902.
45. *Somerset Guardian*, 4 April 1903.
46. *Somerset Guardian*, 9 December 1905.
47. *Somerset Guardian*, 4 November 1910.
48. *Somerset Guardian*, 30 September 1910.
49. Down & Warrington, *op.cit.* p.114.
50. *Somerset Guardian*, 19 November 1904.
51. *Somerset Guardian*, 3 December 1904.
52. *Somerset Guardian*, 4 March 1905.
53. Down & Warrington, *op.cit.*, p.114.
54. *Ibid.*, p.114.
55. *Ibid.*, p.20.
56. *Ibid.*, p.28.

57. E. W. Heppel, 'A Report on the Mines and Minerals remaining unworked at Camerton Colliery', March 1903. RMA RRB33.43
58. Bluhm Bibliography, Introduction.
59. *Victoria History, op.cit.*, p.382ff.
60. *Somerset Guardian*, 30 January 1897.
61. *Somerset Guardian*, 2 July 1898.
62. *Somerset Guardian*, 29 December 1900.
63. *Somerset Guardian*, 5 January 1901.
64. Jevons, *op.cit.*, p.79-80.
65. Down & Warrington, *op.cit.*, p.32 & 114.

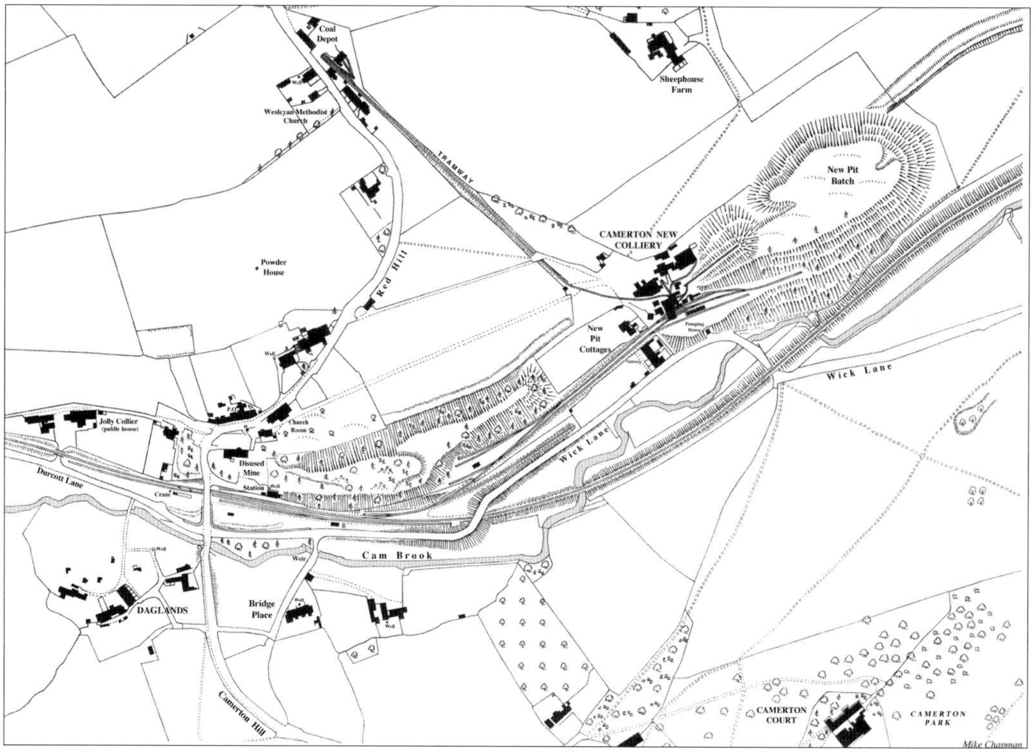

The area of the Camerton Collieries in 1931, compiled from the OS 25-inch maps.

CHAPTER NINE

DECLINE AND CLOSURE – THE FINAL YEARS 1910-1950

Changes of Ownership at Camerton

The mines at Camerton remained in the Jarrett family for almost one hundred years. When Anna and Emily Jarrett succeeded to the estate in 1863 they preferred to work rather than lease the mineral rights, and by the 1880s were running the pits[1]. Although Emily was the younger sister, it was she, in fact, who controlled the pits until her death on the last day of 1911. In its obituary the *Somerset Guardian* mentioned that the Camerton pits then employed three hundred men and boys and that Miss Emily was considered to have been an ideal employer, with a deep, kind-hearted interest in working people and those on her estate. She had helped with the building of the Parish Church, presumably the one at Peasedown St. John, and Camerton School. At the church in Camerton, she was the people's warden and organist, and was known to be a fine horsewoman who never used motor cars.[2] An article published by the same newspaper in 1962 said of her: 'Camerton pit was popular, due to the benevolence of Lady Jarrett who lived at Camerton Court. As owner, no genuine case of illness or trouble went unheeded by her - calling in her carriage on people who were ill or women expecting babies, she left blankets, shawls and delicacies'.[3]

Camerton pit was bought by Sir Frank Beauchamp in 1914, as there were no Jarrett heirs.[4] Within a dozen years he was to become the largest coal owner in the country, having begun by reopening Norton Hill Old Colliery in 1899, closed for forty years, with the sinking of a new shaft. Later he acquired Braysdown, where he had the shafts extended to the lower Farrington series. Following his purchase of Camerton he bought the

An election image of Sir Frank Beauchamp. *Radstock Museum Archive*

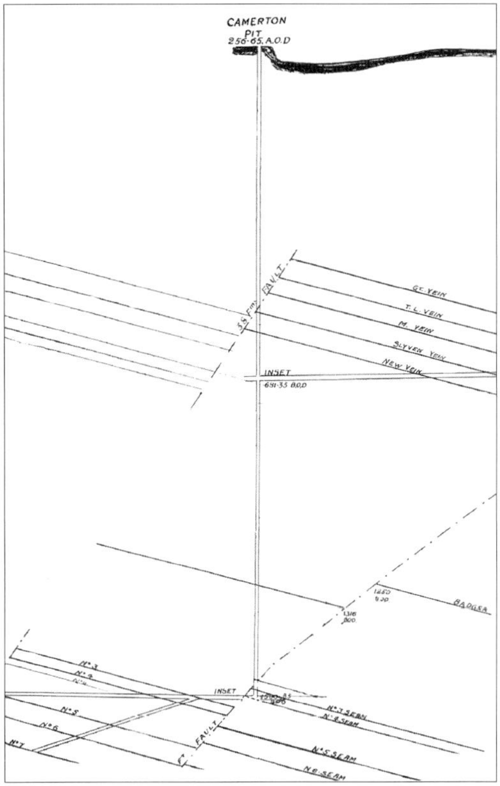

A section of Camerton Pit showing the drivage into the deep Farrington seams which were abandoned after working only a few thousand tons of coal. *John Cornwell collection*

pit at Priston (Tunley) in order to provide coal measures for Camerton, and indeed Camerton did work some Priston coal up until 1938.[5] Nearly all coal from Priston went to the Bath Gas Light & Coke Company.[6]

Sir Frank then bought Clandown and the Earl Waldegrave Collieries at Radstock. It is said that he acquired Dunkerton to prevent the flooding of Camerton and to provide coal reserves for Priston.[7] His objective had always been to amalgamate the collieries into an economical system of working in order to compete with the more favoured mining districts elsewhere in the country. 'No man has risked more … in the development of the mining industry in Somerset … and taken a more personal, deep and active interest in the welfare of the industry.'[8] In 1925 he registered the Somerset Collieries Limited and ten years later formed a new company in which Camerton was one of four working pits employing a total of fourteen hundred men.[9]

Changes in Output

The output of the coalfield rose steadily during the early years of the twentieth century and reached its peak of one and three quarter million tons in the 1920s. Unfortunately the strikes of 1921 and 1926, and the depression which followed, were to prove catastrophic for the industry in this area.[10] In 1920 the amount leaving Camerton was recorded as 11,075 tons.[11] The maximum receipts were £62,208 in 1924.[12] Despite all the efforts to produce more coal the mines in Somerset were starting to decline. Camerton, like Clandown, produced good bituminous coal until well into the twentieth century and it compared well with that mined in the Midlands and Yorkshire, but unfortunately most of the easily accessible coal in the area was of poorer quality and was of use only as house and gas coal.[13] Together with the fact that the cost of working it was relatively high, it meant that it was not really economical to introduce modern mechanical techniques in the pits. The life of the Somerset coalfield was beginning to draw to a close.[14]

The most rapid contraction in the industry took place between 1920 and 1930. In 1920 the pits employed well over seven thousand miners, but this number rapidly decreased.[15] The population of Camerton was recorded as 2,386 in 1911, probably the highest it ever reached, and before miners began to drift away to other coalfields in South Wales and the North of England. The rising population in the village up to this time has been attributed to the stability of employment provided by the Jarrett family over so many years.[16]

Changes in Production at Camerton

There were a number of changes at Camerton in the years before nationalisation but they resulted in little improvement in production. It has been noted that during the 1930s the output was almost exactly the same as it had been a century before. Coal was still being won by hand and most of it was carried in trams or 'tubs' to the bottom of the shaft, giving a daily output of some three hundred tons.[17] By 1920 the Braysdown pumping shaft became the upcast for Camerton, and between 1928 and 1930 an underground roadway was driven from Braysdown to Camerton New Pit.[18] This marked the end of the useful life of the shafts at Old Pit and in 1930 the pithead gear was removed.[19] The chimney at the Old Pit was pulled down around 1930. Jim Hawkins was a pupil at the time and remembers watching from the school playground as some of the lower bricks were removed and replaced with timber. This were then set alight, and when the props gave way the chimney crashed to the ground.[20] The wooden

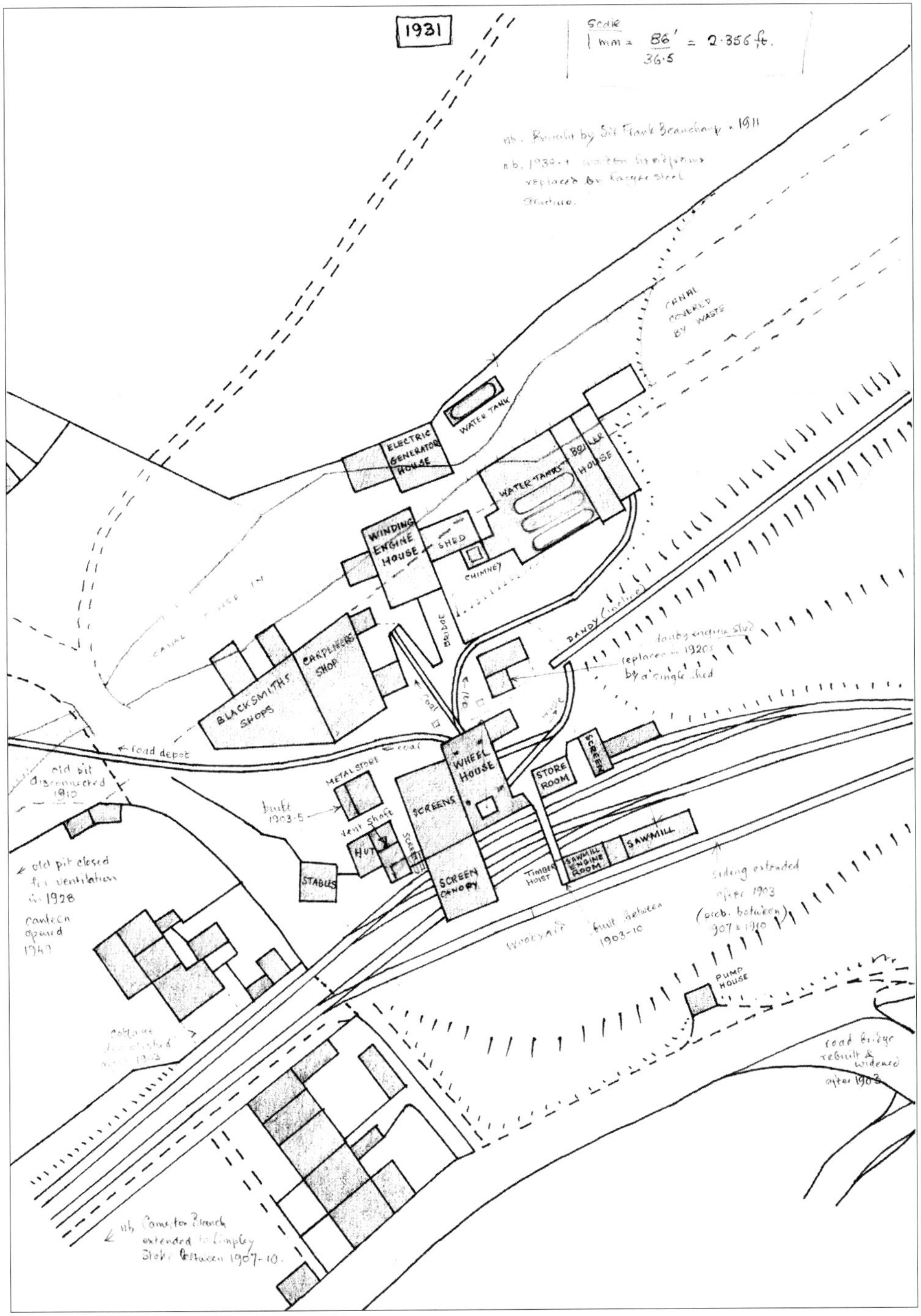

Notes on the layout of Camerton New Pit in c1931, taken from the interviews with the miners in the 1980s.

View of New Pit looking west from the Batch at the time of the filming of *The Ghost Train* in 1931. Since this was taken in the summer season, a great deal of surplus coal has been stacked all around the pit-head buildings. *Radstock Museum Archive*

headgear at New Pit was replaced with steel in 1938.[21] This was for safety reasons due to Government legislation but, even more importantly, because the owners wanted more coal to be raised and therefore a stronger headgear was needed.[22]

The first coal from the second series, the Farrington Series, had been brought up at Camerton in 1913, but the veins were not considered profitable and in 1918 these deeper workings were closed after only 2,015 tons had been brought to the surface. In 1941 Sir Frank was to carry out further development work, but no coal was raised from this series.[23] Some miners still remember it for the 'bad air' that was present at this greater depth.[24] Elsewhere, when the Radstock

Shaftsmen waiting to descend during the construction of the replacement headframe in 1938. *John Cornwell collection*

View of New Pit headframe during its replacement in 1938.
Radstock Museum Archive

An extremely rare photograph of the 1938 replacement of the wooden headframe of New Pit with a larger steel headframe. The new frame was erected over the old one to allow the rope and guides to be changed over a weekend or holiday without interrupting the winding of coal. *John Cornwell collection*

series was exhausted, the pit shafts were deepened and it was from the Farrington series that the last coal was mined in Somerset.

The *Somerset Guardian* reported at some length in 1930 on an interesting wireless experiment that had been made at Camerton Pit by permission of Mr. Don Bennett, manager of the colliery at the time. The test was carried out with a Burndept 4 valve portable set by Mr. Alfred Young. The newspaper reported that others in the party included Mr. J. Greenland, under manager, Mr. Frank Canvin, engineer at the colliery and two ladies. The experiment was judged to be a success. While the cages were running down the shaft, radio signals were practically absent, but they gained strength as the cage was lowered to the bottom of the shaft. Signals from Portishead Post Office station, London Regional and even Radio Toulouse were received at a point one thousand feet below the surface. Before leaving, the party were shown the Great Vein about one and a half miles from the pit shaft, the source of the famous Camerton house coal, 'one of the best house coals in the country'.[25]

A spare sheave waiting to be raised upon the new headframe in 1938. *John Cornwell collection*

Animal Haulage

Miners still recall the introduction of the two 'main and tail' underground winding engines which were able to haul eighteen trams of coal at a time to the pit bottom; 'They were nice engines'. A pony named 'Punch' was used to haul the dead rope into the workings for this new machinery, which dispensed with many of the ponies, previously used to haul some six to eight trams of coal to the bottom of the shaft. There had been three lots of ponies working on one road with change-overs taking place in the lay-bys.[26]

The ponies themselves provided entertainment. They were only brought to the surface during a strike or the long annual holiday. They behaved like children let out of school as they ran wild, prancing around the field above the Post Office. After such an outing they were decidedly frisky when taken back underground to resume work. The trick was to add a couple of extra trams to the train they were pulling until they showed signs of quietening down.[27]

For a number of years shunting had been carried out at New Pit by using two horses to pull the railway wagons under the screens. In 1926, after the closure of the pit at Dunkerton, a small locomotive

A pony with miners at Frank Beachamp's Norton Hill Colliery *Radstock Museum Archive*

with that name was used for a while but it did not prove a success and was sold off. Shunting with horses was resumed, and this continued until nationalisation, the animals being kept in the stable at the bottom of the heapstead. The full wagons ran back down the incline under gravity and were then marshalled into trains for the journey down the valley.[28] There was also a wagon repair works at the foot of the incline. This was a local depot of Messrs Marcroft & Co. Ltd. whose business continued at Radstock until June 1988. They held a contract with Somerset Collieries for the repair of wagons at Camerton.[29]

Accidents

The number of accidents in the last years of the Pit were probably fewer than at any time prev-iously. In January 1911 there was in inquest at the Jolly Collier into the death of Thomas Padfield of Camerton, aged 77, who had been crushed between two railway coal wagons while working on the surface at New Pit. Mr. H. Walker, the Inspector of Mines, Mr. Heppel and Mr. W.F. Garthwaite, the engineer at the colliery, were all present at the inquest. Edward Arthur Wheeler was working with Padfield at 7a.m. loading coal into empty railway wagons. He shunted a wagon under the screens, but three other wagons skidded and moved further than expected. They bumped into Padfield's wagons. Wheeler then went and found Padfield lying between the wagons, apparently dead. It had been a very damp morning and the rails were greasy and slippery, the brakes on the four wagons were on tight. At one stage the wagons had been trigged, but Wheeler had removed the wooden sprags [the blocks or wedges of wood to stop or brake the wheels] to enable him to move them forward. The gradient at the point of the accident was $^3/_8$ inch in the yard and it was known that wagons often skidded three to four feet. A verdict of accidental death was recorded, Padfield having died of a fracture to the base of the skull. His funeral was attended by Sellars, the under manager, and the bailiffs Heal and Greenland.[30]

There was a similar accident, this time underground, in March 1924 when Edward Carter, aged twenty two from Paulton, was killed at Camerton while employed as a carting boy. He was crushed by a runaway tram while he was sitting eating his food at the bottom of a steep incline. On this occasion the inquest was held at the Camerton Inn. A witness, Fredrick Wilson, had been working nearby in the Sylven Vein. He was at the top of the incline and had sent down his own trams, but could not say why the other one had run away. He had not hitched on the rope before knocking out the stop blocks, but he had had no signals from Carter. The jury's verdict was accidental death with some negligence on the part of Wilson for not hitching the rope before knocking out the stop blocks. Mr. Gregory, colliery

View from Camerton Station bridge looking west towards Durcott, with siding and crane on the left. This section of the line, to Hallatrow, was lifted in 1932. The large buildings on the right are the Jolly Collier and its brewery.
Radstock Museum Archive

manager, added that it was the first fatal accident for over fourteen years.[31] The witnesses at the accident included Edward Challenger, examiner at the pit, and Edgar Bourton a motor driver. At this time the Inspector of Mines was Mr. H.T. Evans and Mr. F. Swift, the Somerset Miners' Agent.[32]

This may well have been a good record of safety when it is put alongside the comment from Parfitt that in the first three months of 1926, when the miners were working a seven-hour day, there were three hundred and six deaths in the industry and over twelve hundred were seriously injured. He also pointed out that when the hours were increased to eight hours a day the number of fatalities rose to three hundred and twenty four in the corresponding period for 1927.[33]

One of the last accidents at Camerton is still remembered today. It involved Arthur Windmill, aged thirty of Meadgate, who was working at the pit bottom when he was suddenly drawn into the winding machinery, the 'main and tail'. His right hand was caught in the cogs and had to be amputated in the light of miners' lamps by Dr. Crook of the Laurels at Timsbury before he was taken to Paulton Hospital in the Miners' Welfare Ambulance. The following week the newspaper reported that although Dr. Crook had been underground previously this was his first time in a professional capacity. He was a well-known archaeologist and a cave explorer, and his extensive experience of moving in confined and hazardous places below ground undoubtedly had served him in good stead on this occasion. This accident occurred in March 1936.[34]

Changes on the Railway

There were changes in the fortunes of the Camerton and Limpley Stoke Railway. The passenger service had been suspended during the First World War on the 22nd March 1915. It was the driver of a goods train who brought the news of the end of the war to Camerton and the Cam Valley. He had done this

View taken from Wick Lane of a coal train on the bank to New Pit. *Radstock Museum Archive*

by blowing his whistle continuously as he chugged up the valley. Although the passenger service was reinstated on an experimental basis on the 9th July 1923 it did not last long, and it ceased on the 21st September 1925. A speed limit of ten miles per hour was imposed on all goods trains working the route.[35]

As all the loaded coal trains left Camerton by going down the valley, there was no need for the heavily graded route up to Hallatrow. The section from Camerton to Hallatrow was closed to all traffic on the 8th February 1932 and shortly afterwards the track was lifted from Hallatrow for over three miles, with the result that Camerton again became a terminus. More track was removed in 1937 and the signals and signal box disappeared in 1938.[36] In 1935 only one goods train a day was leaving Camerton Colliery because of the Depression,[37] but the railway found other uses. Arnold Ridley's film *The Ghost Train* was shot on the line in 1931, followed six years later for the filming of the Edgar Wallace thriller *Kate plus Ten*. It was to be used again in 1955 to make the Ealing comedy *The Titfield Thunderbolt*.[38]

A photograph taken during the re-make of *The Ghost Train* in 1941, an Arthur Askey comedy directed by Walter Forde, when Forde's female secretary went down New Pit to see what it was like. In those days it was extremely rare for a woman to go underground. *Radstock Museum Archive*

CAMERTON BRANCH.

Single Line, worked by Train Staff and only one Engine in steam at a time. Staff Stations—Hallatrow, Camerton and Dunkerton.

The speed of Trains in either direction must not exceed 25 miles per hour at any point.

Distances M.	C.	UP TRAINS. STATIONS.		WEEK DAYS. 1	2	3	4	5	6	7	8	9	10	11	12	13	14	15	16	17	18	19	20	SUNDAYS. 1	2	3
					B Mix'd	K Goods	K Goods		B Pass. N			K Goods			K Goods			B Pass.		B Pass.		K Goods W				
					A.M.	A.M.	A.M.		A.M.			P.M.			P.M.			P.M.		P.M.		P.M.				
—	—	Hallatrow ..	dep.	..	8 0	..	9 40	..	11 2	..	..	12 35	..	..	2 30	..	..	4 20	..	5 50	..	6X30	..	..	..	.
2	62	Timsbury Sdg. ..	,,	....	—	....	CR	....	—	....	....	—	....	....	CR	....	....	—	....	—	....	—	....	....	....	...
3	34	Camerton ..	arr.	..	8 13	..	9 55	..	11 12	..	..	12 50	..	..	2 45	..	..	4 30	..	6 0	..	6 45	..	..	..	..
			dep.	....		8 30		....		....	....	12 55	....	....		....	....		....		....	6 55	....	....	....	...
4	56	Dunkerton ..	arr.	..		8 35		..	..	..	..	1 0	..	..	..	..	..	..	..	..	.	7 0	..	..	..	..

DOWN TRAINS. STATIONS.		WEEK DAYS. 1	2	3	4	5	6	7	8	9	10	11	12	13	14	15	16	17	18	19	20	SUNDAYS. 1	2	3
			K Goods	K Goods	B Mix'd			K Goods		K Goods			K Goods			K Goods		B Pass.		K Goods W				
			A.M.	A.M.	A.M.			A.M.		P.M.			P.M.			P.M.		P.M.		P.M.				
Dunkerton	dep.	..	8 50	..	..	..	..	..	..	1 40	..	..	..	..	..	..	..	..	..	7 20	..	..	..	.
Camerton	arr.	....	8 55	....	....	....	....	...	....	1 46	....	....	....	....	....	....	....	....	....	7 25	....	....	....	...
	dep.	..		9 0	10 15	..	..	11 30	..	1 55	..	..	3 10	..	..	4 55	..	6 15	..	7 55	..	..	..	..
Timsbury Siding ..	,,	....	....	CR	—	....	....	CR	....	—	....	....	—	....	....	CR	....	—	....	—	....	....	..	....
Hallatrow	arr.	..	..	9 15	10 28	..	..	11 55	..	2 10	..	..	3 25	.	..	5 10	..	6X25	..	8R10	..	..	..	..

N To run with Brake Van only when there are no Passengers. R Hallatrow and Camerton to arrange if additional trip is required, and in such cases the Engine will work from Hallatrow to Bristol assisting 8.20 p.m. Radstock. W RR on Saturdays.

HALLATROW, CAMERTON AND LIMPLEY STOKE.

Single Line worked by Electric Train Tablet. Intermediate Tablet Stations and Crossing Places :—‡Camerton, Dunkerton Colliery, and ‡Dunkerton. ‡These Stations are only available for crossing two Goods Trains or a Goods and a Passenger Train.

Distances M.	C.	UP TRAINS. STATIONS.		Station No.	WEEK DAYS. 1	2	3	4	5	6	7	8	9	10	11	12K	13	SUNDAYS. 1K	2
					B Rad-stock Motor	K East Depot Goods	K Goods	B Trow-bridge Motor			B Trow-bridge Motor	B Motor	B Motor	K Frome Goods	K Coal.	Radstock & Salisbury Coal		Radstock & Salisbury Coal	
					A.M.	A.M.	A.M.	A.M.			P.M.	P.M.	P.M.	P.M.	P.M.	P.M.		P.M.	
—	—	**Hallatrow**	dep.	1182	8 16	9 30	..	10 55	..	..	1 20	4 8	5 50	6X30	..	11 46	..	11 45	..
2	62	Timsbury Siding	,,	1194	—	CR	....	—	....	....	—	—	—	CR	....	—	....	Saturday nights	....
2	68	Radford and Timsbury Halt	,,	1195	8 23	—	RR	11 2	..	..	1 27	4 15	5 57	—	..	—	..		..
3	4	Stop Board	,,	—	—	P	....	—	....	....	—	—	—	P	....	—	....		....
3	34	Camerton	arr.	1196	8X25	9 50	..	—	..	..	—	—	6 0	6X45	..	—	..		..
			dep.		8 27	11 50	10 30	11 5	....	....	1 30	4 18		7 0	9 55	12 0	....	12 0	....
4	30	Dunkerton Colliery Halt	dep.	—	8 30	—	—	11 8	..	..	1 33	4 21	..	—	—	—	..	—	..
4	44	Dunkerton Colliery	arr.	1197	—	11 55	10 35	—	....	....	—	—	....	7 5	10 0	—	....	—	....
			dep.		CS	12 15		CS	..	..	CS	CS	..	7X40	10 30	12 5	..	12 5	..
6	6	Dunkerton	arr.	1198	—	12 21	....	—	....	....	—	—	....	7 50	—	—	....	—	....
			dep.		8 34½	12 45	..	11 12½	..	..	1 37½	4X25	..	8 8	CS	12 11	..	12 11	..
7	5	Combe Hay Halt	,,	1199	8 37½	—	....	11 15½	....	....	1 40½	4 28½	....	—	—	—	....	—	....
9	22	Midford Halt	,,	1237	8 43½	—	..	11 21½	..	..	1 46½	4 34½	..	—	—	—	..	—	..
10	27	Monkton Combe	,,	1200	8 46½	ST	....	11 24½	....	....	1 49½	4 37½	....	8 33	—	—	....	—	....
11	37	Limpley Stoke ..	arr.	552	8 50	CS	..	11 28	..	..	1 53	4 41	..	CXS	CS	12 36	..	12 36	..
11	72	**Freshford Exchange Sdgs.**	,,	555	....	1 16	....	....	....	....	....	....	....	8 43	10 55	...	....	....	....

DOWN TRAINS. STATIONS.		WEEK DAYS. 1	2	3	4	5	6	7	8K	9	10	11	12	13	SUNDAYS. 1	2	3
		K 5. 0 Sarum Goods			B Motor	K Goods	B Trow-bridge Motor	B Trow-bridge Motor	3.15p.m. Holt Jc. Goods.		B Motor	B Rad-stock Motor	K 5.25 B'istol Goods				
		A.M.			A.M.	A.M.	P.M.	P.M.	P.M.		P.M.	P.M.	P.M.				
Freshford Exchange Sdgs	dep.	7 20	..	..	..	..	....	....	3 45	..	..	..	8 45	..	..	..	..
Limpley Stoke	,,	CS	....	....	10 0	....	12 28	3 23	CS	....	5 0	....	CS	....	....	....	....
Monkton Combe	,,	CR	..	..	10 5	..	12 32	3 27	ST	..	5 4	..	ST	..	..	..	..
Midford Halt	,,	—	....	....	10 8	....	12 37	3 30	—	....	5 7	....	—	....	....	....	....
Combe Hay Halt	,,	M	..	..	10 14	RR	12 43	3 36	—	..	5 14	..	—	..	..	..	..
Dunkerton	arr.	7 40	....	....	—	....	—	—	4 5	....	—	....	—	....	....	....	....
	dep.	7 50	..	..	10 18	..	12 46	3 39	4 10	..	5 18	..	ST	..	..	..	..
Dunkerton Colliery	arr.	7 55	....	....	—	....	—	—	4 15	....	—	....	9 10	....	....	....	....
	dep.	8 5	..	..	CS	10 45	CXS	CS	4 25	..	CS	..	9 20	..	..	..	..
Dunkerton Colliery Halt	dep.	—	....	....	10 22	—	12 50	3 43	—	....	5 22	....	—	....	....	....	....
Camerton	arr.	8X10	..	..	10 25	10 50	—	—	4 30	..	—	..	9 25	..	..	..	..
	dep.	8 30	....	....	10 27		12 53	3 47	4 45	....	5 25	6 15		...	....	....	....
Stop Board	,,	—	..	..	—	..	—	—	4P50	..	—	—	..	..	..	..	..
Radford and Timsbury Halt	,,	—	....	....	10 29	....	12 55	3 49	—	....	5 27	6 17	....	....	....	....	....
Timsbury Siding	,,	—	..	..	—	..	—	—	4 55	..	—	—	..	..	..	..	..
Hallatrow	arr.	8 45	....	...	10 36	...	1 2	3 56	5 5	....	5 34	6 26	....	....	....	....	....

GWR Service timetables for the Camerton Branch railway; in 1909 (above) when Camerton was still a terminus, and in 1923 (below), two years before the passenger service to Limpley Stoke was discontinued. *Colin Maggs*

Camerton Station without its canopy, not needed after the passenger service was stopped. *Colin Maggs*

Camerton Station in 1948, when it served as a storage depôt of war surplus material acquired by Bath businessman Thomas Best for retail in Bath. *Colin Maggs*

Legislation and Strikes

During the early 20th century there were a number of legislative changes which were to have an effect on the working conditions of the men in the pits. The Coal Mines Act and General Regulations of 1911 brought in better safety standards and more efficient working through a more thorough inspection of the mines. Workmen-examiners had been appointed under the Act of 1872 but it was only in 1911 that they were in a sufficiently strong and independent position to do their job properly.[39] The Conciliation Boards had consisted of equal numbers of colliers and owners in the district and they were empowered to fix a percentage above a separately fixed base for every grade of labour in the colliery. Unfortunately this system broke down in 1912 and led to a national coal strike. It resulted in Parliament being forced to establish other means for ensuring a minimum wage for underground workers.

The National Coal Strike of 1912 was a landmark in the history of the coal industry. It led to the passing of the Minimum Wages Act which was brought in because the miner could have many factors working against him before being able to hew sufficient coal to earn a decent wage. These included the conditions at the seam, shortage of trams, rails and timber, or poor ventilation, the presence of water, stone in the coal, soft or broken roofs. In the past these had been overcome by a 'consideration per ton' which was added onto the miner's wage.[40] This strike passed off peaceably in Somerset and resulted in the men obtaining the concrete benefits of the Mines Minimum Wages Act.[41] The Act was not entirely beneficial, however, and was considered to be a great disappointment to many Somerset miners. The strike also showed that the Miners' Federation of Great Britain, formed in the later 1880s, was a stable union representing the industry.[42]

It was a different story in the strike in 1921. This strike, together with the one in 1926, produced much bitterness in the area, as well as being disastrous for the miners themselves. The coal owners and the Government of the day were too strong for the mining community.[43] While the strike of 1921 was in progress the *Somerset Guardian* published the text of a sermon by the Rector of Camerton, the Rev. Dr. Cambie. It may have been based on the text: 'For from within, out of the heart of man come evil thoughts …' Mark 7 v.21. It was entitled 'The Strikers and the Struck'. Like his predecessor John Skinner, Dr. Cambie took a very sensible and impartial stand, pointing out that the country had paid the miners well in the years of the First World War in order to save its skin, and not out of any thoughts of philanthropy. He called for a moderate attitude and asked that the situation be made no worse by people stirring things up further. Finally they should be quite sure that they desired justice for all men and not merely just privileges for themselves. At the same time a Relief Fund was opened in Radstock for the relief of the distress in the area caused by the strike. It was estimated that there were some 5,000 miners in the area of the coalfield.[44]

The strike was followed by a slack time in most of the Somerset collieries and the newspaper reported that a 'short time system' had been arranged at Sir Frank Beauchamp's mines at Norton Hill, Braysdown and Camerton. Men were employed on average for only three days each week so that they could qualify for partial unemployment benefit. The Unemployment Committee which met at Bath passed a strong recommendation that the Ministry of Labour should open a temporary branch office at Peasedown to relieve the large number of men who were having to walk to Midsomer Norton to draw their money. This office was eventually opened.[45]

The struggle to get better working conditions for the miners made slow progress. In 1919 they had appealed for a six-hour day because they believed that this would help to lessen accidents in the pits, but without success.[46] In the same year the Coal Mines Commission, under the chairmanship of Viscount Sankey, recommended that the mines be placed under public ownership[47] and that increases of 2s for a man and 1s for a boy should be paid.[48] In the early part of the 20th century the breakers worked an eight-hour shift, but the carters or carting boys had to stay and finish clearing the coal that was still left at the face. Previous to the Eight Hour Act being passed, breakers had to stay below ground very often to carry out repairs and maintenance which could amount to another half shift, presumably for no extra pay. The men went below between 5 and 6 a.m. and surfaced again between 1 and 2 p.m., but after the Eight Hour Act of 1926 was passed they had to work an extra hour. In effect the Somerset miners were worse off than in the previous years.[49]

A happier note was sounded by the miners' newspaper, the *Somerset Guardian*, in 1924 when it announced that the Camerton Miners' Welfare Committee had obtained a field. The opening ceremony was performed by Sir Frank Beauchamp accompanied by a procession and brass band and with a free tea laid on. There was now a fund to which coal owners contributed ld for every ton of coal raised throughout the country. It was Sir Frank's wish that it should be extended to provide mining scholarships for the men in the pits and that other industries would follow the example then being set.[50]

In 1924 Mr. A. J. Cook, a Somerset man, was elected as the first full-time paid leader of the country's largest trade union, the Miners' Federation of Great Britain. He came to Midsomer Norton in the summer of 1927 where he addressed a large meeting of about two thousand miners and their wives at the Miners' Welfare recreation ground. He gave his assessment of the economic crisis then in existence and he warned Sir Frank Beauchamp to agree to the terms being asked and to end the lock-out at the pits. He believed that the bad state of the coal trade would get worse and he challenged the coal owners to publish the relevant figures. He went on to attack the Government and especially the Prime Minister, Stanley Baldwin, and made it clear that he was in favour of the nationalisation of the industry. His address to the meeting received wide support.[51]

Today many of the old coal waste tips or 'batches' blend in with the landscape, but it was not always so. In January 1926 Sir Frank wrote to the *Somerset Guardian* about the trees he had planted on some of the colliery tips and that in the course of the year he intended to do more. Unfortunately hundreds of the planted trees had been torn up and others cut down. He thought that it might not be entirely the work of children, but he asked parents to warn them. 'Fortunately, I have not an unsightly rubbish tip in front of my house. This cannot be said of the inhabitants of Radstock and they together with the working men who would have been employed this winter in planting the remainder will be the sufferers if the damage continues, as I shall do no more planting unless the practice ceases.'[52]

During the unrest among the miners that summer Sir Frank threatened to close Priston, Dunkerton and Middle Pit at Radstock if the men did not return to work by Midsummer's Day. Dunkerton had actually wound its last coal under the original owner on the 30th May 1925 when Sir Frank acquired the pit but he only managed to raise 4,000 tons before it finally closed in September 1927.[53] Coal had been taken from Priston to the railway siding at Radford by using two Sentinel steam road wagons, until that pit closed in 1927.[54]

In the strike of 1926, which was a lockout in most of the Somerset pits, the men had no special grievances and came out mainly to show their loyalty to the National Federation. It was resisting wage cuts and the imposition of longer hours as these would not reduce the number of accidents in the pits. A settlement finally came at the end of the year.[55] Camerton miners remember it as being a time of great hardship, when men and boys picked over the coal tips to find fuel for their own fires and to sell for a few pence. Finally, when they returned to work – 'We went back for less than when we came out'.[56] It was about this time that Mr. Howard Newth of Timsbury aged 16, tried to get a job at Camerton. He was told 'Too old, my sonny!' but was fortunate to get work at Pensford pit.[57]

The General Secretary of the Federation was back in the area in August 1930, this time at the Miners' Welfare field at Welton. Mr. Cook spoke about the new Coal Mines Bill, maintaining that it was not all that was desired but that it was a step in the right direction. He hoped that there would be a seven-hour day and a five-day week and that an adequate pension would be paid after a miner reached sixty years of age. Another speaker at the meeting said that there was a need for a majority Labour Government which would tackle unemployment, industrial disease, pensions and the nationalisation of the industry. Mr. Fred Swift, secretary of the Somerset Miners' Association at the time, assured Mr.Cook that they had a 96% membership in the Somerset Federation.[58] According to Jevons the Somerset Miners' Association had a membership of 3,893 in 1914 but this would have declined in the intervening years with the contraction of the industry in Somerset.[59]

Fred Swift, Somerset Miners Association agent. *Radstock Museum Archive*

The Guss and Crook

The Somerset miners were unwilling participants in the troubles of 1926, and although the *Somerset Guardian* did not dwell on the strike, it dealt with many issues that affected the miners e.g. strike meetings, negotiations, relief funds, etc. However, it did give much coverage in its pages to the use of the guss and crook in the pits of the area, as this matter was being aired in the House of Commons at the time. The subject came to the fore through an article written by Miss Ellen Wilkinson M.P. in a Socialist newspaper in which she had dealt with the conditions in the Somerset pits.

During a debate in the House she produced a ponderous looking 'leather' girdle to which was attached a chain and hook. Holding it up in full view of the members of the House, she described how the miner in a naked condition with the belt round his waist and the chain passing between his legs, had to crawl along a narrow gallery dragging a tub which was hitched onto the hook at the end of the chain. 'Surely in God's name seven hours are enough when work is carried out in these conditions.'

Miss Wilkinson went on to describe the heat in the gallery being so great that the men wore the barest minimum of clothing, and the filthy ropes soaked with coal dust and perspiration rubbed septic sores on the men's bodies until calluses were caused. Furthermore, she asserted that the Somerset miners were so poor before the lockout that their wives lived on margarine, bread and tea, so that such meat that they could afford should go to the breadwinner of the family. It was her view that the Conservative members of Parliament would not tolerate such conditions for their children for half an hour, yet all they could say was 'Let them work longer for less wages in order that our profits may be safeguarded. I say that it is abominable. Men who vote for longer hours ought not to sleep in their beds until they themselves have done for their country what these men are doing every day'.[60]

Retired Somerset miners have recalled the guss and crook as being the hardest thing about their work, but they did get used to it. They recall how the guss felt cold at the start of the shift with the sweat from the night before and how it rubbed the skin raw in the early days of its use. Back home, in front of the fire the mothers of these young carting boys would bathe the sores and some were known to have worn silk under-drawers to prevent the rubbing of the rope. 'It did make the tears run!'[61]

The Government Commission enquiring into the use of the guss and crook visited Somerset in

September 1927. Three members, accompanied by representatives of the Mines Department of the Home Office saw the guss in actual use and made enquiries among the carting boys and miners themselves. They took evidence from managers, experts and medical men. The Commission also sat at the Victoria Hall in Radstock for the purpose of taking evidence. The meeting was not open to the press or public.[62] The Guss Committee published its report in September 1928 in which it suggested ways of rendering the guss eventually obsolete, but it realised that this was a long-term solution.[63]

Mr. C. Southern, a mining engineer from Writhington Colliery, gave an address to the Bath Rotary Club in 1927 in which he referred to the guss. When he came to Somerset about 1910 he had intended to get rid of the job of carting boy in the pits but he could find little or no injury caused by the guss and crook. In 1914 the Chief inspector of Mines and the Chief Medical Officer had reported that there was no injury caused by wearing it. After questions Mr. Southern said that, in the view of many of the miners concerning the guss, if it were done away with, there would be less men employed in the mines.[64] It is believed that the guss and crook remained in use in the Somerset pits for a number of years. It was still in use at Marsh Lane Pit in 1949.[65]

Towards Nationalisation

At the end of 1935 Sir Frank rearranged his local coal companies. Somerset Collieries Ltd, Radstock, was registered as a public company to acquire and amalgamate the undertakings and assets of Radstock Collieries Ltd which were formerly known as Somerset Collieries Ltd, Norton Hill Collieries Co., Radstock Coal Co., Radstock Wagon Co., and the Radstock Gas Company. The directors were all members of the Beauchamp family.[66]

Even before hostilities began in September 1939 it would have been realised that Great Britain would become even more dependent on the mining industry:

> 'By 1938 the mine numbers had fallen to 1,900 with the annual output reduced to 230 million tons [In Britain]. However the coal industry was still a major industry within the indigenous British economy... The severe economic depression of 1921 led to the Government's hasty decontrol of the industry. However, the ensuing labour unrest and social instability kept the issue of rationalisation to the fore. It was eventually embodied in the Coal Mines Act 1930, which embraced a compulsory marketing scheme, reducing shift hours without loss of pay. As a result, costs increased, necessitating policies to support prices and profit margins.' [67]

During the Second World War the demand for coal would have been as great as ever. 'This brought almost 50,000 conscripts into the coalfields without opposition from the mining workforce or the unions.' [68] These miners became known as Bevin Boys after Ernest Bevin, the Minister of Fuel and Power in the British Government. The pits would have been expected to produce as much coal as possible without the investment in the mines which was sorely needed. The difficulties of mining in this area would have meant that there was little chance of a great increase in production, but every ton was important.

When the National Coal Board was established on the 1st January 1947 there were changes underground which allowed the use of mechanical coalcutters and conveyer belts to take the coal to the bottom of the shaft.[69] Some of this machinery was used at Camerton. The extension of the conveyers underground meant the end of many years of using pit ponies which had been introduced to the area by James McMurtrie. Camerton was the last pit in Somerset to use them.[70] It is said that the last pony to leave the pit was known as 'Archie'.[71] It was all too late for Camerton pit. The South District workings of the mine closed in December 1949 and thirty men were made redundant.[72] Nationalisation had given new hope for Camerton but it proved short-lived as the coal seams were in fact exhausted. The horses in the yard were finally retired from shunting duties, being replaced by a road tractor.

One of the last ponies at New Pit, let out into the field above the colliery. *Radstock Museum Archive*

'Prior to nationalisation in 1945/6 the Ministry of Fuel and Power conducted a review of the Somerset Coalfield and concluded that it could look forward to a long working life. It urged the National Coal Board to take urgent action to increase the volume of recruitment notwithstanding the special war-time measures adopted after 1941 to restrict the movement of personnel out of the mines.'[73] Nevertheless, the fact remained that 'The Somerset coalfield was noted for its technological difficulties and at nationalisation was the least mechanised of the seventeen British coalfields ... At nationalisation in 1947 the workforce had shrunk to under 3,000 who worked in twelve pits and produced only 597,000 tons in that year.'[74] 'Alec Hann recalls that in the post-war period, the country was in a poor economic state, and fuel was desperately needed for British industry. The decision to nationalise was a political one, but for men like himself, it was a sign that money was going to be ploughed into the industry.'[75]

The prospects for the Camerton Colliery were not good at the time of nationalisation. The colliery attracted the lowest valuation of all the pits in the Somerset Collieries Ltd company when it was nationalised, at a sum of £59,935.76 By this time production was often only one hundred and fifty tons a week, which was hardly a viable state under which to remain open.[77]

The Last Days of Camerton Colliery

Finally on the 6th April 1950 the hundred and thirty five men were given their notices and the last coal was wound on the morning of the 14th April. The salvage work at the pit took until August, the pit being officially closed in September when the remaining twenty five men were discharged. The main reason for closure was the exhaustion of accessible reserves. Camerton had been the last pit in Somerset to work the Radstock series, and although efforts had been made to find new reserves, they had been unsuccessful.[78]

The *Somerset Guardian* reported the closure under the headline 'The last shift - End of Camerton Pits - 200 years story.' The newspaper said that there was no ceremony as the last shift came to the surface on that particular Friday. Each man took his personal tools, his pick and shovel, to his new job in one of the pits still working in the area. There were no sackings or redundancies. The bulk of the workforce was transferred to other pits, Braysdown, Norton Hill, Writhlington and Old Mills, being collected by bus from Camerton. Those who were elderly, and some of those partially disabled, retired or took early retirement. It was reported in the *Somerset Guardian* that many of the miners insisted that

Newspaper cutting of Camerton miners coming off the last shift when the colliery was closed on the 14th April 1950. *Radstock Museum Archive*

there was still plenty of workable coal at Camerton. An acute shortage of labour was a contributing cause of the closure. Most of the men were sorry to go. The National Union of Mineworkers had asked for an independent engineer to examine the pit, but he concluded that 'it was the exhaustion of economic coal', and he had been unable to produce any evidence that would have justified keeping the pit open. There was some concern in the community about the 'knock-on' effect of closure on subsidiary industries, such as the wagon works, and fears that the railway service would be curtailed, as it was.[79]

Mr. E. Bourton, one of the twenty five men left for the dismantling work, had been in charge of the winding engine at the pit. His two assistants Mr. P.W. Moon and Mr. J. Hawkins, were among those transferred to other pits. Mr. Bourton had started work forty years before and his assistants had worked there for twenty years. Not only was the pit closing but it meant the end of the railway, which was expected to close in due course.[80] It closed on the 14th February 1951. There had been only one goods train a month after the pit closed. In November 1957 the work of dismantling the remaining track down to Limpley Stoke was started and by the end of the summer of 1958 the task had been completed.[81] During 1955 the chimney at New Pit crashed to the ground and its hundred thousand bricks were bought from the National Coal Board by Mr. Moon, a Timsbury builder.

Today a few bricks mark the site of the workshops at New Pit. The solid concrete anchorage points of the headgear remain among the buddleias and the shafts are capped. The heapstead wall stands above the overgrown sidings where once many thousand tons of coal were loaded, amidst the dirt and dust, into the coal wagons for the journey to distant markets. The birds' song replaces the hiss of steam. There are few reminders of a way of life that has passed away for ever.

Notes to Chapter Nine

Further Reading

Five Arches, the Journal of the Radstock, Midsomer Norton and District Museum Society, on the following subjects:

Francis P. Hillier, 'A Brief History of the Beauchamp Family', Issue 17, 1993.

Colin Dix, 'Memories of Braysdown Colliery', Issue 22, 1995.

Una Pope, 'The Under Manager's Daughter [Braysdown]', Issue 22, 1995.

Ira W. Janes, 'Miners' Wages 1912-1915', Issue 10, 1990.
Oliver G. Janes from 'My Life - Some Memoirs' 1885-1951, Issue 10, 1990.
Ian McInnes, 'The Bevin Boys, Part 1', Issue 48, 2003; Part 2, Issue 49, 2004.
Warwick H. Taylor, 'The Forgotten Conscripts of Sixty Years Ago [Bevin Boys]', Issue 47, 2003.
Ian McInnes, 'Nationalisation: Looking Back Sixty Years On', Issue 57, 2006,
Joe Roberts, 'Memories of a Bevin Boy', Part 1, Issue 63, 2008; Part 2, Issue 64, 2009; Part 3, Issue 65, 2009.
Penny Bonsall, 'Pit Closures, the Attitude of Miners 1947-1973', Issue 12, 1991. See also her fuller version in Southern History, 1990.
Dennis Chedgy and Dick Graham, 'Rambles to Camerton', Issue 12, 1991.
Julie Dexter and Dennis Chedgy, 'Mines, Safety and Rescue in the Somerset Coalfield', Special Issue, 2002.
Julie Dexter (editor), 'Mines and Mining: Memories of the Somerset Coalfield', Special Issue, 2003.

Faults
The whole of the Somerset coalfield is well-known for its faults, the greatest being the Great or Hundred Fathom Fault, which runs through the neighbourhood of Timsbury, Camerton, Clandown and Kilmersdon, and has a throw down to the west varying from 120 to 720 feet. Nearby also is the Farmborough Fault to the north, with a throw of 600 feet.
The Rev. H.H. Winwood in *Handbook to Bath*, The British Association, Pitman, 1888. p.214.
Down & Warrington, *op.cit.*, p.39.

Miners' Wages
Percy Hurd, a Member of Parliament, claimed in a letter to *The Times* that in March 1921 the owners' offer meant an average increase over the rates paid in 1914 of 91%.
RMA RRB.33.24

The Miners' Welfare Fund
The Miners' Welfare Fund was set up by the government in 1920 in response to the growing national concern about social deprivation in the coalfields. It was administered by Miners' Welfare Committees, in the interests of the social well-being, recreation and living conditions of miners and their communities, including education and research but excluding housing. In 1922 the village representative for Timsbury proposed a library and reading room, while the Camerton representative suggested an extension be built on the existing reading room at Meadgate. Public meetings were held subsequently to gather a wider range of opinion, after which both Timsbury, Camerton and another three mining villages applied for the provision of a sports hut and recreation field.
Note to author from Penny Bonsall

Main and Tail Rope System.
'One rope, called the main rope, hauls the full trains out to the shaft; the other, the tail rope, hauls the empty trains in. Two drums are required, one for each rope. Each drum is on a separate shaft and is connected by spur gearing to the engine shaft, and both are so arranged that when one is put into gear or connected to the engine, the other is thrown out of gear'.
Robert Peel, *Coal Mining*, Blackie & Son, 1912, p.257.

Appraisal Report on Camerton Colliery c.1947

Some 300 tons per shift from working the Great Vein, Top Little and Slyven seams. The Report was optimistic about the future into the 1950-70s. Total number of men underground 188, surface 288 men. The machinery included 3 coal cutters 2 gate belts 600yards each, 1 face conveyor 100 yards, 3 Lancashire boilers and a McLane automatic tip. The headgear came from a Bristol colliery in 1938, 2 deck cages. It was erected over the existing wooden headgear so that there was little interruption to the work of the colliery. See the Radstock Museum for example of wooden headgear.
RMA: 2006.3164 M8:box 22

The Extent of the New Pit Workings

'The take of New Pit was very large 2.5 miles from north to south and 1.5 miles east to west. It reached south to the Fosse Way and east to the Dunkerton workings. To the west it was bounded by Upper and Lower Conygre Pits at Timsbury. A succession of upthrow faults to the south of the shafts enabled the main haulage road from the pit bottom to run southwards with little or no dip, which reduced the cost of the dip workings. The coal reserves were almost exhausted by nationalisation. There was little modernisation following nationalisation, some undercutting machines and conveyors were brought in. The output of the final years was low:

1947 - 32,264 tons of saleable coal
1948 - 32,238 tons of saleable coal
1949 - 34,494 tons of saleable coal

John Cornwell, *The Collieries of Somerset and Bristol*, Landmark Publishing 2001.

Losses at Camerton, 1949

NATIONAL COAL BOARD
OUTPUT & COSTS COMMITTEE
SOUTH WESTERN DIVISION - BRISTOL AND SOMERSET AREA
Collieries losing on an average more than 15/- per Ton (at Inland Prices) in the Half Year to 30 June, 1949.
COLLIERY Summary of Divisional Comments on future of Colliery

CAMERTON The coal reserves at this pit are rapidly nearing exhaustion and the pit will probably be closed within the next twelve months. Men to be transferred to Norton Hill as soon as pit room is available.

YEAR 1948

Loss per Ton	Amount	Saleable Output
20/4	£32,814	32,238 tons

JANUARY TO SEPTEMBER 1949

Loss per Ton	Amount	Saleable Output
18/11	£23,916	25,196 tons

Compensation at Nationalisation

The National Coal Board paid £597,000 for the whole Somerset coalfield on 1 January 1947. The main coal owners were: Somerset Collieries Ltd (Beauchamp) received £250,244; Wm Evans (Old Mills Collieries) Ltd, £138,816; Pensford and Bromley Collieries (1921) Ltd, £85,760; and Writhlington Collieries Ltd, £60,000; etc.
Down & Warrington, *op.cit.*, p.27.

The Jarrett Sisters

The daughters of John Jarrett, who had died in 1863, were Anna Mary Jarrett 1838-1893, and Emily Elizabeth 1840-1911.

Colonel Sir Frank Beauchamp CBE JP 1866-1950

Frank Beauchamp's father, William, changed his family name from Beachim to Beauchamp in 1876. In addition to his coal mines he owned Pennant Stone Quarries at Cloud Hill, Hallatrow. On his death in 1894 he was succeeded by Frank Beauchamp who started to modernise the industry. He bought the Camerton Coal Company after the death of Emily Jarrett and lived at Woodborough House which later became the local headquarters of the National Coal Board for a few years.
Down & Warrington, *op.cit.*, p.212.

Ernest Bevin 1881-1951

He was born in Winsford, Exmoor, Somerset the son of poor parents, his father is not known, and his mother died when he was 8. With little education he left school aged 9 and was a farm labourer at 11. In 1899 he moved to Bristol and worked as a driver. Later he joined the Dockers' Union and became a Trade Union official and its Secretary in 1911. He was the National Organiser for the Union in 1914. In the 1918 General Election he was the unsuccessful Labour Candidate for Bristol Central. Winston Churchill invited him to join the coalition government in 1940 as Minister of Labour 1940 and National Service. He was appointed Foreign Secretary by Attlee in the post war government but poor health led to his death in 1951.
Oxford Dictionary of National Biography

Acts of Parliament

1910 Mines Accidents (Rescue and Aid) Act:
Its purpose was to make provision for the organisation of rescue and aid in the case of accidents in the mines.

1911 Coal Mines Act:
The Act was to consolidate and amend the law relating to coal mines and certain other mines. It was a great advance on any previous mining legislation and gave the Secretary of State power to issue 'Orders' for the prevention of accidents. The Act introduced major legislation and was innovative inasmuch as it allowed for ongoing new regulations to be introduced as required. This would include Stone Dusting to combat dust explosions (1920, 1924, 1939 & 1949); Lighting, (1927, 1934); Winding & haulage (1937); plus various regulations on the use of explosives & fire precautions (see Royal Commission on Safety in Coal Mines 1935-38). Some previous Acts were repealed in part or entirely. (Peel, p.366.)

With regard to coal dust, the Act required that 'The floor, roof, and sides of the roads shall be systematically cleared so as to prevent as far as practicable coal-dust accumulating' (Peel, p.340.)
Robert Peel, *Coal Mining*, Blackie & Son, 1912

1912 COAL MINES (MINIMUM WAGE) ACT.

1915 Formation of the Coal Mining Organization Committee which regulated coal prices (1915); state control of Welsh coal mines (1916); state control of all UK coal mines (1917). Withdrawn in 1921.

1919 COAL MINES ACT:
Amended all Coal Mine Acts from 1887 to 1914 with respect to hours worked underground.

1923 EXPLOSIVES ACT.

1926 MINING INDUSTRY ACT:
This Act promoted the second Somerset Collieries Ltd. which included Camerton along with Norton Hill, Braysdown and Ludlows Mines.
Down & Warrington, *op.cit.*, p.214.

1930 COAL MINES ACT:
Introduced a quota system. Aimed to protect wages, mitigate competition and protect consumer interests. 'The Coal Mines Reorganisation Commission was constituted under the Coal Mines Act of 1930 and, after its partial failure, was replaced by the Coal Commission. Formed under the Coal Act 1938, with the object of unifying coal royalties … this body likewise failed to equalise royalties. Down & Warrington, p.25. 'The Act also embraced a compulsory marketing scheme, reducing shift hours without loss of pay. As a result, costs increased, necessitating policies to support prices and profit margins.'
Ian McInnes, 'Nationalisation: Looking Back Sixty Years On', *Five Arches*, Issue 57, 2006,

1937 & 1948 FACTORIES ACTS.

1938 COAL ACT:
Nationalisation of the mining industry was announced in the Coal Act 1938. The Act created the Coal Commission (5 people appointed by the Board of Trade) which enacted all Board of Trade requests in the national interest, specifically during the Second World War. All seams & mines came under its control in 1942 and it was not repealed until the following Act.

1946 COAL INDUSTRY NATIONALISATION ACT 12 JULY:
This established the public ownership and control of all the coal mining industry and allied activities and established the National Coal Board.

1951 THE WORKMEN'S COMPENSATION (SUPPLEMENTATION) ACT:
Provided for the payment of allowances out of the Industrial Injuries Fund to supplement workmen's compensation where the accident happened before 1924.
Pears Cyclopaedia 63rd edition 1954-55 p.152.

1946, 1949 & 1951 NATIONAL INSURANCE ACTS.

1946, 1948 NATIONAL INSURANCE (INDUSTRIAL INJURIES) ACTS.

1950 COAL MINING (SUBSIDENCE) ACT.

'Digging in a Somerset Mine'
by B. Eves. A poem from December 1920, from the collection of the Radstock Museum:

Down! Down! Digging in a Somerset Mine,
Down where the sun or stars never shine,
Down where no flower of beauty doth grow,
We Lads are digging out the coal below.

Dig! Dig! Digging in a Somerset Mine,
Lamp, pick and shovel; digging all the time,
Down where the light of day never gleams,
We Lads are working in the black coal seams.

Down! Down the shaft in an old coal mine,
Down where we risk our lives, all the time,
Down where the bird or girl never sings,
We Lads are busy till our shift begins.

Hew! Hew! Hewing in an old coal mine.
Lamp, pick and shovel; hewing all the time,
Down where the props stay the wooden beams,
We Lads are carting from the black coal seams.

Down! Down! Picking in a Somerset Mine,
Down where the bells are never heard chime,
Down where the coal tumbles, bit by bit,
We Lads are working in the old Coal Pit.

Pick! Pick! Picking in a Somerset Mine,
Lamp, pick and shovel; clicking all the time,
Down with the Ponies, black from head to sole,
Putts and tallow candles in an old Coal Hole.

References to Chapter Nine

1. Down & Warrington, *op.cit.*, p.113.
2. *Somerset Guardian*, 5 January 1912.
3. *Somerset Guardian*, 7 September 1962, 'Mineworkers life over fifty years ago', by G.A. Hillier; article in five instalments.
4. Down & Warrington, *op.cit.*, p.213.
5. *Ibid.*, p.125.
6. Richard Kelham, *British Railway Journal, op.cit.*, p.339-341.
7. Down & Warrington, *op.cit.*, p.125.
8. *Somerset Guardian*, 26 March 1926.
9. Down & Warrington, *op.cit.*, p.213.
10. Clew, *op.cit.*, p.38.
11. Maggs & Beale, *op.cit.*, p.59.
12. Down & Warrington, *op.cit.*, p.114.
13. Buchanan & Cossons, *op.cit.*, p.78.
14. H.G. Jeffries, *A Geography of Somerset*, A. Wheaton & Co. 1931, p.53-54.
15. Coysh, *op.cit.*, p.219ff.

16. Down & Warrington, *op.cit.*, p.37.
17. Down & Warrington, *op.cit.*, p.115.
18. Down & Warrington, *op.cit.*, p.202.
19. *Ibid.*, p.114.
20. Conversation with J. Hawkins and F. Sellars, 5 November 1986.
21. Collection of John Cornwell.
22. Comment by Dennis Chedgy
23. Down & Warrington, *op.cit.*, p.117.
24. Conversation, Hawkins & Sellars, 5 November 1986.
25. *Somerset Guardian*, 21 March 1930.
26. Conversation, Hawkins & Sellars, 5 November 1986.
27. *Ibid.*
28. Maggs & Beale, *op.cit.*, p.62.
29. *Ibid.*, p.55.
30. *Somerset Guardian*, 27 January 1911.
31. *Somerset Guardian*, 7 March 1924.
32. *Somerset Guardian*, Ibid.
33. Parfitt, *op.cit.*, p.41.
34. *Somerset Guardian*, 27 March 1936 and 3 April 1936; Conversation, Hawkins & Sellars, 5 November 1986.
35. Clew, *op.cit.*, p.139 and 140.
36. Maggs & Beale, *op.cit.*, p.59.
37. *The Monktonian* XXI, April 1935, No.5, p.245f; see also Maggs and Beale, op.cit., p.104.
38. Maggs & Beale, *op.cit.*, p.111.
39. Jevons, *op.cit.*, pp.404ff and 842ff.
40. *Ibid.*, p.499-503.
41. Down & Warrington, *op.cit.*, p.32.
42. Comment to author from Penny Bonsall
43. Parfitt, *op.cit.*, Introduction and p.48.
44. *Somerset Guardian*, 29 April 1921.
45. *Somerset Guardian*, 23 June 1922.
46. Parfitt, *op.cit.*, p.41.
47. Jevons, *op.cit.*, p.viii.
48. Parfitt, *op.cit.*, p.40.
49. Parfitt, *op.cit.*, p.16.
50. *Somerset Guardian*, 4 July 1924.
51. *Somerset Guardian*, 1 July 1927.
52. *Somerset Guardian*, 15 January 1926.
53. *Somerset Guardian*, 18 June 1926; see also Maggs & Beale, *op.cit.*, p.65.
54. Clew, *op.cit.*, p.140.
55. Down & Warrington, *op.cit.*, p.32.
56. Conversation, Hawkins & Sellars, 13 November 1986.

57. *Ibid.*, 31 October 1986.
58. *Somerset Guardian*, 22 August 1930.
59. Jevons, *op.cit.*, p.480.
60. *Somerset Guardian*, 2 July 1926.
61. Conversation, Hawkins & Sellars, 13 November 1986.
62. *Somerset Guardian*, 7 October 1927.
63. Down & Warrington, *op.cit.*, p.53-55.
64. *Somerset Guardian*, 3 June 1927.
65. Williams, *op.cit.*, p.20.
66. *Somerset Guardian*, 13 December 1935.
67. Ian McInnes, 'Nationalisation: Looking Back Sixty Years On', *Five Arches* Issue 57, 2006, p.8
68. *Ibid.*, p.8.
69. Conversation, Hawkins & Sellars, 5 November 1986.
70. Maggs & Beale, *op.cit.*, p.62.
71. Robin Atthill, *The Curious Past*, The Wessex Press 1955, p.7ff.
72. Down & Warrington, *op.cit.*, p.115.
73. Innes, *Ibid.*, p.9.
74. Innes, *Ibid.*, p.12.
75. Innes, *Ibid.*, p.9.
76. Kelham, *op.cit.*, p.339-341.
77. Down & Warrington, *op.cit.*, p.115.
78. *Ibid.*, p.115.
79. Comments to author from Penny Bonsall
80. *Somerset Guardian*, 21 April 1950.
81. Clew, *op.cit.*, p.145.

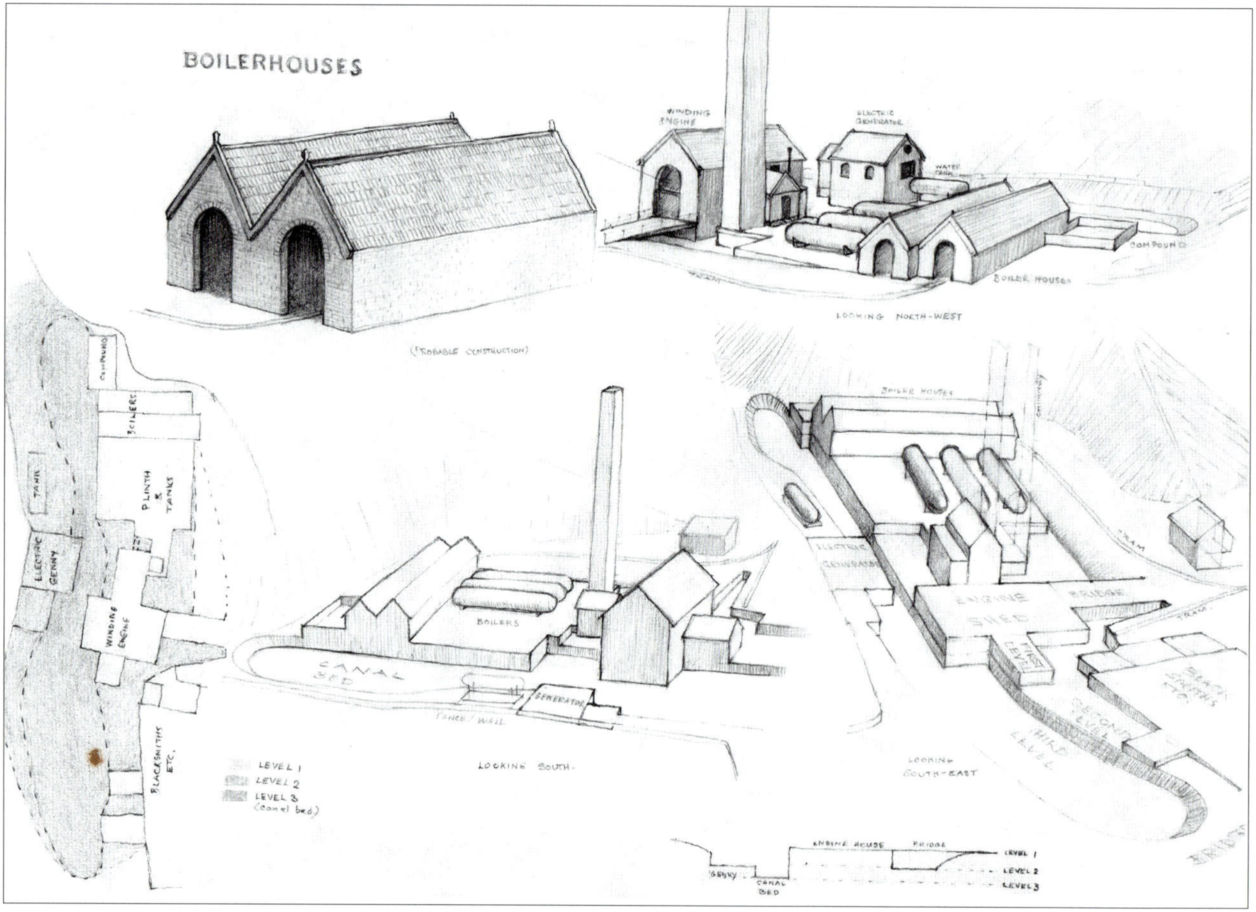

Sketches of Camerton New Pit made from photographs towards the construction of a model of the pit.

CHAPTER TEN - POSTSCRIPT

Miners Remember 'back in them days'

In the autumn of 1986, with the kind help of Mr. and Mrs. Ken Taylor, I was privileged to meet Redvers Emery, Jim Hawkins, Fred Sellars and Jack Sellars, all of whom had worked in Camerton Pit and whose memories of life in those days remain vivid. I have tried to record their memories in the following paragraphs, although at the time our conversation ranged widely over life in general as it affected them from day to day. My thanks are due to all these people and to Mr. and Mrs. Brian Emery for the time they gave.

Getting a job

It was not easy to get work in Camerton Pit; because of its popularity the managers could pick and choose whom they would employ. Jim Hawkins received the reply from the under-manager, Mr. Greenland, *'Ye want some work? Go down and dig that garden!'*. In the early twenties he went to ask Mr. Greenland every day for several months before getting his first job at the pit at the age of fourteen.

One way of obtaining work was by doing odd jobs for the owner. There was a lad who dug potatoes and even then had to go on asking for twelve months before being taken on. Others started on the local farms at the age of twelve but at thirteen changed to the pits where the pay was better. Jack Sellars started in the early years of the century at one shilling (5p) a day.

Getting to work

The present network of local footpaths criss-crossing the surrounding fields were the short-cuts used by miners getting to and from work. Many lived at Timsbury, Paulton and Peasedown. Others travelled on bicycles, storing them under the screens or beside the 'Little Hut' until their shift ended. Others were on the road walking from Paulton by around four in the morning. It was the start of a long day, with considerable distances to walk underground. By the end of the Pit's working life men were taking three quarters of an hour to walk from the pit bottom to the face being worked.

'If anybody were coming down Red Hill when the hooter did blow they'd just turn round and go back home.'(JH) That blast on the hooter at 6 a.m. was the first of many; by that time the men were expected to be underground. Camerton's hooter, quite distinct from that of all the other collieries, could be heard far and wide across the Cam valley.

Getting ready to go below

The men congregated in the 'Little Hut' where they left their outer clothes before going underground:

'That's where the men did go in the mornings, when they did come early and there's a big fire in there,

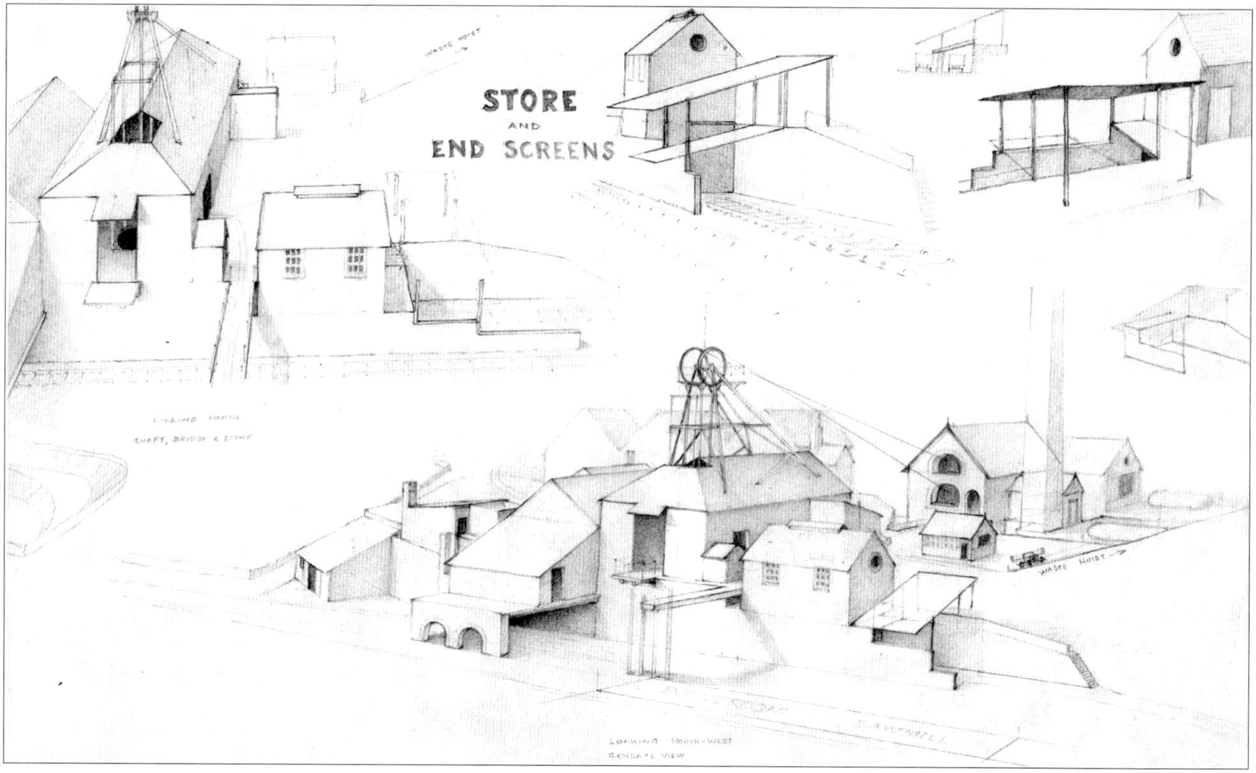

Sketches of Camerton New Pit made from photographs towards the construction of a model of the pit.

in what the men did call the little hut place. The men did go in there and have their food. Then we did go in there and do the snails, bake 'taters and all'. (FS)

The 'Little Hut' was the scene of a strange practice. Not only did the men bake potatoes, warm and dry themselves by the fire, but they also roasted snails on shovels. This delicacy was known as 'wallfruit'! *'Once they did hop, he were finished, he were done, he were ready!',* Not all the miners could stomach this particular treat! Some of the snails were gathered from the wall of the old canal, and the slime from the snails, kept in a jar, was also used as an ointment for their legs.

Nearby was the Candle House where *'we did get out lamps or candles in the morning.'* (JS) Each man gathered his tools. His pickhead, marked with his own sign, had been left for sharpening in the blacksmiths' shop at the end of the previous shift. He hoped to get the same one back in the morning:

> *'The hardest tool I worked with in the pit was the guss and crook. That was the hardest thing I had. You did get used to it. You had to. Where you made the rope go round your body, the sweat and that. Come the next morning it was like putting on an iceberg, wet through from the day before with sweat. You had it on and you did get warm again'.* (FS)

Jack Sellars mentioned having a double rope at the back so that *'It eased your back, didn't cut so much',* while Redvers remembered that *'it used to stick to your back and pull the skin off'.* Finally, before going below ground each man took his tally disc off the board; it remained with him until he reached the surface again.

The shift began at 6 a.m. and lasted until 2 p.m. A second shift, which did not cut coal, carried out repairs between 1.30 p.m. and 10 p.m. when all the lights at the pithead were put out. This was a sign to the local lads that they should be in home by then. Speaking of this late shift, Fred recalled;

'The night shifts had to go and do the roads. We had to fire the roadways, you had to get the roadways cleared to be able to start the work the next morning. If you didn't clean up they'd lose a lot of coal. So that's what the night workers did do, they did drive the road by night and put up the arches an all'. (FS)

Clay from the pits near the top of Red Hill was used for packing the shot when firing down the rock underground. It was fetched from the clay pits by a horse and cart being sent up from the colliery.

The miners also took their food for the shift. It was mainly sandwiches carried in their 'tommy bag'. No wonder the mice underground did well! They may have come in with the fodder for the ponies. Some of the miners caught them and put them down their shirts. They also took two pints of cold tea or water, some of which was used for their carbide lamps which needed recharging several times during the working day. As Camerton was not a 'gassy' pit, naked lights were allowed using carbide, fat or plain candles, and the men were also permitted to smoke. They often worked bare-footed, or wore hob-nailed boots, although these had the disadvantage that their feet got so hot that they could tip the sweat out of them!

It was generally agreed that Camerton was a good pit in which to work. *'They were good times. Every miner were a friend. Everybody was in the same boat. We did all help each other.'* (FS) Fred Newth was quoted as having said, *'Never a better lot of chaps than the Camerton Pit'. 'Camerton were a lot better than any I were in, and not so hot underground.'* (RE)

Getting the coal

The Timsbury seams were worked in the North District of the pit, while in the South it was the Braysdown seams. *'In the Miners' Welfare Field you'll see a dip all the way across the field. They do say that's the fault, what's parting Camerton from Braysdown seams.'* (FS)

The men worked the Top Series, especially the Great Vein which was about two feet thick in places, in what was known as 'Drift and Topple Mining':

'You'd have a drift, then you did turn off the top and go up and then you did go up with that topple until you came to a fault, then you'd go about twenty yards in and the topples did have what they call about a twenty yard seam to work.' (FS)

They worked in a team of four, with two breakers and two carters:

'We used to have a six yard stint marked off every morning. You had to clear that up, clear the coal out, timber it up, ready for the cutter to go up through on the night shift. That's where a lot of overtime come in, because some may have a bit of rough ground than what the others did, the roof come in, and he couldn't get his coal off. They did stop down then and help him get that coal off.' (FS)

The breakers were paid seven shillings and sixpence (37½p) and the carters six shillings and two pence (31p) a day. They would load their putts with between two and five hundredweight of coal depending on the height of the seam at the place where they were working. Then working together they would push or haul the putt to the tub or tram. *'When there was a low place you were in, and your back did drag along, all the little bits did get in there and did rub. That did make the tears run.'* (RE) If there were very steep slopes, a windlass with two handles, with a big cog and rachet, was used to move the coal up and down to the main tramways.

As each tub, carrying about ten hundred weight, was filled, it was marked.

> *'All the coal that did go in the tubs, they had numbers on their tubs. Well, when that do go up to be weighed at the pit top, all that were tallied up at the end of the day. That did go up on the board, all that they did send, all that company did send up that certain day. Every company had a number. The number was put on the top of the board ... Just before the men did rise he'd write them all up that certain number had sent during the shift. Then Thursday all that were tallied up and then that did go to the office. That were ready then for the men to collect it Saturdays.'* (JH and FS)

The main means of haulage for many years were six ponies with names like 'Beauty' and 'Punch', which could draw from five to six tubs and sometimes as many as eight. The man in charge of this train was on top of the first tub lying down. *'I never had any control over the horse, none whatever. He was going on. He knew where he had to go.'* (JH) If he went off too fast, sprags were put in the wheels to slow him down. *'When I were driving a horse we had a little crook about a third of the normal one so that you could push it in your pocket.'* (RE) Redvers used this to lift a loaded tram back onto the track if it became derailed. Every year the ponies had a special treat when they came above ground during the long annual holiday, or during a strike. They were allowed to run wild in the Powder House field behind the Post Office.

Getting injured

There were many minor accidents because all the work was dangerous. Broken arms and collar bones were not uncommon. The main danger was from falling roofs. It had been known for one man to be pushed into the soft ground underneath by the debris falling from the roof! There was also the danger from tubs of coal, running amok down some of the steep roadways. Coal dust was an ever-present danger. Even after thirty to forty years out of the pit some men still have traces of coal dust in their lungs. Pneumonicosis did cause minor lung damage to perhaps a majority of miners but, in addition, Somerset had the highest incidence of silicosis, apart from South Wales and Monmouthshire. This was caused by the silica in the frequently occurring 'greys', the bands of sandstone separating the coal seams. Research by Penny Bonsall has shown that between the wars the Somerset Miners' Association's most successful campaign was to get the Workmen's Compensation Act amended to include recognition of silicosis as an industrial disease of miners. Both Fred and Jim remembered the accident mentioned previously when a man had to have an amputation when caught in the 'main and tail' haulage machinery.

Abrasive sores were many. In time the men became hardened to them. *'My eldest brother he did come home and he'd be raw all over his body. 'Twas on the bare skin, you see, and his knees were sore. I seen my old mother bathe his knees hundreds of times when he was in Camerton New Pit'.* (JH)

Getting air and getting out

A large fire at the bottom of the ventilation shaft created a draught which pulled the air through the workings, the airflow being directed by the brattice curtains and the walls of rubbish, built where the coal had been extracted. There were also electrically driven fans to assist the ventilation, and up until 1939 canaries were kept in the pit to warn of bad air, which did happen at times. *'You couldn't get a flame on the candle. You did not want no sleeping pills.'* (JS) On one occasion Jack was so drowsy underground that he fell asleep for the whole of the late shift and did not come round until ten o'clock in the evening, due to the staleness of the air.

Camerton was not liable to flooding, and although wet in places, it was generally considered to be a dry pit. Pumping, using two big pumps at the pit bottom, started at 4 a.m. and continued for two hours because there was not enough electrical power for all the needs of the colliery. The waste water was discharged into the Cam brook by the lane.

The shaft at Old Pit was kept in working order as an escape route, with one winding wheel and one cage, until New Pit was linked underground with Braysdown in 1930. *'At the finish it was possible to walk from Camerton to Braysdown then on to Writhlington, Radstock, Kilmersdown and Norton Hill, all underground.'* (FS) Both Redvers and Jack remembered the wooden bridge crossing the canal basin opposite the Post Office. Coal was hauled across this bridge from New Pit to keep the Old Pit engine going up until 1930.

Getting to know the colliery

All the power that the colliery required was supplied by four Lancashire boilers, three being in use and the fourth on maintenance, being cleaned and cleared out. The large amount of ash was taken away by Keelings of Keynsham who used it in the making of concrete products. Two horses, which were kept in the stable near the top of the 'Slope', were used to pull the empty railway wagons up into the spare sidings from which they were allowed to run back under the screens controlled by their brakes. The wagons had been pushed so far up the gradient from the station by the locomotive.

> *'When they were loaded they were let down under their brakes down to where the main engine did get them from the station. Sometimes they had forty or fifty loads of coal. I can mind when there were sixty tubs [railway wagons] of coal on the back of that engine pulling towards Bath by Dunkerton.'* (FS)

It was very dusty under the screens and the men claimed that you got blacker there than down the Pit! Two wagons at a time were filled under the screens, one for lump and the other for small. The 'Lump', or large coal, was sold mainly for house coal, while the small was sent to the gas works. Another screen, nearer the batch, was for 'brushed' coal which was not sorted in any way.

A corner of the Blacksmiths' Shop still stands and it was here that new cages were made, the crooks fashioned, and the tools sharpened. This was the place where all the metal repairs and requirements of the colliery were taken care of. At first there were only two cages in the shaft, later a third was added.

The man on the winding engine often had fun at his workmates expense by making the cage rise or fall in the shaft at faster than normal rates. The winding engine was steam-driven, only being replaced by an electrical one near the end of the Pit's life. This was one of the jobs that Jim Hawkins carried out at Camerton.

Jack Sellars worked in the saw mill for many years after having to take a surface job. He said it was a good place to be in winter. *'Your hands used to stick to the iron saw bench because of the amount of resin that gathered on it.'* Most of the timber that was used in the Pit was fir *'because it did give a bit, and not snap'.* (JS)

The 'batch' or dirt tip which today dominates the site of New Pit and gives a superb view of the area, was constantly being added to, first by the 'Dandy'. This was steam-driven and took one tub of waste or shale to the top where it was tipped by hand. The men who spent long hours on the top spreading the waste had a little hut to shelter from the worst of the weather. Later the 'Dandy' was

The McLane tipper, and (right) a close-up view. *Radstock Museum Archive*

replaced by the electrically-driven McLane Tipper, possibly about 1920. This carried two buckets of coal waste at the end of its two gantries and discharged them automatically when it hit two pieces of wood at the top of the batch.

Up behind the Post Office there was the 'little ammunition hut' in what was known as Powder House Ground. The detonators and explosives for underground blasting were kept here, well away from the main parts of the colliery. *'When the deputies, when they wanted their stuff they did go right round there and get that. They weren't allowed outside that hut, not unless they were carrying the proper containers.'* (FS)

At the Pump House, or 'Donkey House' as some called it, beside Wick Lane, water was pumped up from the brook for the boilers. *'That's where the women did come out to get their hot water for doing the washing.'* Steam from the boiler came down and condensed in a tank, hence it was known locally as 'steam water'. *'The women used to come out the cottages, fight out who was going to get there first and get the hot water.'* (KT) *'You'd see six or seven buckets lined up there, specially when we came, off at one o'clock shift.'* (RE) As the water was distilled, it was pure enough to be used by Sammy Coombes and others for topping up accumulators which people used in those days to power their radios. Sammy Coombes collected the water in his car and took it back to his garage.

Getting the coal away

All the coal that was not discharged into railway wagons under the screens was sent up the 'Gugg' to the land sales depot on Red Hill. The coal carts that came from Bath and elsewhere were all loaded carefully by stacking the largest lumps of coal around the outside of the cart. Ken Taylor recalled that a black Shire Horse, belonging to his grandfather, which had eleven inch shoes, was used as a trace-horse to give assistance up Tunley Hill, near Tunley Farm, on the road to Bath. In those days, taking a load of coal to Bath by horse and cart was a whole day's work.

Bill Coles was in charge of the horses in the shunting yards, and between 1.30 pm and 3.30 pm he would use them to deliver the best coal from the pit to the local gentry.

Getting paid or not

Although the basic wage was seven shillings and six pence a day for breakers, the men were paid 'on ton'. *'There were a lot were on 'non ton'. Besides, some of it was so hard they couldn't get enough out, all they had was seven and six a day.'* (JH)

What happened if the owners did not want any coal dug, because there was coal in stock or there was a shortage of railway wagons? *'They blowed the hooter three times if they didn't want us to work next day.'* (FS) If it was blown four times it meant that the men had to go to Peasedown to collect their dole money. Times were such that it was not uncommon to have three days work and three days on the dole. The excess coal was stacked in every available space; around the pithead, where the canteen was later to be built, in the timber yard, and even on the batch itself. Before the coal offices were built beside the present Post Office, the men used to go along to the Jolly Collier on Saturdays to collect their pay.

A recent photograph of the pit canteen building which was erected after nationalisation.

Getting cleaned up

There were no pithead baths at Camerton, so some men used the brook. The more usual practice was for the women folk to have plenty of hot water ready for the miners coming in, and they would get washed beside the fire. Fred remembered the many occasions *'My mother had five coming in. All the hot water would be ready for the baths. My mother did put on her washing boiler every day and she had to carry it into the kitchen and we did wash beside the fire.'* For others who lived nearer the pit there was the 'steam water' from the colliery boiler to help with this never-ending chore.

Getting better conditions and pay

There are still vivid memories of the 1926 lockout. Fred and his father, along with others, gleaned over the batch looking for pieces of coal and selling it at a shilling (5p) a bag. He reckoned that coal was stacked on the batch at this time, *'people dug everywhere for coal.'* (FS)

Despite the long months of hardship caused by the lockout it achieved very little good for the miners. They generally lost as a result of it. *'We went back for less than we came out.'* (RE) It was a hard time with no money coming in for six months.

The Somerset Miners' Association worked to improve pay and conditions for the miners and Redvers recalled paying his sixpence a week to the local union agent. Everyone at Camerton was in the union and they held their meetings in the club house at Meadgate behind the public house.

Getting extra cash

With only a shilling a day as the starting wage, the miner was often short of money. Sometimes, as in the days of Skinner, they earned extra money by helping in the fields with the haymaking. They would also catch rabbits and moles. The moleskins would be stretched out to about seven by five inches and these were used to make pads for the knees of their trousers and known as 'fustin'.

Then there was the fishing. Before the serious pollution of the waters of the Cam brook it was well stocked with a variety of fish. Near the foot of the batch there was a pond, probably forming part of the old canal, which seemed full of frogs and was also a place to go fishing. Jack Sellars claimed that you did not even need a hook, just a worm on a piece of cotton and you could *'just pull 'em out'*.

Gardens were very important to the mining families. They needed big ones to grow as much food as possible to eke out the low wages of the times. If they were householders they did get a weekly coal allowance of two hundredweight from the pit. This was known as 'bag coal', and was delivered by Archie Gray with his horse and cart. It was dumped outside the cottages and had to be shovelled and barrowed into the coal store. Much of it would be burnt to provide the large amount of hot water that was needed every day.

Getting up to mischief

'We made our own fun!' They had to. There was very little to do in the village after work was finished for the day. They discovered that with the help of a penny and a piece of bent wire, chocolate bars could be removed from the machine that stood on the station platform. They got a thrill when fog detonators, 'nabbed from the hut by the railway' were put under a train! Long before that, in the days of the canal, the coal boats used to tie up for the night along towards Radford. The local lads would creep down and put sacking or turfs on the chimney tops of the barges, with disastrous results for the poor bargees.

Getting away from it all

The miners had their times of relaxation and recreation. For many years pigeon racing was very popular. There was football played at the Recreation Ground owned by the Miners' Welfare since the early twenties. On those Saturday afternoons when there was a match the men started their shift at 4 a.m. and then came up early. *'If you could play football pretty good, you could get a job at Camerton.'* (JS) As they were in the Bath and District League it meant that they could get away from the village for a few hours.

A statue of a coalminer which formerly stood outside the Jolly Collier, since removed to the site of Old Pit, now a nature reserve. This is one of two statues which were produced for the Festival of Britain in 1951, cast in modern fibreglass. The other statue was acquired by the Headingly football club.

In the days of the railway, when the steam motor train ran, *'we used to nip in and have a penny ride down to Dunkerton'*.(JS) *'When we had a penny, that was!'* (RE) There were visits to Bath on Wednesdays and Saturdays by bicycle. These would be left at Odd Down Corner, near St. Martin's Hospital, and the tram taken down into Bath. Sometimes they cycled all the way down into Bath and left their cycles behind Furze's Restaurant in Southgate Street while they 'went on the town'.

Every year the Miners, Welfare would arrange a day trip to Weston-super-Mare, leaving by train from Camerton. Eventually, probably in the thirties, there was a break during the last week of July and the first part of August, when the men could take time off, but without pay.

For two weeks the dust, dirt and the darkness could be forgotten.

GLOSSARY OF TERMS USED IN COAL MINING

Local areas may use other terms than the ones here

Back-shift The second set of miners working in any spot each day.

Banksman The man who receives the coal at the top of the shaft.

Batch A spoil heap or tip containing the waste material from the mine.

Brakesman The man in charge of the winding engine.

Brattice A partition made of wood, canvas, strong tarred cloth or other material hung from the roof to the floor of the roadways, used to direct currents of air to provide ventilation in the mine. These were often opened and shut by boys to allow the passage of trams or tubs.

Carting Boys Young boys who pulled the putt of coal from the face to the main tramways. On steep inclines (upgrades) a second boy would either push the putt or, on steep descents (downgrades) use the hook on his guss to act as a brake at the back of the putt.

Coal Measures Seams of coal and rocks, mudstones and shales.

Corve or Corf A square frame of wood for carrying or sliding coal upon at the bottom of the mine, similar to a putt.

Dial A kind of compass for taking bearings underground where a magnetic compass would not work be reliable.

Dip The amount of slope of the vein or bed of coal.

Dipple A heading driven from the main roadway downwards towards the dip or deep.

Downcast The downward current of air in the mine which could be increased by allowing water to also descend the shaft.

Down Dip The area where the seams dip down away from the surface.

Dressing The act of separating coal from the waste.

Drift Any working underground which is horizontal or a sloping tunnel driven into the coal seams.

Engine Shaft The shaft up which the drainage water of the mine is raised to the surface.

Fault A disturbance of the strata. If it is upwards it is called an upthrow or leap; if downwards a downthrow or slide.

Gin or Whim A machine for raising coal from a mine, usually powered by a horse.

Goaf or Gob Parts of the mine from which the coal has been extracted and often filled with the waste.

Gugg A system of pulleys at the top and bottom of an incline to raise or lower putts.

Guss & Crook A girdle of rope or leather with a hook attached to it which was used to drag the putt.

Heading A small gallery driven in advance of a main road.

Heapstead The buildings and works around a mineshaft.

Longwall Mining A method of working coal by which the coal is extracted in one working.

Pillar A column of rock left to support the roof or walls.

Pitch The limit of the ground set to be worked by the miner.

Poll-pick A miner's pick, having one end sharp and the other formed into a hammer.

Putt A box-like structure or sledge without wheels which was dragged by a carting boy. The container on top was made of hazel rods wrapped round iron pins.

Rise and Dip To work upwards towards the surface. Workings going 'to the rise' are going up the inclination or slope of the seam. Those going 'to the dip' are going down.

Screen A grading device like a sieve for separating the various-sized pieces of coal from the mine.

Seam A bed of coal.

Sink An excavation in a downward direction. Those who dug new shafts were called sinkers.

Sprag A short prop of wood to give support above where coal is being undercut to prevent a fall of coal.

A chock of wood to restrict the moving of a tram or coal wagon as a form of brake.

Sump At the bottom of the engine shaft a pit lower than the deepest level which collects the water that drains from the workings. From here the water is pumped to the surface.

Timbering The fixing of timber in the mine to support the roof and walls of the levels or the sides of the shaft.

Tippler A machine to discharge coal from trams into the screens or onto the heap of waste.

Topple A heading driven from the main roadway upwards towards the rise.

Trams The small wagons used to take the coal to the surface, also known as tubs.

Upcast The upward current of air in the mine created by the natural heat in the mine, sometimes with the addition of a furnace.

Winding engine An engine used to raise the coal in the trams and to take the miners to and from the bottom of the shaft.

BIBLIOGRAPHY

AIHCAM, Journal of Avon industrial Buildings Trust.

Albert, W., *The Turnpike Road System in England 1663-1840*, CUP 1972.

Anstie, J., *The Coalfields of Gloucestershire and Somersetshire and their resources*, 1873 (Kingsmead Reprints 1969).

Arlett, M., *The Railways of Midford*, Somerset and Dorset Railway Trust 1983.

Arlett, M., *The Somerset and Dorset at Midford*, Millstream Books 1986.

Aston, M., & Burrow, I., *The Archaeology of Somerset*, Somerset County Council, 1982.

Astell, J., *Somerset at Work, 1870-1950*, Redcliffe Press 1982.

Atthill, R.A., *The Curious Past*, Wessex Press 1955,

Atthill, R.A., *Old Mendip*, David and Charles 1971.

Atthill, R.A., *The Somerset and Dorset Railway*, David and Charles 1985.

Barber, Ross *The Dramway*, Avon Industrial Buildings Trust, 1986.

Bath Chronicle.

Bath Herald.

Bath Journal.

Journal of the Bristol Industrial Archaeological Society.

Billingsley, J., *General View of the Agriculture of the County of Somerset*, Bath 1797.

Bluhm, R.K., *A Bibliography of the Somerset Coalfield*, Library Association 1968.

Bluhm, R.K., 'The Somerset Coalfield, 1790-1820', *A Second Somerset Miscellany*, Bath & Camerton Archaeological Society 1971.

Bluhm, R.K., [Article] *Industrial Archaeology*, Vol.3, 1966.

Brice, S.W., *The Coalfield of North Somersetshire*, Bemrose and Lothian 1867.

Buchanan, R.A., & Cossons N., *Industrial Archaeology of the Bristol Region*, David and Charles 1969.

Buckland, W., & Coneybeare, W.D., 'Observations on the South Western Coal District of England', *Trans. of the Geological Society*, 2nd Series,Vol.1, part 2.

Bulley, J., 'To Mendip for Coal, a study of the Somerset Coalfield before 1830', *Journal of the Somerset Archaeological & Natural History Society*, 1951-52, No.97 Part I, No.98 Part II.

Camerton and Limpley Stoke Railway, *GWR Magazine*, No.22, 1910.

Clew, K., *The Kennet and Avon Canal*, David & Charles 1985.

Clew, K., *The Somersetshire Coal Canal and Railways*, Bran's Head 1986.

Clutton Local History Group, *A Brief History of Coalmining at Clutton.*

Collier, Peter, *Colliers Way*, Ex Libris Press 1986.

Collins J.H., *Principles of Metal Mining*, Wm Collins 1875.

Collinson, J., *The History of Somersetshire*, 1791.

Coombes, N., & Bax, A.N., eds., *Journal of a Somerset Rector 1803-1834: John Skinner*, OUP 1984.

Cornwell. *John Collieries of Somerset and Bristol*, Landmark 2001.

Coysh, A.W., Mason, E., & Waite, V., *The Mendips*, Robert Hale 1971.

Davies, P., A.J.Cook, David Parker, Hartcliffe Community Centre, Bristol.

Dobson, D.P., *The Archaeology of Somerset*, Methuen 1931.

Down, C.G., & Warrington, A.J., *The History of the Somerset Coalfield*, David and Charles 1971.

Dunning, R.W.A, *History of Somerset*, Somerset County Library 1978.

The Engineer, Journal of the Institute of Civil Engineers, Vols.103 & 107, 1907 & 1909.

'The Colliers' Story', *Folk News*, Summer No.1, 1974.

Flower, Fred, *Somerset Mining Life*, Millstream Books 1990.

Ministry of Fuel and Power, *Regional Survey Report, Bristol and Somerset Coalfield*, HMSO 1946.

Galloway, R.L.A, *History of Coal Mining in Great Britain*, 1882, David and Charles Reprints 1969.

Gilson, R.G., & Quartley, G.W., 'Some aspects of the Somersetshire Coal Canal Tramways', *Industrial Archaeology*, Vol.5, 1968.

Gould, Shane, *The Somerset Coalfield*, Somerset Industrial Archaeological Society Survey No.11 1999.

Greenwell, G.C., & McMurtrie, J., *The Radstock Portion of the Somersetshire Coalfield*, Lambert 1864.

Greenwood, C.& J., *Somersetshire Delineated*, 1822 (Reprinted by Alan Sutton Publications Ltd. 1980).

Griffin, A.R., *The British Coalmining Industry*, 1977; The Collier, Shire Books 1982.

Hadfield, C., *The Canals of Southern England*, Phoenix 1955.

Hadfield, C., *The Canals of South & Southeast England*, David and Charles 1969.

Handley, C., *The Railways and Tramways of Radstock*, Somerset and Dorset Railway Trust, 1979.

Howell, C., *Round Here in them days*, Fosseway Press 1980.

Hutton, E., *Highways and Byways of Somerset*, Macmillan 1919.

Jeffries, H.G., *A Geography of Somerset*, Wheaton 1931.

Jevons, H.S., *The British Coal Trade*, 1915, David and Charles 1969.

Kelham, R., [Article], *British Railways Journal*, Vol.9, August 1985.

Locke, R., *Supplement to Collinson's History of Somersetshire*, Taunton 1939.

McMurtrie, J., [Article] on the working of small seams, *Proceedings of the South Wales Institution of Engineers*, Vol.12, No.5.

Maggs, C.G., & Beale, G., *The Camerton Branch*, Wild Swan Publications1985.

Maggs, Colin, 'Seventy five years since the opening of Camerton-Dunkerton Railway', *Bath Chronicle* 25 August 1982.

The Monktonian, Magazine of Monkton Combe School, 1935 and 1954.

National Coal Board, Plan for Coal; the NCB's Proposals 1950.

Owen, A.V., *The Delectable Valley*, Fyson's 1952.

Parfitt, A., *My Life as a Somerset Miner*, 1930, Somerset Miners' Association 1968.

Peel, Robert, *An Elementary Text Book of Coal Mining*, Blackie 1912.
Railway Magazine [Article on the filming of the Titfield Thunderbolt], No.99, 1953.
Savage, R.J., ed., *Geological Excursions in the Bristol Area*, University of Bristol 1977.
Skinner, J., See Coombes and Bax.
Somerset Guardian.
Stuart, D.M.D., 'Coal Dust - An Explosive Agent', *The Colliery Manager*, London 1894.
Stuart, D.M.D., *The Origin and Rationale of Colliery Explosions*, Wright and Co., Bristol 1895.
Torrens, H., The Caisson Lock at Combe Hay, *Bristol Industrial Archaeological Society Journal*, No.8, 1975.
Tunstall, J., *Rambles about Bath*, 1847.
Victoria History of the Counties of England, Somerset, Vol.2, 1911.
Walker, F., *The Bristol Region*, Nelson 1971.
Warner, R., *A Walk through some of the Western Counties of England*, 1800.
Warner, R., *The History of Bath*, 1801.
Warner, R., *Excursions from Bath*, 1811.
Warnock, D., *The Bristol & North Somerset Railway 1863 -1884*, Temple Cloud 1978.
Warnock, D., & Parsons, R.G., *The Bristol and North Somerset Railway since 1884*, 1979.
Wedlake, W.J., *Excavations at Camerton, Somerset, 1926-1958*, Camerton Excavation Club 1958.
Wedlake, W.J., 'Tithe Disputes at Camerton, Somerset, 1800-1830', *A Second Somerset Miscellany*, Bath and Camerton Archaeological Society 1971.
Wells, W.C., *Historical Review of the Bristol and Somerset Coalfields*, Mardon Flexible Packaging Ltd., Midsomer Norton, 1977.
Wesley, J., *The Journals of the Revd. J. Wesley*, edited 1909-1916.
Williams, W.J., *Coalmining in Bishop Sutton - North Somerset, c.1799-1929.*
Winwood, H.H., Section on Geology in British Association *Handbook to Bath*, Pitman 1888.
Wood & Cunningham (printers) *The improved Bath or Picture of Bath and its environs*, Bath, c.1809.
Winchester, Simon, *The Map that Changed the World*, Viking-Penguin 2001.

SOURCES

Museum of Bath at Work
Tapes of Camerton Miners recorded in 1986.
Model of Camerton New Pit.

Radstock, Midsomer Norton and District Museum
Records of Braysdown and Camerton Collieries deposited by Una (Stevie) Pope.
Documents, Photographs and Artefacts etc relating to Camerton Mines.

Kingswood Heritage Museum
Cossham Map of the Bristol and Somerset Coalfields.

Bristol Coal Mining Archives, Hallatrow
Jenny Cornwell.

Somerset Record Office, Taunton.

University of Bristol
Records of the Somerset Miners' Association

ACKNOWLEDGEMENTS

Camerton Parish Council; Nick Turner the Curator, and Volunteers at the Radstock, Midsomer Norton and District Museum; Patience Barnes; Penny Bonsall; Dennis Chedgy; Alfred Church; Ron Fullager; Roger Halse; Alec Hann; Jeremy Hogwood; Muir McKean; Sylvia Macmillen; Stevie Pope; Tom Randall; Dennis Rendell; Ken Taylor; Jacky Walters; staff of the Museum of Bath at Work.

APPENDIX

Extract from William Smith's description of Mearns Pit in High Littleton, with definition of mining terms.
(Smith MS, Oxford University)

1. The Pitt 100 Yard deep where the Coal is landed by a Machine turned by a Horse which consists of a large upright Axle (and braces) – feet high on the upper part of which is fixed a Drum wheel – feet Diam: and – feet thick at the Curcumference having a rim or Board on it's upper and lower edges projecting out – and another round the middle which divides it in two parts round which coils two Ropes running over two Rollers and two little Wheels – feet Diam: just over the Pitt to the ends of these two Ropes the Baskets (called Bushells) are hooked on and as the empty one goes down on one Rope the full one comes up on the other to the top when the full one is unhook'd at Top and the empty one at Bottom. And the Horse turns and drives the Machine the contrary way which lets down the empty one and draws up the full one as before and so on alternately –

2. A Standing – is a place by the side of the Bottom of the Pitt at the top of the Gugg abt.8 or 10 feet high where is fixed a Windlass (turnd by Men) with a large Balance wheel on it round the Axle of which coils two Ropes to the ends of which are hook'd two 3 Bushell Carts (on four low Wheels) which run up and down the Guggs the empty one going down and the full one coming up at the same time which is pitch't down in the standing and loaded into the Bushell Baskets that come down the Pitt.

3. A Gugg – is a common Road about 4 feet high and – wide and 55 yards long – Pitches abt. 9 Inches in a Yard in the Bottom lies Timber framed together down which are two Roads on four Rutts made for the Wheels of the Carts to run in so as to pass one by the other going up and down.

4. A Twinway – a common Road from the Bottom of the first Gugg to the Standing at the top of the Second about 4 feet high – feet wide and 40 Yards long and nearly on the level. The 3 Bushell Carts that are wound up the Second Gugg are Drawn along here to the bottom of the first by a Man down on his hands and feet, bare, with a Cord round his Waist, to which is fastened a Chain that comes between his legs and hooks to the fore part of the Cart.

INDEX

PLACES

PEOPLE

COMPANIES

MINES

TOPICS